First World War
and Army of Occupation
War Diary
France, Belgium and Germany

24 DIVISION
73 Infantry Brigade
Royal Sussex Regiment
9th Battalion
21 August 1915 - 31 May 1919

WO95/2219/2

The Naval & Military Press Ltd
www.nmarchive.com
Published in association with The National Archives

Published by

The Naval & Military Press Ltd

Unit 10 Ridgewood Industrial Park,

Uckfield, East Sussex,

TN22 5QE England

Tel: +44 (0) 1825 749494

www.naval-military-press.com

www.nmarchive.com

Contents

Document type	Place/Title	Date From	Date To
Heading	WO95/2219/2		
Heading	France 9th Battalion Royal Sussex Regt. 1915 Aug-1919 May		
Heading	9th Battn. The Royal Sussex Regiment. August And September (21.8.15 to 30.9.15) 1915		
War Diary	Woking	21/08/1915	21/08/1915
War Diary	Embrey & Rimboral France	03/09/1915	16/09/1915
War Diary	Ramboral & Embrey	17/09/1915	21/09/1915
War Diary	Laires	22/09/1915	23/09/1915
War Diary	Beuvry	24/09/1915	24/09/1915
War Diary	In The Trenches	25/09/1915	28/09/1915
War Diary	Sailly Les Bourses	29/09/1915	29/09/1915
War Diary	Norrentes Fontes	30/09/1915	30/09/1915
Heading	24th Division 9th. Royal Sussex Vol 2 Oct 15		
War Diary	Norrentes Fontes	01/10/1915	02/10/1915
War Diary	Herzeele	03/10/1915	05/10/1915
War Diary	Proven	06/10/1915	11/10/1915
War Diary	Rosenhill	12/10/1915	13/10/1915
War Diary	Trenches	14/10/1915	19/10/1915
War Diary	Rosenhill	20/10/1915	27/10/1915
War Diary	In The Trenches	28/10/1915	31/10/1915
Heading	24th Division 9th. Royal Sussex Vol. 3 Nov 15		
War Diary	In The Trenches	01/11/1915	02/11/1915
War Diary	Rosenhill	03/11/1915	06/11/1915
War Diary	In The Trenches	07/11/1915	12/11/1915
War Diary	Rosenhill	13/11/1915	15/11/1915
War Diary	Dickebusch	16/11/1915	16/11/1915
War Diary	In The Trenches	17/11/1915	22/11/1915
War Diary	Rosenhill	23/11/1915	23/11/1915
War Diary	On The March	24/11/1915	26/11/1915
War Diary	Houlle	27/11/1915	30/11/1915
Heading	24th Div 9th. Roy. Sussex Vol. 4 December 1915		
War Diary	Houlle	01/12/1915	31/12/1915
Heading	9th Battalion Royal Sussex Regiment. January 1916.		
Heading	24th 9th. Roy. Sussex Vol. 5 73rd Inf Bde		
War Diary	Houlle	01/01/1916	07/01/1916
War Diary	Camp C.	08/01/1916	15/01/1916
War Diary	Belgian Chateau	16/01/1916	18/01/1916
War Diary	In The Trenches	19/01/1916	22/01/1916
War Diary	Belgian Chateau	23/01/1916	26/01/1916
War Diary	In The Trenches	27/01/1916	30/01/1916
War Diary	Camp F	31/01/1916	31/01/1916
War Diary	9th Battalion Royal Sussex Regiment. February 1916		
Heading	War Diary of 9th Royal Sussex Regt from 1/2/16 to 29/2/16		
War Diary	Camp F	01/02/1916	08/02/1916
War Diary	Ypres Cellars	09/02/1916	11/02/1916
War Diary	Trenches	12/02/1916	24/02/1916
War Diary	Poperinghe	25/02/1916	29/02/1916
Heading	9th Battalion Royal Sussex Regiment. March 1916.		

Heading	War Diary of 9th Battalion Royal Sussex Regiment from March 1st 1916 to March 31st 1916		
War Diary	Poperinghe	01/03/1916	03/03/1916
War Diary	Belgian Chateau	04/03/1916	07/03/1916
War Diary	Trenches	08/03/1916	11/03/1916
War Diary	Belgian Chateau	12/03/1916	15/03/1916
War Diary	Camp E.	16/03/1916	19/03/1916
War Diary	Meteren	20/03/1916	24/03/1916
War Diary	Trenches	25/03/1916	31/03/1916
Heading	9th Battalion Royal Sussex Regiment. April 1916		
Heading	War Diary of 9th (Service) Battn. Royal Sussex Regt. From April 1st 1916 To April 30 1916		
War Diary	Kortepyp	01/04/1916	05/04/1916
War Diary	Trenches	06/04/1916	11/04/1916
War Diary	Red Lodge	12/04/1916	17/04/1916
War Diary	Trenches	18/04/1916	23/04/1916
War Diary	Kortepyp	24/04/1916	30/04/1916
War Diary	Trenches		
Heading	9th. Battalion Royal Sussex Regiment. May 1916		
Heading	War Diary Of 9th Royal Sussex Regt. From. May 1st 1916 To May 31st 1916		
War Diary	Trenches	01/05/1916	05/05/1916
War Diary	Red Lodge	06/05/1916	11/05/1916
War Diary	Trenches	12/05/1916	17/05/1916
War Diary	Kortepyp	18/05/1916	25/05/1916
War Diary	Trenches	26/05/1916	31/05/1916
Heading	9th Battalion. Royal Sussex Regiment. June 1916		
Heading	War Diary of 9th Bn Royal Sussex Regt. From 1.6.16 To 30.6.16		
War Diary	Trenches	01/06/1916	03/06/1916
War Diary	Red Lodge	04/06/1916	11/06/1916
War Diary	Trenches	12/06/1916	17/06/1916
War Diary	St Jans Cappel	18/06/1916	20/06/1916
War Diary	Wakefield Huts.	21/06/1916	27/06/1916
War Diary	Trenches	28/06/1916	30/06/1916
Heading	9th Battn. The Royal Sussex Regiment. July 1916		
Heading	War Diary 9th. Bn. Royal Sussex Regt. From 1.7.16 To 31.7.16		
War Diary	Trenches	01/07/1916	01/07/1916
War Diary	Wakefield Huts	02/07/1916	06/07/1916
War Diary	Kemmel Shelters	07/07/1916	07/07/1916
War Diary	Dranoutre	08/07/1916	10/07/1916
War Diary	Trenches	11/07/1916	20/07/1916
War Diary	Fletre (Coq de Paille)	21/07/1916	24/07/1916
War Diary	Montagne	25/07/1916	31/07/1916
Heading	9th Battalion. Royal Sussex Regiment. August 1916		
Heading	War Diary of 9th Royal Sussex Regt For Month Of August 1916		
War Diary	Corbie-Sur-Somme	01/08/1916	01/08/1916
War Diary	Sailly-le-Sec	02/08/1916	02/08/1916
War Diary	Happy Valley	03/08/1916	07/08/1916
War Diary	The Citadel	08/08/1916	10/08/1916
War Diary	The Craters	11/08/1916	15/08/1916
War Diary	The Citadel	16/08/1916	18/08/1916
War Diary	Attach on Outskirts of Guillemont	18/08/1916	20/08/1916
War Diary	The Craters	20/08/1916	31/08/1916

Heading	9th Battalion. Royal Sussex Regiment. September 1916		
Heading	9th Royal Sussex War Diary for month of September 1916		
War Diary		01/09/1916	30/09/1916
Heading	9th Battalion Royal Sussex Regiment. October 1916		
War Diary		01/10/1916	30/10/1916
Heading	9th Battalion Royal Sussex Regiment. November 1916		
Heading	9th Royal Sussex Regt War Diary for month of November 1916		
War Diary		01/11/1916	30/11/1916
Heading	9th. Battalion Royal Sussex Regiment. December 1916		
Heading	War Diary Of 9th Royal Sussex Regt For Month Of December 1916.		
War Diary		01/12/1916	31/12/1916
Heading	War Diary Of 9th Royal Sussex Regiment For The Month Of January 1917.		
War Diary		01/01/1917	31/01/1917
Heading	9th Bn. The Royal Sussex Regiment. War Diary For The Month Of February 1917		
War Diary		01/02/1917	24/02/1917
Heading	War Diary For The Month Of March 1917. Of 9th Battalion The Royal Sussex Regiment.		
War Diary		01/03/1917	31/03/1917
Heading	9th Royal Sussex Regiment 73rd Infantry Brigade 24th Division April 1917		
Heading	9th. Royal Sussex Regiment For The Month Of April 1917		
War Diary		01/04/1917	29/04/1917
Heading	War Diary Of 9th Battalion Royal Sussex Regt For The Month Of May 1917		
War Diary		01/05/1917	31/05/1917
Heading	War Diary Of 9th Battalion The Royal Sussex Regt For Month Of June 1917		
War Diary		01/06/1917	30/06/1917
Heading	War Diary Of 9th Battalion Royal Sussex Regiment For Month Of July 1917		
War Diary	In The Field	01/07/1917	31/07/1917
Heading	9th. Battalion Royal Sussex Regiment For The Month Of August 1917.		
War Diary		01/08/1917	31/08/1917
Miscellaneous	Special Order. 9th. Battalion Royal Sussex Regiment.	07/08/1917	07/08/1917
Heading	9th Battalion Royal Sussex Regiment For The Month Of September 1917		
War Diary	In The Field	01/09/1917	30/09/1917
Heading	9th Battalion The Royal Sussex Regiment For The Month Of October 1917 Vol 2		
War Diary	Field	01/10/1917	30/10/1917
Heading	9th. Battalion Royal Sussex Regiment. For The Month Of November 1917		
War Diary	Field	01/11/1917	30/11/1917
Heading	9th Battalion Royal Sussex Regiment For The Month Of December 1917		
War Diary	Field	01/12/1917	31/12/1917
Operation(al) Order(s)	9th Royal Sussex Regiment Operation Order No. 196	04/01/1918	04/01/1918
Heading	9th Battalion Royal Sussex Regiment For The Month Of January 1918		

War Diary	Field	01/01/1918	31/01/1918
Heading	9th. Bn Royal Sussex Regiment For The Month Of February 1918		
War Diary		01/02/1918	25/02/1918
Heading	9th Battalion Royal Sussex Regiment March 1918		
Heading	9th Bn. Royal Sussex Regiment For The Month Of March 1918.		
War Diary	Field	01/03/1918	31/03/1918
Miscellaneous	Diary of Lt. Col. M.V.B. Hill March 21st-27th 1918		
Miscellaneous	Written By Captain H.A. Saxon. M.C. commanding C. Company of 9th Royal Sussex Regiment after his return from Germany, in December 1918.		
Heading	9th Battn. The Royal Sussex Regiment. April 1918		
Heading	9th Bn. Royal Sussex Regt For The Month Of April 1918		
War Diary	Field	01/04/1918	30/04/1918
Miscellaneous	Casualty Lists.		
Miscellaneous	Battalion Orders By Captain C.V. Newton. M.C. Commanding 9th Royal Sussex Regiment.	10/04/1918	10/04/1918
Heading	9th Bn The Royal Sussex Regiment For The Month Of May 1918		
War Diary	Field	01/05/1918	31/05/1918
Heading	War Diary For Month Of June. 9th Battalion Royal Sussex Regt.		
War Diary	Field	01/06/1918	29/06/1918
Operation(al) Order(s)	Battalion Order No 5 by Lieut. Colonel. N.I. Whitty. D.S.O. Commanding 24th Bn, Machine Gun Corps.	01/06/1918	01/06/1918
Miscellaneous	Appendix To Battalion Order No 5		
Miscellaneous	Table "A"	01/06/1918	01/06/1918
Map	Rgt. Battn.		
Operation(al) Order(s)	73rd. Infantry Brigade Order No. 194	01/06/1918	01/06/1918
Miscellaneous	Operation Orders by Lieut. Colonel S.F. Stallard, C.M.G., D.S.O. Commanding Left Group Artillery.	02/06/1918	02/06/1918
Miscellaneous	Operation Orders by Lieut. Col W.R. Corrall. M.C. for a Raid on enemy trenches on night 3rd/4th June 1918	31/05/1918	31/05/1918
Heading	9th Bn Royal Sussex Regiment For The Month Of July 1918		
War Diary	Field	01/07/1918	31/07/1918
Heading	9th Bn Royal Sussex Regiment For The Month Of August 1918		
War Diary	Field	01/08/1918	31/08/1918
Heading	9th Royal Sussex Regt War Diary.		
War Diary	Field	01/09/1918	30/09/1918
Heading	9th Bn Royal Sussex Regiment For The Month Of October 1918		
War Diary	Field	01/10/1918	31/10/1918
Miscellaneous	Summary Of Operations. October 5th to October 17th 1918.	27/10/1918	27/10/1918
Heading	9th Bn The Royal Sussex Regiment For The Month Of November 1918		
War Diary	Field	01/11/1918	30/11/1918
Miscellaneous	9th Royal Sussex Regiment Appendix to War Diary November 1918		
War Diary	Field	01/12/1918	31/12/1918
Heading	9th Bn Royal Sussex Regiment For The Month Of January 1919		

War Diary	Field	31/01/1919	31/01/1919
Miscellaneous			
Heading	War Diary 9th Bn Royal Sussex Regt		
War Diary	Taintegnies	01/02/1919	28/02/1919
War Diary	Taintignies Belgium	01/03/1919	31/03/1919
War Diary	Creplaine France	01/04/1919	31/05/1919

73RD BRIGADE
24TH DIVISION

FRANCE

9TH BATTALION

ROYAL SUSSEX REGT.

~~JAN - MAY 1919~~

1915 AUG — 1919 MAY

73rd Inf.Bde.
24th Div.

Battn. disembarked
Havre from England
1.9.15.

WAR
DIARY

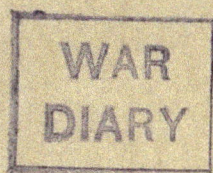

9th BATTN. THE ROYAL SUSSEX REGIMENT.

AUGUST AND SEPTEMBER

(21.8.15 to 30.9.15)

1 9 1 5

Instructions regarding War Diaries and Intelligence Summaries are contained in F. S. Regs., Part II. and the Staff Manual respectively. Title pages will be prepared in manuscript.

WAR DIARY
or
INTELLIGENCE SUMMARY.
(Erase heading not required.)

Place	Date	Hour	Summary of Events and Information	Remarks and references to Appendices
Woking	21/8/15		During the week following the 21st August 1915 the Regiment was ordered to proceed over-seas. On Aug 31st the Regiment left Woking for Southampton in three parties and embarked on the S.S. "La Marguerite" disembarking at Havre on the morning of the 1st September 1915 and marching to Camp No 5 Havre. After remaining for 24 hours the Regiment entrained at Havre during the afternoon of the 2nd inst	
	do		and detrained at Marenquel on the morning of the 3rd inst, marching to the billeting area assigned to the Battalion at Embrey and Rimboval arriving at the latter places at 4.0 pm and 4.30 pm respectively. The weather was very bad and it rained in torrents	
Embrey & Rimboval France	3/9/15		the whole day. The leather equipment stood the wet weather very badly and does not appear to be very durable	J.H.L.
	4/9/15		Still very wet. Every effort was made to increase the comfort of the billets of which were mostly in barns and outhouses, the day being occupied in inspection of rifles, iron rations, feet etc, digging of latrines and other necessary duties.	J.H.L.
	5/9/15		Being Sunday Church Services were held at Rimboval and Embrey and the day being fine clothes blankets etc were able to be dried.	J.H.L.
	6/9/15		(Monday) Was again fine and the Battalion settled down to a fixed programme of work for the week, comprising trench digging musketry, taking trenches by compass at night, bomb throwing route marching etc. In the afternoon at 12.0 pm the Officers of	

8353 Wt. W2544/1454 700,000 5/15 D. D. & L. A.D.S.S./Forms/C. 2118.

Instructions regarding War Diaries and Intelligence Summaries are contained in F. S. Regs., Part II. and the Staff Manual respectively. Title pages will be prepared in manuscript.

or

INTELLIGENCE SUMMARY.

(Erase heading not required.)

Place	Date	Hour	Summary of Events and Information	Remarks and references to Appendices
			the Regiment met the Corps Commander (Lieut Gen Haking commanding the 11th Corps) at Headquarters 73rd Brigade. Gen[l] Haking congratulated them on their arrival in France and expressed his pleasure at meeting them.	
	7/9/15		(Tuesday) Again fine and the Battalion carried out the programme of gen[eral] syllabus. Nothing further of interest to record.	
	8/9/15		(Wed) Fine weather again today and still in billets at Rimboval and Embry. Sites were arranged for ranges at Rimboval and Embry for A & B Companies and C & D Companies respectively. Special courses of bomb throwing and machine gun fitting arranged. The following Officers were ordered for a 24 hour tour of the trenches and left Brigade Head Quarters today at 9.30 am:- Major Langdon, Capt. McIvor and Capt. Holloway. Special pockets were issued for carrying smoke helmets.	
	9/9/15		(Thur) Weather very hot. Progress made on both ranges and special courses. Nothing of importance to record.	
	10/9/15		(Fri) Fine weather and very warm. Special courses carried out and ball cartridge at rate of 100 rounds per N.C.O. and man allowed. Special rifle course with ball ammunition commenced. A key	

Instructions regarding War Diaries and Intelligence Summaries are contained in F. S. Regs., Part II. and the Staff Manual respectively. Title pages will be prepared in manuscript.

or

INTELLIGENCE SUMMARY.

(*Erase heading not required.*)

Place	Date	Hour	Summary of Events and Information	Remarks and references to Appendices
			on range at Rimboval and 6-bay on range at Embry. 2nd Lieut Armytage appointed Reserve Machine Gun Officer in place of 2nd Lieut Kirkpatrick. Revolver practice carried out at Rimboval by all Officers. The C.O. and all Officers also + N.C.O's by battery (?) attended a demonstration at Divisional Head Quarters at Royon at 10.30 am. A lecture was given first on the effects of gas. All ranks were then ordered to put on their smoke helmets and were passed through a trench into which gas was being driven. The helmets proved their complete efficiency. JHL	
	11/9/15		(Sat) Fine weather and very hot. The Battalion attended Divisional manoeuvres and formed up at the rendezvous at 8.0 am facing N.W. on the north of the Embry - Rimboval road. An assault was carried out by the 72nd Brigade which was ordered to attack Petit Mesnil ~~and~~ the 73rd Brigade being in reserve. The 7th Northants and 12th Fusiliers were ordered up in support and at 11.30 am the 13th Middlesex and 9th Royal Sussex were ordered to support in the direction of Henneville. JHL The operation ceased at 1.30 pm and the Battalion marched back to billets. Troops paraded without packs.	

*353 Wt. W2544/1454 700,000 5/15 D. D. & L. A.D.S.S./Forms/C. 2118.

Instructions regarding War Diaries and Intelligence Summaries are contained in F. S. Regs., Part II. and the Staff Manual respectively. Title pages will be prepared in manuscript.

or

INTELLIGENCE SUMMARY.

(Erase heading not required.)

Place	Date	Hour	Summary of Events and Information	Remarks and references to Appendices
			in shirt sleeves and wore skeleton marching order with rifles and ammunition. All machine gunners, bombers, transport, signallers and other specialists paraded with the Battalion. 1st line Transport was taken. JHS	
	12/9/15		(Sunday) Fine and very hot. Church of England services held at Rimbovel and Embry by the Chaplain. Non-Conformist service at Embry & Roman Catholic service at Church Rimboval. After Church Service recruits of "A" & "B" Companies fired on the Rimboval range and the recruits of "C" & "D" Companies on the range at Embry. Nothing further to record. JHS	
	13/9/15		(Monday) Fine and hot. All Companies continued to carry out the rifle course with ball ammunition on their respective ranges. Cpl Reed Guards Brigade Instructor in bombing commenced a course of instruction in bombing at 9 am this morning. 2nd Lieut Stewart & 2nd Lieut Hangland visited the Grenade School at St. Omer for a short course of inst. then leaving Rimboval at 4.30 am. JHS	
	14/9/15		(Tuesday) Wet. Divisional exercise at Bourbers les Hesmond. The Battalion fell in at 7.30 am and marched to the place of	

#353 Wt. W2544/1454 700,000 5/15 D. D. & L. A.D.S.S./Forms/C. 2118.

Instructions regarding War Diaries and Intelligence Summaries are contained in F. S. Regs., Part II. and the Staff Manual respectively. Title pages will be prepared in manuscript.

or

INTELLIGENCE SUMMARY.

(Erase heading not required.)

Place	Date	Hour	Summary of Events and Information	Remarks and references to Appendices
			rendezvous in rear of the 12th Royal Fusiliers arriving at 9.15 am. Owing to the inclement weather the operations were postponed and the Battalion marched back to billets. Lieut Heneage, Grenadier Guards delivered a lecture at the Headquarters of the 12th Royal Fusiliers at Embry at which the Bombing Officer and Bombing N.C.O's were present. At 5.30 pm he gave another lecture at Brigade Head Quarters at Torcy at which the C.O., 2nd in Command and Adjutant were present. A reading and writing room for N.C.O's and men was opened for the first time by the Chaplain.	JHS
	15/9/15		(Wed) Fine. Companies carried out Musketry course as arranged on ranges at Rimboval and Embry. All machine gunners, bombers, signallers, snipers and other specialists underwent special instruction. Transport practised daily. Lieut Godwin and 2nd Lieut Armitage, Machine Gun Officers left for a tour of 24 hours in the trenches and were attached to the Canadian Division. Nothing further to record	JHS
	16/9/15		(Thurs) Fine. Musketry was again carried out (bombing, sniping, consolidating trenches by night, wood fighting). Nothing further to record	

Instructions regarding War Diaries and Intelligence Summaries are contained in F. S. Regs., Part II. and the Staff Manual respectively. Title pages will be prepared in manuscript.

or

INTELLIGENCE SUMMARY.

(*Erase heading not required.*)

Place	Date	Hour	Summary of Events and Information	Remarks and references to Appendices
Rimboval & Embrey	17/9/15		Friday Fine. The days programme was identical with that of yesterday & there is nothing of interest to report.	JLeS
	18/9/15		Saturday Fine. Musketry was again carried out on both ranges, together with special courses for bombers & snipers. 2nd Lieut Stewart, two N.C.O's & 6 men were detailed to attend a course at the Divisional Grenade School at QUILEN and left at 3.0 o'clock. A lecture was given by Col. Stewart to the Officers at Royal Fusiliers Head Quarters at Embrey. Nothing further of interest transpired.	JLeS
	19/9/15		Sunday Fine. Church Parades were carried out. The Battalion was thoroughly practised in "embussing" and "debussing" at Embrey, special attention being paid to the best method of allotting men fully armed & equipped to busses & getting them on and off in a rapid and orderly manner. Average time taken for loading 35 seconds.	JLeS
	20/9/15		Monday Fine. Route march to Hucqueliers (?). 1st Line Transport exercised with the Battalion. It was with deep regret that news was received that 2nd Lieut Stewart had been killed by the explosion of a bomb at the school at QUILEN. He was a very promising & gallant Officer and his death will be a great loss to the Regiment. Orders were received in the course of the afternoon that the Battalion would move from billets the following day and preparations were made for the move.	

8353 Wt. W2544/1454 700,000 5/15 D. D. & L. A.D.S.S./Forms/C. 2118.

Instructions regarding War Diaries and Intelligence Summaries are contained in F. S. Regs., Part II. and the Staff Manual respectively. Title pages will be prepared in manuscript.

or

INTELLIGENCE SUMMARY.

(Erase heading not required.)

Place	Date	Hour	Summary of Events and Information	Remarks and references to Appendices
Rimboval & EMBREY	21/9/15		Tuesday Fine. The Battalion marched from billets at 6.15 pm joining up with the Brigade at CREQUY & marched to LAIRES arriving there at 1.0 am the following morning.	[illegible]
LAIRES	22/9/15		Wednesday Fine. The Battalion left LAIRES at 7.30 pm marching into billets at BUSNES arriving at 2.30 am the following morning. It was a very trying march a great part of the way being over pavé and the Battalion behaved excellently.	[illegible]
LAIRES	23/9/15		Thursday Wet. The Battalion changed billets remaining in the same area.	
BEUVRY	24/9/15		Friday Fine. The Battalion marched into billets at BEUVRY arriving there at about 2.0 a.m. on the morning of 25th	[illegible]
IN THE TRENCHES	25/9/15		Saturday Fine. Orders were received at 10 am for the Battalion to march and the Regiment proceeded to SAILLY LES BOURSES. On arrival there the Brigadier was informed that it had been transferred to the 9th Division and was ordered to proceed via VERMELLES to the trenches, arriving there at 12.30 pm. An attack had been carried out by the Highland Brigade and at about 3.0 pm in the afternoon the Regiment was ordered to take cover in the support trenches near K1 where it remained until 9.30 pm when a Staff Officer came with the Brigade Major and ordered the Battalion to advance with the Fusiliers on FOSSE 8. This was carried out in column of Companies with 50 paces interval	

2353 Wt. W2544/1454 700,000 5/15 D. D. & L. A.D.S.S./Forms/C. 2118.

Instructions regarding War Diaries and Intelligence Summaries are contained in F. S. Regs., Part II. and the Staff Manual respectively. Title pages will be prepared in manuscript.

or

INTELLIGENCE SUMMARY.

(Erase heading not required.)

Place	Date	Hour	Summary of Events and Information	Remarks and references to Appendices
NTHE TRENCHES			The Battalion arrived at the FOSSE at about 11.30 pm and formed up while the guiding officer and the Adjutant Capt. Stokes went forward round the EAST side of the FOSSE to reconnoitre and to further guide the Regiment. The guiding Officer & Capt. Stokes returned about 12.30 am, A. Co then started round the EAST side of the FOSSE to occupy trenches there. Meanwhile Brig Gen'l Oswald came up and directed the remaining 3 Companies right over the FOSSE to occupy stated positions on the left of A Company. The order of the Companies was then from the left B, D, C and A. The Battalion Head Quarters was established just in rear of the East end of the FOSSE. Major Porter proceeded with B D & C Companies. Both machine guns under Lt. Godwin were with A Company. Several attacks were made by the enemy during the night of 25th Sept '15 and the morning of the 26th, the enemy snipers & bombers being particularly active. Orders were received that the FOSSE was to be held at all costs and notwithstanding the fact that the men were without food or water the position was held until the evening of 27th when orders were received that the Brigade was being relieved by the 85th Brigade. During the whole of the period of occupation of the FOSSE the Regiment was subjected to incessant artillery & machine gun fire and notwithstanding the losses sustained the Battalion behaved with the utmost gallantry.	

Instructions regarding War Diaries and Intelligence Summaries are contained in F. S. Regs., Part II. and the Staff Manual respectively. Title pages will be prepared in manuscript.

~~WAR DIARY~~
or
INTELLIGENCE SUMMARY.
(Erase heading not required.)

Place	Date	Hour	Summary of Events and Information	Remarks and references to Appendices
			It is regretted that before being launched into such a desperate action steps had not been taken to accustom the men to war conditions.	
	27/9/15		At about 5.0 am at dawn on the 27th the enemy made an assault on the left of A Co on Cabaret No 3. Notwithstanding rifle & machine gun fire a good number of the enemy got into Cabaret No 3 from which they opened enfilade fire down the trench occupied by A & B Companies. The position of A Company then became untenable and they were obliged to retire to the original support trench of the [illegible] Germans. The lack of bombs was a great handicap and L/Cpl Stokes succeeded in securing 70 which were passed up to A Company. Both machine guns were blown up in action but whilst they were serviceable the machine gunners worked them with good effect.	JMS
	28/9/15		During the night of the 27th and the early morning of the 28th Sept the Battalion was withdrawn from the trenches to the bivouac at ~~[illegible]~~ SAILLY LES BOURSES. At 10 am on 28/9/15 a roll was called and the following were found to be missing, killed and wounded:- Major W.R. Pooler, Major A.R.M. Woodlaw, Capt F.J. Godman, Capt A.R. McIvor, Capt J.G. Clarke, Capt B.H. Holloway	JMS

Instructions regarding War Diaries and Intelligence Summaries are contained in F. S. Regs., Part II. and the Staff Manual respectively. Title pages will be prepared in manuscript.

WAR DIARY
or
INTELLIGENCE SUMMARY.
(Erase heading not required.)

Army Form C. 2118.

Place	Date	Hour	Summary of Events and Information	Remarks and references to Appendices
			Capt H. Bury, Lt G. M. Shackil, Lt L. W. Kennelly, Lt A. A. Clowe, Lt H. R. Helderton, Lt F. G. Pelford, Lt F. R. Bring, 2nd Lieut D. W. Armitage, 2nd Lieut H. B. Pennington, 2nd Lieut D. Langlands, 2nd Lieut J. R. Kirkpatrick, 2nd Lieut J. S. Borrodaile, Lieut N. S. Whitton (RAMC) and 362 Other Ranks.	
CAILLY LES BOURSES	29/9/15		Wednesday Wet. At 8.30 pm the Battalion marched in very bad weather to the NOEURY LES MINES Station entraining for BERGUETTE and marching to billets at village of NORRENTS FONTES arriving there at 2.30 am.	JRS
NORRENTES FONTES	30/9/15		Thursday Fine. The Battalion rested in billets at NORRENTES FONTES. One officer (2nd Lieut Rogerson) and 23 men rejoining the Battalion from the trenches.	JRS

24th Division

121/7517

73/24

9th Royal Sussex
Vol 2

Oct 15

2.I.
12 sheets

Instructions regarding War Diaries and Intelligence Summaries are contained in F. S. Regs., Part II. and the Staff Manual respectively. Title pages will be prepared in manuscript.

WAR DIARY
or
INTELLIGENCE SUMMARY.
(Erase heading not required.)

Army Form C. 2118.

October 1915 — 9/Royal Sussex.

Place	Date	Hour	Summary of Events and Information	Remarks and references to Appendices
NORRENTES-FONTES	1/10/15		Friday Fine. The Battalion again rested in billets	
	2/10/15		Saturday Fine. The Battalion left the billets at 11.45 am marched to BERGUETTE Railw. Station entraining for GODEWAER-SVELDE and marching from there to billets at HERTZEELE arriving at 8.15 pm.	

8353 Wt. W2544/1454 700,000 5/15 D. D. & L. A.D.S.S./Forms/C. 2118.

T2134. Wt. W708—776. 500000. 4/15. Sir J. C. & S.

Instructions regarding War Diaries and Intelligence Summaries are contained in F. S. Regs., Part II. and the Staff Manual respectively. Title pages will be prepared in manuscript.

WAR DIARY
or
INTELLIGENCE SUMMARY.
(Erase heading not required.)

Army Form C. 2118.

9th Royal Sussex Reg

Place	Date	Hour	Summary of Events and Information	Remarks and references to Appendices
HERZEELE	3/10/15		Sunday. Wet. In billets at HERZEELE. Church Parades was held. Efforts were made to re-equip the Battalion. Nothing further to record.	JHL
	4/10/15		Monday. Fine. Still in billets at HERZEELE. Parades under Company Commanders. Inspection of rifles & equipment.	JHL
	5/10/15		Tuesday. Fine. In billets at HERZEELE. Men exercised in fire control & fire discipline. Machine gun & bombing sections underwent instruction.	JHL
PROVEN	6/10/15		Wednesday. Wet & cold. The Battalion left the trench [?] & marched via HOUTKERQUE into billets at PROVEN arriving at 4 o pm. 6 Officers & 400 O.R. proceeded by motor bus for a period of 48 hours in the trenches near YPRES. 4 Officers from 7th Northants Regiment were attached for duty.	JHL
	7/10/15		Thursday. Fine. In billets at PROVEN. Special classes were held for machine gunners & bombers. Draft of 20 O.R. were received from 10th Battn Royal Sussex Reg together with the following officers:- 2nd Lieut A L H O'Beirne, G. L. de Wolf, A F L Beverly	JHL

2353 Wt. W2544/1454 700,000 5/15 D. D. & L. A.D.S.S./Forms/C. 2118.

Instructions regarding War Diaries and Intelligence Summaries are contained in F. S. Regs., Part II. and the Staff Manual respectively. Title pages will be prepared in manuscript.

WAR DIARY
or
INTELLIGENCE SUMMARY.
(*Erase heading not required.*)

Army Form C. 2118.

9th Royal Sussex Reg

Place	Date	Hour	Summary of Events and Information	Remarks and references to Appendices
PROVEN	8/10/15		Friday Fine. Still in billets at PROVEN. 2 Officers + 50 O.R. passed through course of instruction in hand grenades. The trench party returned at 12 o midnight. Two casualties were reported during period of occupation of trenches. - 3536 Pte A. Sandall killed, 2558 Pte H. Grainger slightly wounded	J.H.S.
do	9/10/15		Saturday Fine. In billets at PROVEN. Complete inspection of the Battalion in Arms, Ammunition, clothing, equipment, feet etc. Special instruction classes in bombing and machine gun. Nothing further to report	J.H.S.
do	10/10/15		Sunday Fine. Church parades for all denominations at PROVEN. Battalion route march at 2.0 pm	J.H.S.
	11/10/15		Monday Fine. Battalion marched from PROVEN at 9.30 am to Camp C at ROSENHILL near RENINGHELST and took over Camp arriving at 3.0 pm. Nothing further to report.	J.H.S.

8353 Wt. W2544/1454 700,000 5/15 D. D. & L. A.D.S.S./Forms/C. 2118.

Army Form C. 2118.

WAR DIARY
or
INTELLIGENCE SUMMARY.
(Erase heading not required.)

Instructions regarding War Diaries and Intelligence Summaries are contained in F. S. Regs., Part II. and the Staff Manual respectively. Title pages will be prepared in manuscript.

9th Royal Sussex Reg

Place	Date	Hour	Summary of Events and Information	Remarks and references to Appendices
ROSENHILL	12/10/15		Tuesday Fine In Camp All Companies practised in fitting trenches. Special instruction to machine gunners bombers & signallers and representatives of Companies in use of periscope	
	13/10/15		Wednesday Fine Still in Camp @ ROSENHILL Brigade Route march. In the afternoon all Companies in fire discipline & fire direction. Special courses for bombers signallers machine gunners & range finders. O.C. Companies and four N.C.O's per company went to trenches occupied by Duke of Cornwall's Light Infantry viz O24 O25, O26 for the purpose of inspecting trenches to be taken over by their various Companies. C.O., 2nd in Command & Adjutant made a tour of the trenches and made arrangements with the O.C. the Duke of Cornwall's Light Infantry for the relief	

Instructions regarding War Diaries and Intelligence Summaries are contained in F. S. Regs., Part II. and the Staff Manual respectively. Title pages will be prepared in manuscript.

Army Form C. 2118.

WAR DIARY
or
INTELLIGENCE SUMMARY.
(Erase heading not required.)

9th Royal Sussex Reg

Place	Date	Hour	Summary of Events and Information	Remarks and references to Appendices
TRENCHES	14/10/15		Thursday Fine. Battalion left Camp at 4.0 pm and proceeded via DICKEBUSCH to the relief of trenches which were taken over from the DUKE OF CORNWALL'S LIGHT INFANTRY and the relief completed at 9.40 pm. D Company took over O 24 C Company took over O 25 and O 26 with two platoons of B Co in support. A and B Companies less two platoons of B Co being in support at BATTn Headquarters at CANAL BANK KINGSWAY	JHd
do	15th to 19/10/15		Eight officers joined the BATTn today from the 10th BATTn. Friday to Tuesday } Fine. The Battalion held these trenches during this period the enemy being particularly quiet, the parapets & parados of all trenches being in a bad condition, considerable work was carried out, an average of about 2000 sand bags being placed in position each 24 hours. Enemy's artillery active at intervals but were promptly silenced by the Batteries in support particularly the BELGIAN Battery which did effective work. The rebuilding of dugouts	JHd

2353 Wt. W2544/1454 700,000 5/15 D. D. & L. A.D.S.S./Forms/C. 2118.

Instructions regarding War Diaries and Intelligence Summaries are contained in F. S. Regs., Part II, and the Staff Manual respectively. Title pages will be prepared in manuscript.

WAR DIARY
or
INTELLIGENCE SUMMARY.
(Erase heading not required.)

Army Form C. 2118.

9th Royal Sussex Regt

Place	Date	Hour	Summary of Events and Information	Remarks and references to Appendices
			was also carried out at BATTn HEADQUARTERS. Casualties were extremely small, only 5 OTHER RANKS being wounded during period of occupation, none fatally.	[illegible]
	19/10/15		Tuesday Fine. The Battalion was relieved on the evening of the 19th by the 6th E SURREY REGT the relief being completed by 8.30 pm and marched by companies to C CAMP, ROSENHILL the last company arriving at 1.0 am on the morning of 20th	[illegible]
ROSENHILL	20/10/15		Wednesday Fine. In camp at ROSENHILL. A thorough inspection of rifles ammunition clothing equipment etc was held. In the afternoon half the Battalion marched to the BATHS at RENINGHELST where each man had a hot bath and a change of underclothing. Nothing further to report.	[illegible]
	21/10/15		Thursday Fine. Still in camp at ROSENHILL. Inspection of the BATTn by the Commanding Officer. The remaining	

Instructions regarding War Diaries and Intelligence Summaries are contained in F. S. Regs., Part II. and the Staff Manual respectively. Title pages will be prepared in manuscript.

WAR DIARY
or
INTELLIGENCE SUMMARY.
(Erase heading not required.)

Army Form C. 2118.

9th Royal Sussex Regt

Place	Date	Hour	Summary of Events and Information	Remarks and references to Appendices
			half of the BATTN marching to the BATHS at RENINGHELST Special instruction given to Machine gunners bombers & signallers & nothing further to report	
ROSENHILL	22/10/16		Fine. In camp at ROSENHILL. Battalion carried out a route march in morning and fire discipline and fire control in the afternoon. Nothing of importance to record	JHL
do	23/10/16		Saturday fine. In camp at ROSENHILL. Special instruction given to Bombers Snipers Signallers and all other specialists daily. Battalion found a working party of 10 officers and 300 other Ranks for the trenches. Nothing further to record	JHL
do	24/10/16		Sunday Wet. Church Parades for all denominations was held in the morning. Nothing further to report	

8353 Wt. W2544/1454 700,000 5/15 D. D. & L. A.D.S.S./Forms/C. 2118.

Instructions regarding War Diaries and Intelligence Summaries are contained in F. S. Regs., Part II. and the Staff Manual respectively. Title pages will be prepared in manuscript.

WAR DIARY
or
INTELLIGENCE SUMMARY.
(Erase heading not required.)

Army Form C. 2118.

9th Royal Sussex Reg

Place	Date	Hour	Summary of Events and Information	Remarks and references to Appendices
ROSENHILL	25/10/15		Monday Wet. In camp at ROSENHILL. Rifle inspection parades and usual routine. Instruction of all specialists. Work on hut construction.	[illegible]
do	26/10/15		Tuesday Fine. Still in camp at ROSENHILL. Company Commanders & Platoon Commanders visited the line of trenches to be taken over from the 1st Bn LEINSTER REGT, and remained in trenches. Inspection of all arms, equipment, ammunition etc prior to leaving for the trenches.	[illegible]
do	27/10/15		Wednesday Wet. Marched into trenches and took over from 1st Bn LEINSTER REGT and were disposed as follows: A Co on right, B Co on the left, ~~C~~ with D Co less two platoons in the centre. C Co in support with remaining two platoons of D Co	[illegible]

Instructions regarding War Diaries and Intelligence Summaries are contained in F. S. Regs., Part II. and the Staff Manual respectively. Title pages will be prepared in manuscript.

WAR DIARY
or
INTELLIGENCE SUMMARY.
(Erase heading not required.)

Army Form C. 2118.

9th Royal Sussex Reg

Place	Date	Hour	Summary of Events and Information	Remarks and references to Appendices
			the relief being completed at 9.0 p.m. Situation normal.	
IN THE TRENCHES	28/10/15		Thursday Wet. Great difficulty with drainage. Parapets & parados falling into trenches. All available men working to rebuild with sand bags. Situation normal. Slight shelling at intervals during the 24 hours.	
do	29/10/15		Friday Wet. Trenches in a worse condition than ever. Small river running near supports rising rapidly. Attempts being made to relieve pressure of water. 5000 sand bags placed in position on parapets & parados of front line trenches. Communication trench in very bad state. Two men killed on this date. One by a sniper & one by a stray bullet. Situation normal.	

8353 Wt. W2544/1454 700,000 5/15 D. D. & L. A.D.S.S./Forms/C. 2118.

Instructions regarding War Diaries and Intelligence Summaries are contained in F. S. Regs., Part II. and the Staff Manual respectively. Title pages will be prepared in manuscript.

WAR DIARY
or
INTELLIGENCE SUMMARY.
(Erase heading not required.)

Army Form C. 2118.

9th Royal Sussex Reg

Place	Date	Hour	Summary of Events and Information	Remarks and references to Appendices
IN THE TRENCHES	30/10/15		Saturday Fine. Work proceeded with rapidly on parapets & parados also on communication trench. Men thoroughly exhausted as they were working for whole of time repairing damage caused by rain. Enemy very quiet during this period.	JHL
do	31/10/15		Sunday Wet. Great difficulty again with drains and parapets. No revetting ever having been done in the trenches these fall in without any warning and entail a never ceasing vigilance. ~~D~~ Support dug-outs all fallen in and therefore there was no shelter for the men. Enemy shelled supports at various times during the 24 hours.	JHL

2353 Wt. W2544/1454 700,000 5/15 D. D. & L. A.D.S.S./Forms/C. 2118.

24th Division

Q

9th Royal Sussex
Vol: 3

121
7693

Nov 15

Instructions regarding War Diaries and Intelligence Summaries are contained in F. S. Regs., Part II. and the Staff Manual respectively. Title pages will be prepared in manuscript.

WAR DIARY
or
INTELLIGENCE SUMMARY.
(Erase heading not required.)

9th Bn Royal Sussex Regt

Army Form C. 2118.

Place	Date	Hour	Summary of Events and Information	Remarks and references to Appendices
IN THE TRENCHES	1/11/15		Monday Wet. Still in trenches. Situation normal with exception of slight shelling of support trench. Enemy snipers active. Nothing further to record	JHS
do	2/11/15		Tuesday Wet. Situation normal. Great difficulty again experienced with drainage etc. Parapets & parados giving a great deal of trouble as they were continually falling in. Relieved at 8.30 pm by 2nd LEINSTER Reg and marched back via DICKEBUSCH to REST CAMP at ROSENHILL arriving there at 10.30 pm. 2nd Lt C.D.L. HILL and 2nd Lt G.R.A. DEACON joined from Cadet School	JHS
ROSENHILL	3/11/15		Wednesday Fine. In Camp at ROSENHILL. Usual Camp routine carried out	JHS
do	4/11/15		Thursday Fine. In Camp at ROSENHILL. 7.0 am Roll call & physical drill. 10.30 am Battalion Parade in skeleton marching order for inspection by Commanding Officer. Inspection of all drafts who have joined the Regiment since the action at LOOS. Nothing further to report	JHS

2353 Wt. W2544/1454 700,000 5/15 D. D. & L. A.D.S.S./Forms/C. 2118.

Instructions regarding War Diaries and Intelligence Summaries are contained in F. S. Regs., Part II. and the Staff Manual respectively. Title pages will be prepared in manuscript.

WAR DIARY
or
INTELLIGENCE SUMMARY.
(Erase heading not required.)

Army Form C. 2118.

Place	Date	Hour	Summary of Events and Information	Remarks and references to Appendices
ROSENHILL	5/11/15		Friday Fine Usual parades, including rifle and ammunition inspection. 3129 L/cc Sgt DENNET W.C. awarded the Distinguished Conduct Medal	
do	6/11/15		Saturday Fine Battalion paraded at 2.45 pm and proceeded to trenches to relieve 2nd LEINSTER REG. & took over trenches P_1, P_2, P_3, P_4, P_{4b} including S_8 Q_3 in support. 21st CANADIANS on our right and 1st MIDDLESEX on our left. Relief completed at 8.0 pm	
IN THE TRENCHES	7/11/15		Sunday Fine Quiet day in trenches. Our snipers active which did not provoke any retaliation. Nothing of interest to record.	
do	8/11/15		Monday Wet Enemy's artillery active about 11.0 am and 3.0 pm shelling support trench. retaliation given by our artillery which silenced them. Work done on drainage etc and repair of parapets	
do	9/11/15		2nd Lt R.J.M. ELIAS joined and 40 O.R. Tuesday Wet Considerable difficulty with parapets and parados. 18th CANADIANS relieved 21st CANADIANS on our right. Enemy quiet. Nothing further to report	

Instructions regarding War Diaries and Intelligence Summaries are contained in F. S. Regs., Part II. and the Staff Manual respectively. Title pages will be prepared in manuscript.

WAR DIARY
or
INTELLIGENCE SUMMARY.
(Erase heading not required.)

Army Form C. 2118.

Place	Date	Hour	Summary of Events and Information	Remarks and references to Appendices
IN THE TRENCHES	10/11/15		Wednesday Fine Considerable activity among our aeroplanes. Sniping active on both sides. Enemy's artillery fired at intervals during the afternoon until silenced by our guns. Great difficulty in support trenches on account of water. Nothing further to report	JCL
do	11/11/15		Thursday Fine Progress made with work in trenches, parapets & parados rebuilt. CANADIANS and ourselves at work rebuilding communication trench which had fallen in in places. Enemy quiet.	JCL
do	12/11/15		Friday Fine Relieved in trenches by 8th ROYAL WEST KENT REGT. Relief not complete until a very late hour. Battalion marched back to camp at ROSENHILL via DICKEBUSCH arriving in camp at 2.30 am	JCL
ROSENHILL	13/11/15		Saturday Wet In camp at ROSENHILL. Usual parades & inspections & specially the condition of men's feet. Nothing further to report	JCL

2353 Wt. W2544/1454 700,000 5/15 D. D. & L. A.D.S.S./Forms/C. 2118.

Instructions regarding War Diaries and Intelligence Summaries are contained in F. S. Regs., Part II. and the Staff Manual respectively. Title pages will be prepared in manuscript.

WAR DIARY
or
INTELLIGENCE SUMMARY.
(Erase heading not required.)

Army Form C. 2118.

Place	Date	Hour	Summary of Events and Information	Remarks and references to Appendices
ROSENHILL	14/4/15		Sunday Wet In camp at ROSENHILL. Church parade at YMCA hut at RENINGHELST Rifle & ammunition inspection. 2nd Lt C.E. GOAD joined	
do	15/4/15		Monday Fine. Battalion ordered into BRIGADE RESERVE at DICKEBUSCH & took up billets there. "B" COMPY proceeding into dug outs at SPOIL BANK; they incurred six casualties - all wounded - while marching in, being fired on by the enemy with shrapnel.	
DICKEBUSCH	16/4/15		Tuesday Fine In billets at DICKEBUSCH Battalion engaged in finding fatigues for work in trenches. Enemy shelled DICKEBUSCH with long range guns. Light & high explosive shells falling within a radius of 30 yards of the billets occupied by "C" Coy. no damage was done	
IN THE TRENCHES	17/4/15		Wednesday Wet Battalion marched to trenches and relieved 2nd LEINSTER REGt. relief being complete at 8 30 pm. 21st CANADIANS on our right & 1st MIDDLESEX on our left. Nothing further to record	

2353 Wt. W2544/1454 700,000 5/15 D. D. & L. A.D.S.S./Forms/C. 2118.

Instructions regarding War Diaries and Intelligence Summaries are contained in F. S. Regs., Part II. and the Staff Manual respectively. Title pages will be prepared in manuscript.

WAR DIARY
or
INTELLIGENCE SUMMARY.
(*Erase heading not required.*)

Army Form C. 2118.

Place	Date	Hour	Summary of Events and Information	Remarks and references to Appendices
IN THE TRENCHES	18/11/15		Thursday Wet. Quiet day in trenches. Pouring with rain all day. 13th MIDDLESEX on our left relieved by 7th NORTHANTS. Nothing further to report	
do	19/11/15		Friday Fine. Difficulty again experienced with drainage. All dugouts in firing line collapsed. Rebuilding of dugouts & parapets carried out. Enemy's artillery active during morning but were replied to by our guns and quickly silenced	
do	20/11/15		Saturday Fine (frost & fog) our artillery fired continuously during the day bombarding the enemy's positions in rear of firing line, enemy did not reply. Sniping on both sides active	
do	21/11/15		Sunday Very foggy, no rain. Quiet all along our sector. Good work done to parapets. Nothing of interest to report	
do	22/11/15		Monday Fine slightly foggy. Our artillery particularly active and snipers of both sides. Battn relieved by 1st ROYAL SCOTS FUSILIERS. Relief complete at 9.0 pm. Marched back to ROSENHILL camp arriving at 11.0 pm	

2353 Wt. W2544/1454 700,000 5/15 D. D. & L. A.D.S.S./Forms/C. 2118.

Instructions regarding War Diaries and Intelligence Summaries are contained in F. S. Regs., Part II. and the Staff Manual respectively. Title pages will be prepared in manuscript.

WAR DIARY
or
INTELLIGENCE SUMMARY.
(Erase heading not required.)

Army Form C. 2118.

Place	Date	Hour	Summary of Events and Information	Remarks and references to Appendices
ROSENHILL	23/11/15		Tuesday Wet. In camp at ROSENHILL. Inspection of rifles, ammunition feet clothing etc. Nothing of interest to report	[initials]
ON THE MARCH	24/11/15		Wednesday Wet. Battalion commenced march into DIVISIONAL rest and left camp at 4.0 pm marching with units of 72nd BRIGADE to STEENVOORDE	[initials]
do	25/11/15		Thursday Fine. Battalion paraded and marched to ARNEKE via CASSEL arriving ARNEKE 6.0 pm	[initials]
do	26/11/15		Friday Rain snow & hail. Battalion left ARNEKE at 9.00 am & arrived in Rest Area at 3.30 pm (HOULLE) 3 Companies in billets at MALTERY, one Company in farms adjoining. Billets good	[initials]
HOULLE	27/11/15		Saturday Fine. Battalion parade, inspection of arms, equipment & clothing, ammunition & kits. Nothing of interest to record.	[initials]

2353 Wt. W2544/1454 700,000 5/15 D. D. & L. A.D.S.S./Forms/C. 2118.

Instructions regarding War Diaries and Intelligence Summaries are contained in F. S. Regs., Part II. and the Staff Manual respectively. Title pages will be prepared in manuscript.

WAR DIARY
or
INTELLIGENCE SUMMARY.
(Erase heading not required.)

Army Form C. 2118.

Place	Date	Hour	Summary of Events and Information	Remarks and references to Appendices
HOULLE	28/11/15		Sunday Fine. Church of England parade at 10 a.m. Non conformists & Presbyterians at 11 a.m. Voluntary service for all denominations at 6 p.m. Celebration of Holy Communion at 7 a.m. First leave party left at 5 a.m. LT GODWIN appointed BDE M.G. 73rd BRIGADE with rank of Captain dated Nov 10th 1915	
HOULLE	29/11/15		Monday Wet. Close order drill was carried out by Companies. Sites for rifle range, machine gun range, bombing & bayonet courses chosen. All gas helmets handed in after inspection	
do	30/11/15		Tuesday Fine. Company & Platoon drill. Instruction in fire discipline, physical drill etc. Nothing of interest to report	

24th Div

9th Roy: Sussex

Vol: 4

December 1915

121
7910

E.M.3

H.I.
7 sheets

Instructions regarding War Diaries and Intelligence Summaries are contained in F. S. Regs., Part II. and the Staff Manual respectively. Title pages will be prepared in manuscript.

WAR DIARY
or
~~INTELLIGENCE SUMMARY.~~
(*Erase heading not required.*)

9th Royal Sussex Regt.

Army Form C. 2118.

Place	Date	Hour	Summary of Events and Information	Remarks and references to Appendices
HOULLE	1/12/15		Wednesday Showery. There was a BRIGADE Route march through MOULLE WATTEN and back to EPERLECQUES. Draft of 120 O.R. arrived on 30/11/15	WCN
do	2/12/15		Thursday. Fine. Training carried out by Companies according to programme submitted, as also under Specialist Officers.	WCN.
do	3/12/15		Friday. Wet. Training under Company Commanders and specialists as per programme submitted. The new draft was inspected by G.O.C. 24th Division. A Coy had use of range in the morning and B Coy in the afternoon. Lt Col. J.A.G. Rainsford proceeded to England on leave. Capt. N.C. NORTON appointed Adjutant in place of CAPT. STOKE appointed 2nd in command. MAJOR LANGDON took command of Battalion.	WCN
do	4/12/15		Saturday. Wet. Training under Coy. Commanders and specialists as per programme submitted. B Coy had use of range in the morning.	WCN
do	5/12/15		Sunday. Fine. 10% of companies attended Church Parade in the School Room HOULLE at 11.30 am. Non Conformists & Presbyterians at 11.0 am. Holy Communion at 7.30 am.	WCN
do	6/12/15		Monday. Showery. Training under Company Commanders & specialist Officers according to programme. B Coy had use of Range in the morning and C Coy in the afternoon. 40 All ranks started on a 3 day course with the R.E. 2nd Lt. C.H. Dudeney joined the Battalion.	WCN

Instructions regarding War Diaries and Intelligence Summaries are contained in F. S. Regs., Part II. and the Staff Manual respectively. Title pages will be prepared in manuscript.

WAR DIARY
or
~~INTELLIGENCE SUMMARY.~~
(Erase heading not required.)

Army Form C. 2118.

Place	Date	Hour	Summary of Events and Information	Remarks and references to Appendices
HOULLE	7/12/15		Tuesday. Showery. Training under Company Commanders & Specialist Officers according to programme. Nothing of interest to report.	WCN
do	8/12/15		Wednesday. Fine. Brigade route march. The route was HOULLE, MORINGHEM, INGLINGHEM, HOULLE. First line transport did not go.	WCN
do	9/12/15		Thursday. Wet. Training under Company Commanders as per programme. Capt. J. L. Stokes proceeded to England on leave from 8th to 15th inclusive. Vacancies for leave was considerably curtailed in order to give more vacancies to the regular Battalion of the Brigade.	WCN
do	10/12/15		Friday. Showery. Companies are trained by their Commanders in Company drill &c. 8 O.R. were returned to the base as medically unfit for service. vide DGMS 445/1/1 D/d 10/9/15. A divisional inter company Shooting Competition was inaugurated.	WCN.
do	11/12/15		Saturday. Wet. Brigade route march. C Company were not on parade as they were isolated on account of a case of measles. First line transport accompanied the Battalion. The Brigade marched past the G.O.C. Lt 2c Mr proceeded on leave to England from 11th to 18th inclusive.	WCN

2353 Wt. W2544/1454 700,000 5/15 D. D. & L. A.D.S.S./Forms/C. 2118.

Instructions regarding War Diaries and Intelligence Summaries are contained in F. S. Regs., Part II. and the Staff Manual respectively. Title pages will be prepared in manuscript.

WAR DIARY
or
INTELLIGENCE SUMMARY.
(Erase heading not required.)

Army Form C. 2118.

Place	Date	Hour	Summary of Events and Information	Remarks and references to Appendices
HOULLE	12/12/15		Sunday. Fine. 7 30 am Holy Communion in School room HOULLE. 11 30 am Church of England Service in the Courtyard of the Malterie. Non-conformists + Presbyterians at 11.0 am at the School room. Voluntary Service at 6 30 pm for all denominations at reading room HOULLE. 2nd Lieuts C.V. NEWTON and H. TREACHER joined the Battalion.	WCN
do	13/12/15		Monday Fine. There was a practice Brigade parade in anticipation of an inspection by ~~SIR JOH~~ Field Marshall SIR JOHN FRENCH. 2nd Lieuts R.A. BAZELEY and J.A. FLOWERS joined the Battalion.	WCN
do	14/12/15		Tuesday Fine. Training under Company Commanders + specialist officers. 2nd Lt. J.S. CASSELLS joined the Battalion.	WCN
do	15/12/15		Wednesday Fine. Brigade route march. Capt W.C. NORTON proceeded to England on leave from 15th to 22nd inclusive. The C.O. 3 Company Commanders and M.G.O. attended a lecture on machine guns at NORDAUSQUES.	WCN
do	16/12/15		Thursday Fine. Battalion paraded for a gas demonstration. Sgt E.R. SWANN proceeded to Cadet School BLENDECQUES on 15th as a candidate for a Commission.	WCN
do	17/12/15		Friday Fine. Training under Company Commanders and Specialist officers. Nothing further of interest to report.	WCN

Instructions regarding War Diaries and Intelligence Summaries are contained in F. S. Regs., Part II. and the Staff Manual respectively. Title pages will be prepared in manuscript.

WAR DIARY

or

~~INTELLIGENCE SUMMARY.~~

(Erase heading not required.)

Army Form C. 2118.

Place	Date	Hour	Summary of Events and Information	Remarks and references to Appendices
HOULLE	18/12/15		Saturday. Showery. A Brigade Transport Competition was inaugurated. This was held at 2.30 pm. The Battalion being third in the Brigade. 2nd LEINSTERS being first. Capt GODMAN and Capt BURY officially reported wounded and prisoners of war in GERMANY.	WCN
do	19/12/15		Sunday. Showery. 7.30 am Holy Communion in school room HOULLE. 9.0 am Church parade in Courtyard of MALTERIE. Non conformists & Presbyterians service at 11.0 am. Sgt HAWKINS proceeded to England on leave from 18th to 25th inclusive.	WCN
do	20/12/15		Monday. Fine. Battalion route march. 4 officers per company attended a lecture by LT. COL. SKINNER of 7th NORTHANTS on the campaign in S.W. AFRICA.	WCN
do	21/12/15		Tuesday. Fine. The Battalion held a practice attack on model trenches at the Quarries HOULLE. Draft 35 OR joined the Battalion.	WCN
do	22/12/15		Wednesday. Wet. Training under Company Commanders as per programme. Special order of the day by Field Marshall SIR JOHN FRENCH on relinquishing command of the British Army in FRANCE was issued.	WCN
do	23/12/15		Thursday. Showery. Battalion had a practice attack on model trenches. A thorough inspection of rifles was held and defective rifles were repaired by the Armourer Sergeant.	WCN

Instructions regarding War Diaries and Intelligence Summaries are contained in F. S. Regs., Part II. and the Staff Manual respectively. Title pages will be prepared in manuscript.

WAR DIARY
or
~~INTELLIGENCE SUMMARY.~~
(Erase heading not required.)

Army Form C. 2118.

Place	Date	Hour	Summary of Events and Information	Remarks and references to Appendices
HOULLE	24/12/15		Friday. Wet. Training under Company Commanders as per programme. There was a Sergeants dinner and concert held in the evening to which the C.O. 2nd in Command, ADJT & 4 O.C. Companies were invited. This proved a great Success.	WCN
do	25/12/15		Saturday. Showery. Christmas day 7.30 am Voluntary Holy Communion 11.30 am Church parade in the MALTERIE yard. 10.30 am Non-conformists Wesleyans & Presbyterians in the School room HOULLE. The Battalion appeared to thoroughly enjoy the arrangements made for their benefit.	WCN
do	26/12/15		Sunday. Wet. 7.30 am Voluntary Holy Communion. 9.30 am Church parade 10.30 am Non conformists Wesleyans & Presbyterians church parade.	WCN
do	27/12/15		Monday. Wet. Battalion had practice in the model trenches.	
do	28/12/15		Tuesday wet & windy. Training under Company Commanders as per programme. C Company had use of Range in the morning.	WCN WCN
do	29/12/15		Wednesday. Showery. Training in Company & extended order drill under Company Commanders as per programme. B.G.C presented the Military Cross ribbon to CAPT GODWIN and the D.C.M ribbon to SGT. DENNETT.	WCN
do	30/12/15		Thursday. Showery. Battalion practised open country manoeuvres. The sum of Fcs 1393 was collected in the Battalion for the Sussex Prisoners of War Fund.	WCN
do	31/12/15		Friday. Showery. Brigade inspection & Brigade Transport inspection by G.O.C. 24th Division. 2nd LT. V. DELAMHURST joined the Battalion.	WCN

2353 Wt. W2544/1454 700,000 5/15 D. D. & L. A.D.S.S./Forms/C. 2118.

73rd Brigade.
24th Division

9th BATTALION

ROYAL SUSSEX REGIMENT.

January 1 9 1 6.

M. M.

5 I.
9 sheets

9th Roy: Sussex
Vol: 5

13th July [illegible]

24

Army Form C. 2118.

Instructions regarding War Diaries and Intelligence Summaries are contained in F. S. Regs., Part II. and the Staff Manual respectively. Title pages will be prepared in manuscript.

WAR DIARY
or
~~INTELLIGENCE SUMMARY.~~
(Erase heading not required.)

9th Royal Sussex Regt.

Place	Date	Hour	Summary of Events and Information	Remarks and references to Appendices
HOULLE	1/1/16		Saturday. Wet. There was a Battalion parade on which the Commanding Officer read out two letters. One from G.O.C and one from Bishop of Manchester. 2nd LT. A.W. COLLINGBOURNE was appointed Transport Officer to date from 18/12/15, in place of 2nd LT. W.J.F. AUSTIN, posted to A Company for duty.	WCN.
do	2/1/16		Sunday. Wet. 7.30 am Voluntary Holy Communion. 9.30 am Church Parade. 11.0 am Non-Conformists Presbyterians & Wesleyans at School room HOULLE.	WCN.
do	3/1/16		Monday Fine. Battalion paraded at 9.0 am for practice on the model trenches at which the G.O.C and B.G.C were present. The G.S.O.1 17th Division gave a lecture at NORDAUSQUES on the new front to be held by 24th Division. The general impression given by him was that the line to which we were going was the worst bit of the worst section of the whole western front.	WCN.
do	4/1/16		Tuesday. Showery. Parade under Company Commanders & specialist Officers according to programme submitted. There was a short Battalion parade at 11.30 am on which the Commanding Officer gave a short address on the lecture of the previous day. Privates PEPPER and COTTRELL were tried by F.G.C.M.	WCN

Instructions regarding War Diaries and Intelligence Summaries are contained in F. S. Regs., Part II. and the Staff Manual respectively. Title pages will be prepared in manuscript.

WAR DIARY
or
~~INTELLIGENCE SUMMARY.~~
(*Erase heading not required.*)

Army Form C. 2118.

Place	Date	Hour	Summary of Events and Information	Remarks and references to Appendices
HOULLE	5/1/16		Wednesday. Showery. The Battalion paraded at 9.30 a.m. for a Brigade Route March. Nothing further of interest to report.	WCN.
do	6/1/16		Fine. Training was carried out under Company Commanders and Specialist Officers as per programme arranged. LT. E.R. DAVIES left to take up his duties on the Water Line Transport and was struck off the strength of the Battalion.	WCN.
do	7/1/16		Wet. The Battalion paraded at 9.50 a.m. less 1 platoon of A Company which left with the Transport at 7.15 a.m. and marched to ST. OMER. With the band in front the Battalion marched out from the rest billets to ST. OMER where the train was taken to QUINTIN. The Battalion detrained here and marched via POPERINGHE to camp C at G18a (Sheet 28) which was reached at 6.30 p.m.	WCN.
CAMP C.	8/1/16		Fine. The day was taken up by cleaning of rifles + equipment after the move from rest billets at HOULLE.	WCN.
do	9/1/16		Sunday. Fine. 9.30 am to 12.30 p.m. Voluntary Church Parades were held by companies each company provided 1 hut. As the Battalion was under 1 hours notice to move, no N.C.O. or man was allowed out of camp except under exceptional circumstances. Smoke helmets were now worn day and night.	WCN.

Instructions regarding War Diaries and Intelligence Summaries are contained in F. S. Regs., Part II. and the Staff Manual respectively. Title pages will be prepared in manuscript.

Army Form C. 2118.

WAR DIARY
or
~~INTELLIGENCE SUMMARY.~~
(Erase heading not required.)

Place	Date	Hour	Summary of Events and Information	Remarks and references to Appendices
CAMP. C	10/1/16		Monday. Showery. Parades were held under Company Commanders, and special attention was paid to the inspection of Rifles, Gas Helmets and feet. 2nd LT. W. J. F. AUSTIN was posted as 2nd in Command of A Company.	WCN.
do	11/1/16		Tuesday. Fine. The morning was given up to making improvements in the camp which was in a very muddy condition. There was no parade in the afternoon. 2nd LT. W. J. F. AUSTIN and 3 other ranks proceeded on leave to ENGLAND from 11th to 18th inst. inclusive. The practice of wearing the goggles on the hat which had become prevalent was ordered to be discontinued.	WCN.
do	12/1/16		Wednesday. Fine. Inspection of rifles, gas helmets &c by Companies and work on camp improvement in the morning. There was no parade in the afternoon. During the morning two TAUBES passed over the camp travelling N.W. towards POPERINGHE. Two bombs were dropped which fell about 200 yards from the camp on open ground. No damage was done.	WCN.
do	13/1/16		Thursday. Wet. Inspection of rifles equipment &c, especial attention being paid to feet and work on camp improvement was carried on. Specialists paraded for instruction under their officers. A F.G.C.M. was held at Battalion H.Q., at 10.0 a.m. 3798 PTE. FISHER G. "C" Company was tried. The C.O. machine gun officer and 1 officer per Company visited BELGIAN CHATEAU and inspected the camp which the Battalion was to take over later.	WCN

Instructions regarding War Diaries and Intelligence Summaries are contained in F. S. Regs., Part II. and the Staff Manual respectively. Title pages will be prepared in manuscript.

WAR DIARY
or
~~INTELLIGENCE SUMMARY.~~
(Erase heading not required.)

Army Form C. 2118.

Place	Date	Hour	Summary of Events and Information	Remarks and references to Appendices
CAMP C	14/1/16		Friday. Fine. The 5th LABOUR BATTALION's Baths at H 14 a 4.6. were allotted to the Battalion today. Only men who were going to the trenches bathed. The R.A. Band from England played for an hour at 3.0 p.m. on the camp parade ground, and was much appreciated. PTE. UPTON A. D Company was wounded whilst on a working party.	WCN
do	15/1/16		Saturday. Fine. The morning was spent in cleaning up huts and camp preparatory to moving. The Battalion less 50 men per company paraded at 2.30 pm and marched to BELGIAN CHATEAU which was reached about 6.0 p.m. No packs were carried by the men. 1 officer per company and the Grenadier officer left camp at 10.0 am for BELGIAN CHATEAU for the purpose of taking over stores &c. The following message was received from 24th Division:— G.O.C. much pleased at report received from C.R.E on work done by working party A. Company, 9th Royal Sussex Regt. The B.G.C. (73rd Brigade) is much gratified and congratulates all ranks of the company concerned on receiving such a good report.	WCN
BELGIAN CHATEAU	16/1/16		Sunday. Fine. The morning was spent in cleaning huts rifles equipment &c. One H.E. Shell dropped in the open fields in the vicinity of the camp, but no damage was done.	WCN
do	17/1/16		Monday. Showery. Feet rifle equipment inspections during the day. The Battalion found 300 men for fatigue at GORDON FARM.	WCN

8353 Wt. W2544/1454 700,000 5/15 D. D. & L. A.D.S.S./Forms/C. 2118.

Instructions regarding War Diaries and Intelligence Summaries are contained in F. S. Regs., Part II. and the Staff Manual respectively. Title pages will be prepared in manuscript.

WAR DIARY
or
~~INTELLIGENCE SUMMARY.~~
(Erase heading not required.)

Army Form C. 2118.

Place	Date	Hour	Summary of Events and Information	Remarks and references to Appendices
BELGIAN CHATEAU	18/1/16		Tuesday. Wet. Relieved the 13th MIDDLESEX in trenches B8 and C1. Headquarters were situated in ZOUAVE WOOD. B Company in the front line A company in support C company local reserve and D company in reserve.	WCN.
In the Trenches	19/1/16		Wednesday Fine. Work on improvements in the trenches was carried on as much as possible. In the morning starting about 8.30 am both enemy and our own artillery were very active. REGENT STREET seeming to receive special attention with H.E. and shrapnel from the enemy. The bombardment did not last more than an hour, only desultory firing taking place later. B Company had two O.R. wounded.	WCN.
do	20/1/16		Thursday Showery. A quiet day as concerned artillery. Enemy Snipers were busy + were replied to by our own snipers. In the evening A company relieved B company in the front line, who went into support. No casualties	WCN.
do	21/1/16		Friday Fine. A quiet day again. Snipers are most active at night, while the artillery works by day. C company had one man wounded	WCN.

2353 Wt. W2544/1454 700,000 5/15 D. D. & L. A.D.S.S./Forms/C. 2118.

Instructions regarding War Diaries and Intelligence Summaries are contained in F. S. Regs., Part II. and the Staff Manual respectively. Title pages will be prepared in manuscript.

WAR DIARY
or
~~INTELLIGENCE SUMMARY.~~
(Erase heading not required.)

Army Form C. 2118.

Place	Date	Hour	Summary of Events and Information	Remarks and references to Appendices
IN THE TRENCHES	22/1/16		Saturday. Fine. Relieved in the trenches by 13th MIDDLESEX. The Battalion marched back to BELGIAN CHATEAU by Companies, changing their gum boots at the ASYLUM on the way. At 10 pm our artillery in the vicinity of the CHATEAU was very active for ¼ of an hour. A Company had one sergeant wounded, and C Company one man.	WCN.
BELGIAN CHATEAU	23/1/16		Sunday. Fine. Cleaning up of rifles equipment &c after the turn in the trenches. Nothing of importance to report.	WCN.
do	24/1/16		Monday. Fine. Inspection of rifles gas helmets feet &c was carried out. The Battalion found a fatigue party of 400 OR for work in the trenches. LT. R J M LIAS was evacuated sick to hospital.	WCN.
do	25/1/16		Tuesday. Fine. Several enemy aeroplanes flew over the camp, evidently trying to locate the batteries in the vicinity. Our anti-aircraft guns were very active. Several of our aeroplanes went up and the enemy disappeared. A fatigue party of 500 OR was again found by the Battalion for work in the trenches.	WCN.
do	26/1/16		Wednesday. Fine. During the day the Battalion drew gum boots from the ASYLUM. Starting at 5.0 pm we relieved the 13th MIDDLESEX in the same trenches, B8 and C1. D Company in the front line, C Company in support, A Company in local reserve and B Company in reserve.	WCN.

Instructions regarding War Diaries and Intelligence Summaries are contained in F. S. Regs., Part II. and the Staff Manual respectively. Title pages will be prepared in manuscript.

WAR DIARY
or
~~INTELLIGENCE~~ SUMMARY.

(*Erase heading not required.*)

Army Form C. 2118.

Place	Date	Hour	Summary of Events and Information	Remarks and references to Appendices
IN THE TRENCHES	27/1/16		Thursday wet. Headquarters in ZOUAVE WOOD were shelled at 11.0 am with H E for ½ hour. Sniping and rifle fire being active as usual mostly at night. C Company had one O.R. wounded. 2nd LT FLOWERS was wounded in the arm in a bomb accident which might ~~Friday Fine.~~ have proved fatal but for the presence of mind of No. 3154 L/C T.E. HOARE, who picked up the bomb & threw it over the parapet.	WCN.
~~do~~	~~28/1/16~~			
do	28/1/16		Friday fine. A good deal of sniping took place and 2nd LT. R.A BAZELEY was killed. C Company lost one man killed and two wounded, one of whom died later. C Company relieved D Company in the front line, who went into support.	WCN.
do	29/1/16		Saturday fine. At 2.30 pm and 3.30 pm enemy artillery was very active for 10 minutes, many H.E. shells falling round headquarters and SANCTUARY WOOD. No casualties occurred at H.Q. A Company lost 1 man killed and C Company 1 man wounded.	WCN
do	30/1/16		Sunday fine. Battalion was relieved in the trenches by 12th FUSILIERS and marched by companies back to the ASYLUM where gum boots were changed and 2 cookers supplied tea and thence to CAMP F at H.19.6.	WCN
CAMP F	31/1/16		Monday fine. Cleaning of rifles equipment &c after the turn in the trenches. Nothing further of interest to report.	WCN

2353 Wt. W2544/1454 700,000 5/15 D. D. & L. A.D.S.S./Forms/C. 2118.

73rd Brigade.
24th Division

9th BATTALION

ROYAL SUSSEX REGIMENT.

February 1 9 1 6.

Confidential.

War Diary

of

9th Royal Sussex Regt.

from 1/2/16 to 29/2/16

W. C Norton
Capt. Adjt.
for O.C. 9th Royal Sussex Regt.

Instructions regarding War Diaries and Intelligence Summaries are contained in F. S. Regs., Part II. and the Staff Manual respectively. Title pages will be prepared in manuscript.

WAR DIARY
or
~~INTELLIGENCE SUMMARY.~~
(Erase heading not required.)

Army Form C. 2118.

Place	Date	Hour	Summary of Events and Information	Remarks and references to Appendices
AMP F.	1/2/16.		Fine. Companies proceeded with programme of work already submitted to the Brigade. Specialists working under their own arrangements. The G.O.C. 24th Division came round the camp, much admiring the drying room. We began on company's washing with fair success. Drying takes some time as the weather is not dry though fine. However washing and drying socks like this is better than relying on Divisional arrangements.	W.C.N.
	2/2/16.		Fine. We had the use of the Baths at POPERINGHE. The remainder of the day being taken up by company training and specialist training. The Battalion received a gift of numerous tins of Sausages and peppermints from the Sussex Soldiers Cigarette and Comforts fund through the Hon Sec Miss Adams of St Leonard's on Sea. This fund has also given to the regiment at various times as many as 66,000 Woodbine Cigarettes.	W.C.N.
	3/2/16.		Fine. The companies went on a routemarch except D Company who had the use of the baths at POPERINGHE. The Brigadier came round the camp. In the afternoon there was a regimental concert at the Recreation room of the Labour Battalion. The Colonel sang and the concert was a great success. It had to be cut rather short as the Labour Battalion wanted the use of the room.	W.C.N.

(B353) Wt. W2544/1454 700,000 5/15 D. D. & L. A.D.S.S./Forms/C. 2118.

Instructions regarding War Diaries and Intelligence Summaries are contained in F. S. Regs., Part II. and the Staff Manual respectively. Title pages will be prepared in manuscript.

WAR DIARY
or
~~INTELLIGENCE SUMMARY~~.
(Erase heading not required.)

Army Form C. 2118.

Place	Date	Hour	Summary of Events and Information	Remarks and references to Appendices
CAMP F	4/2/16.		Fine. Companies carried on with their programme of work. The Grenadiers drew 100 live Grenades and practised bomb-throwing. In the evening there was a fire in the camp opposite the quartermaster's stores of R.F.A. The R.F.A were afraid [of] catching fire and an outhouse burnt right out. So bright was it that the Germans might open fire on it but this did not happen.	WCN.
	5/2/16.		Fine. Companies continued their training except D Coy who were detailed to be responsible for the drainage of the camp and other work in it. At 10.45 pm the Battalion was ordered to Stand To ready to Move at an hours notice. This was not well done as several men did not have their iron rations nor waterbottles filled. The Transport situated about 2 miles away turned out very well and were round at the camp well under the hour. The Brigadier came round but did not stay long as he was not satisfied.	WCN.
	6/2/16.		Fine. Church of England Service was held at Labour Battalion Canteen; however only 400 men could be accomodated. Services for other denomination were held.	
	7/2/16.		Cloudy. Inspections of rifles ammunition etc were held by companies. A draft of 46 arrived a great many of whom were old Sussex men who had been wounded at Loos, and sick since then. At 10 pm the Battalion had to stand to. This was much better done. The Brigadier was very pleased. After the hour the Battalion was dismissed.	WCN

Instructions regarding War Diaries and Intelligence Summaries are contained in F. S. Regs., Part II. and the Staff Manual respectively. Title Pages will be prepared in manuscript.

WAR DIARY
or
~~INTELLIGENCE SUMMARY~~
(Erase heading not required.)

Army Form C. 2118

Place	Date	Hour	Summary of Events and Information	Remarks and references to Appendices
~~[illegible]~~ CAMP F	8/2/16		A & B Companies and Bombers went up to trenches. These were billeted in YPRES in cellars. As there was not room for the whole battalion C & D Coys were left behind at Camp F under Major Stokes. These two Companies had to find a working party. We relieved 8th Queens at 6.45pm.	WCN.
YPRES cellars	9/2/16		The Battalion had to find 250 men for working party. A & B Coys and Bombers were used all officers going too. No casualties.	WCN.
	10/2/16		The same working party had to be found. Aeroplanes were active. YPRES was shelled slightly but no damage done in our quarter.	WCN.
	11/2/16		C & D Coys and Machine Gunners came up from Camp F and rested for the day in the Cavalry Barracks. At 6.30pm the Battn marched to the trenches by companies to take over from 13th Middlesex. Relief complete about 10.30 pm. A & B Coys in firing line and support. C & D Coys in reserve trench and cellars on the Menin Road.	WCN.
TRenches.	12/2/16		Fine. A fairly quiet day, not much shelling. The C O went to advanced HQ to stop there for the remaining time in the Trenches. Major Stokes and Adjutant stopped at HQ on the Menin Road.	WCN.
	13/2/16		Fine. A very heavy bombardment took place lasting for 8½ hours. A great deal of damage was done to the front line trenches. There were about 30 Casualties. 2nd Lt Tisdall was killed while ~~trying~~ to digging a man out who had been buried alive by the shelling. A Company was relieved by D as they had had a very bad time.	WCN.

1875 Wt. W593/826 1,000,000 4/15 J.B.C. & A. A.D.S.S./Forms/C. 2118.

Instructions regarding War Diaries and Intelligence Summaries are contained in F. S. Regs., Part II. and the Staff Manual respectively. Title Pages will be prepared in manuscript.

WAR DIARY
or
INTELLIGENCE SUMMARY
(Erase heading not required.)

Army Form C. 2118

Place	Date	Hour	Summary of Events and Information	Remarks and references to Appendices
Trenches	14/2/16		Wet. A considerable amount of shelling took place all through	
			the day and at 5.45 pm, the enemy blew up two mines on	
			our front line. These were immediately seized by B and D Coys and	
			a German attack was repulsed. A platoon of D Company was	
			completely buried alive with 2nd Lt Hill. B Coy also suffered	
			heavily. The C.O showed remarkable gallantry and coolness and gave	
			3 cheers for the Germans when they attacked. The night was spent	
			in digging themselves in on the craters. 2nd Lt DeWolf was	
			killed, 2nd Lts Shaw and Good were wounded. Capt Ardy wounded at duty.	WCN
	15/2/16		Fine. A fairly quiet day and not much shelling. Were relieved	
			by 13th Middlesex. The Battalion went back to cellars in YPRES	
			Total Casualties 2 officers killed, 3 wounded, 134 O.R Casualties.	WCN
	16/2/16		Wet. Spent in resting. We did not have to find any working	WCN
			parties for which we were very grateful.	
	17/2/16		Fine. We had to find 200 men for working parties which we	
			found considerable difficulty in finding as an enormous amount	WCN
			of men went sick and were sent to hospital.	WCN
	18/2/16		Wet. Another working party had to be found.	
	19/2/16		Fine. We relieved the 13th Middlesex again in the same trenches. A & C	
			Coys were in firing line and support. Major Stoker went to advanced	WCN
			HQ. The C.O and Adjutant remained at HQ on Menin Rd.	

Instructions regarding War Diaries and Intelligence Summaries are contained in F. S. Regs., Part II. and the Staff Manual respectively. Title Pages will be prepared in manuscript.

WAR DIARY
or
INTELLIGENCE SUMMARY
(Erase heading not required.)

Army Form C. 2118.

Place	Date	Hour	Summary of Events and Information	Remarks and references to Appendices
Trenches	20/2/16.		Fine. A fairly quiet day. Nothing unusual occurred on our front.	WCW.
	21/2/16		Fine. A quiet day.	WCW.
	22/2/16.		Wet. A quiet day. B Company relieved A Coy. Some snow fell.	WCW.
	23/2/16		Wet. A quiet day. Lt Lion was killed in the early morning. A hard frost.	WCW.
	24/2/16		Fine. A quiet day. Relieved by the 1st K.S.L.I. Relief was suspended but took place at 12 midnight. We went by train to POPERINGHE and were billeted there. Very comfortable though cold.	WCW.
POPERINGHE	25/2/16.		Fine. The day was taken up by resting and reequipping. Companies reorganised in the afternoon.	WCW.
	26/2/16		Fine. Companies continued their inspections.	WCW.
	27/2/16		Fine. There were no Church Services.	WCW.
	28/2/16		Fine. The G.O.C addressed the Battalion congratulating them on the splendid work they had done, during the last tour in the trenches.	WCW.
	29/2/16.		Wet with snow. Company training according to programme already submitted to the Brigade.	WCW.

73rd Brigade.
24th Division.

<u>9th BATTALION</u>

<u>ROYAL SUSSEX REGIMENT.</u>

<u>March 1 9 1 6</u>

9th R Sussex

Vol 7

24

Confidential

War Diary of

9th Battalion Royal Sussex Regiment

From March 1st 1916 to March 31st 1916

L.A.

7. I.
3 sheet

Army Form C. 2118

Instructions regarding War Diaries and Intelligence Summaries are contained in F. S. Regs., Part II. and the Staff Manual respectively. Title Pages will be prepared in manuscript.

WAR DIARY
or
INTELLIGENCE SUMMARY
(Erase heading not required.)

Place	Date	Hour	Summary of Events and Information	Remarks and references to Appendices
POPERINGHE	1/3/16		Companies carried on training	J. T. L.
"	2/3/16		" "	J. T. L.
"	3/3/16		Battalion left POPERINGHE for the trenches, going by train at 8.30 P.M. We relieved 8th Queens. Relief complete very late. We occupied BELGIAN CHATEAU. Quiet night.	J. T. L.
BELGIAN CHATEAU	4/3/16		Quite quiet all day. A great deal of snow fell. There was some shelling on & round about the dug-outs but no damage done. H.Q. was moved from huts to Farm House since we were there last. We had to find 200 men for working parties.	J. T. L.
"	5/3/16		Snow fell. There was some shelling. We had to find working parties again	J. T. L.
"	6/3/16		More shelling than usual, 4 dug-outs were blown in. Only one or two casualties	J. T. L.
"	7/3/16		Not much shelling. We moved up to relieve 13th Middlesex, leaving at 7.0 P.M. Relief complete at 11.45 P.M.	J. T. L.
TRENCHES	8/3/16		Quite quiet all day	J. T. L.
	9/3/16		" " " "	J. T. L.
	10/3/16		" " " "	J. T. L.
	11/3/16		There was a very heavy strafe lasting from about 2.0 to 4.0 p.m. on our left and on our front. Little damage was done except to a small portion of our front line. The shelling went on intermittently for some time. We were relieved by 13th Middlesex and went back to BELGIAN CHATEAU.	J. T. L.
BELGIAN CHATEAU	12/3/16		Very quiet, we found working parties	J. T. L.
"	13/3/16		Quiet, we found working parties	J. T. L.
"	14/3/16		Rather more shelling than usual	J. T. L.
"	15/3/16		We were relieved by 8th Queens at BELGIAN CHATEAU and went back to CAMP E. We had to find working parties.	J. T. L.
CAMP E.	16/3/16		Inspections were held.	J. T. L.

1875 Wt. W593/826 1,000,000 4/15 J.B.C. & A. A.D.S.S./Forms/C. 2118.

Instructions regarding War Diaries and Intelligence Summaries are contained in F. S. Regs., Part II. and the Staff Manual respectively. Title Pages will be prepared in manuscript.

WAR DIARY
or
INTELLIGENCE SUMMARY
(Erase heading not required.)

Army Form C. 2118

Place	Date	Hour	Summary of Events and Information	Remarks and references to Appendices
CAMP E	17/3/16		We had the baths all day	J.T.L.
"	18/3/16		Companies had route marches.	J.T.L.
"	19/3/16		Moved by road to METEREN where we relieved a Canadian Battalion in billets. We marched through RENNINGHELST, WESTOUTRE and SHAEXKEN	J.T.L.
METEREN	20/3/16		Company training and route marches. Battalion rather soft after having not much marching.	J.T.L.
"	21/3/16		Company training.	J.T.L.
"	22/3/16		Company training.	J.T.L.
"	23/3/16		Moved up to RED LODGE where we relieved 13th Canadian Battalion. This was Brigade Reserve. Dug-outs and huts.	J.T.L.
	24/3/16		Moved up to trenches 135-140 inclusive relieving 14th Canadian Battalion. Relief complete 9.0 P.M. Very quiet night.	J.T.L.
TRENCHES	25/3/16		Some shelling on our left where the 7th Northants held the line	
"	26/3/16		Some shelling on our front in early morning. We had 10 casualties 2nd Lt Vidler [?] joined for duty	J.T.L. J.T.L.
"	27/3/16		Quiet all day 2nd Lt Prince joined for duty.	
"	28/3/16		Quiet except for some shelling in the afternoon on Reserve Company	J.T.L.
"	29/3/16		Very quiet day. Weather fine	J.T.L.
"	30/3/16		Very quiet day Weather fine	J.T.L.
"	31/3/16		Very quiet. We were relieved by 13th Middlesex Battalion. Relief complete by 10.0 P.M. The Battalion marched back to KORTE PYP.	J.T.L. J.T.L.

1875 Wt. W593/826 1,000,000 4/15 J.B.C. & A. A.D.S.S./Forms/C. 2118.

73rd Brigade.
24th Division.

9th BATTALION

ROYAL SUSSEX REGIMENT.

April 1 9 1 6

XXIV

9 Sussex
Vol. 8

Confidential.

War Diary.

of

9th (Service) Battn. ~~of~~ Royal Sussex Regt.

From April 1st 1916 To April 30 1916

John F. P. Langdon Lt. Col.
Comm: 9th Royal Sussex Regt.

4. 5. 16.

M.D.

8 I
4 sheets

Instructions regarding War Diaries and Intelligence Summaries are contained in F. S. Regs., Part II. and the Staff Manual respectively. Title Pages will be prepared in manuscript.

Army Form C. 2118

WAR DIARY
or
INTELLIGENCE SUMMARY
(Erase heading not required.)

Place	Date	Hour	Summary of Events and Information	Remarks and references to Appendices
KORTEPYP.	1/4/16.		The day was occupied in kit inspections etc and generally cleaning up after the tour in the trenches. Nothing of interest to Report. Draft of 21 men arrived.	WCN.
	2/4/16.		Companies proceeded with the programme of work as sent in to Brigade Office. Baths were allotted to the Battalion at Neuve Eglise.	WCN.
	3/4/16		Companies proceeded with their training. A small manoeuvering scheme was carried out. G.O.C Division supervised the operations. The Battalion had to find 200 men for working parties on burying cable. Neuve Eglise was shelled.	WCN
	4/4/16.		Programme of work proceeded with. A regimental concert was held in a Y.M.C.A. hut close to the camp which proved a great success. Some working parties. The Commanding Officer proceeded on leave.	WCN.
	5/4/16		Programme of work proceeded with. Nothing further of interest to report.	WCN.
TRENCHES	6/4/16		Battalion relieved 13th Middlesex in the line. All quiet.	WCN.
	7/4/16		Quiet day.	WCN.
	8/4/16		Quiet day	WCN.
	9/4/16.		The Breastworks were shelled. All men except two wounded left without further casualties. Otherwise quiet.	WCN.
	10/4/16.		Quiet. Minnenwerfer fired on Fabion Farm but no material damage done.	WCN.
	11/4/16		Quiet.	WCN.
RED LODGE	12/4/16		Relieved by 13th Middlesex. Battalion moved back to Red Lodge in Brigade Reserve.	WCN.
	13/4/16.		Working parties were employed by day on making slits in the side of the hill as protection in case of being shelled. Working parties at night had to be found for work up the line.	WCN.

1875 Wt. W593/826 1,000,000 4/15 J.B.C. & A. A.D.S.S./Forms/C. 2118.

Army Form C. 2118

Instructions regarding War Diaries and Intelligence Summaries are contained in F. S. Regs., Part II. and the Staff Manual respectively. Title Pages will be prepared in manuscript.

WAR DIARY

~~or~~

~~INTELLIGENCE SUMMARY~~

(Erase heading not required.)

Place	Date	Hour	Summary of Events and Information	Remarks and references to Appendices
RED LODGE	14/4/16		Work carried on as the day before. Working parties by day and night. The Commanding Officer returned from leave.	WCN.
	15/4/16.		All leave stopped and men supposed to be recalled. This was not done in our case as our men were returning on 15th the day all had to be back. It was afterwards discovered that this order only referred to troops in England and our leave should never have been stopped. Capt McNair V.C who was to have gone to England to be decorated could not go.	WCN.
	16/4/16.		Work carried on as the day before.	WCN.
	17/4/16		Work as before.	WCN.
TRENCHES.	18/4/16.		Relieved 13th Middlesex Regt. Early relief, complete by 10.15 pm. All quiet.	WCN.
	19/4/16.		All quiet.	WCN.
	20/4/16.		Trench 140 received a little attention, 4 parts of the trench being breached. No great damage done however.	WCN. WCN
	21/4/16		Quiet day.	WCN
	22/4/16		Quiet day.	
	23/4/16		Quiet day. Relieved by 13th Middlesex Regt. All quiet	WCN.
KORTEPYP	24/4/16		Day spent in kit inspection and cleaning up generally.	WCN
	25/4/16		Programme of work as submitted to Brigade Office proceeded with.	WCN.
	26/4/16.			
	27/4/16		Programme of work proceeded with. ~~[illegible]~~	WCN.

Instructions regarding War Diaries and Intelligence Summaries are contained in F. S. Regs., Part II. and the Staff Manual respectively. Title Pages will be prepared in manuscript.

WAR DIARY
or
INTELLIGENCE SUMMARY
(Erase heading not required.)

Army Form C. 2118

Place	Date	Hour	Summary of Events and Information	Remarks and references to Appendices
KORTEPYP.	28/4/16	1.30am	Gas alarm was spread all over the country. Battalion turned out and stood to. After waiting some little time, battalion stood down and turned in again. It was a false rumour spread by division on our right Training proceeded with during the day. A game of football was played in	WCN.
	29		the afternoon Officers versus the Rest. Officers won 3-2. A small operation was carried out with Lewis guns and scouts with one	
	29/4/16		Company. B.G.C. watched the operations. At 12.45 am Gas alarm again went. Battalion stood to and at 2.30 am	WCN.
	30/4/16		had the Order to Move. Battalion moved into Divisional Reserve. At KORTEPYP we had about 20 minutes' warning for. As the Battalion had plenty of time to put on gas helmets, no serious effects were felt. We arrived at Assembly point of Divisional reserve at 4.30 am. After being there for some time, we marched back again to Camp. The Germans attacked our left Brigade of Division but were driven back.	
TRENCHES.			Relieved 13th Middlesex Regt in front line. They had had about 70 casualties through gas and shell fire.	WCN.

1875 Wt. W593/826 1,000,000 4/15 J.B.C. & A. A.D.S.S./Forms/C. 2118.

73rd Brigade.
24th Division.

9th BATTALION

ROYAL SUSSEX REGIMENT.

May 1916

9 Sussex

XXIV Vol. 9

CONFIDENTIAL

WAR DIARY

OF

9th ROYAL SUSSEX REGT

From May 1st 1916 To May 31st 1916

In the Field.
1.6.16.

John F.P. Langdon
Lt Col.
Comdg 9th Royal Sussex Regt.

9. I
3 sheets

Instructions regarding War Diaries and Intelligence Summaries are contained in F. S. Regs., Part II. and the Staff Manual respectively. Title Pages will be prepared in manuscript.

WAR DIARY
~~or~~
~~INTELLIGENCE SUMMARY~~
(Erase heading not required.)

Army Form C. 2118

Place	Date	Hour	Summary of Events and Information	Remarks and references to Appendices
TRENCHES	1/5/16.		All was quiet except some shelling on STINKING FARM.	WCN
	2/5/16		Quiet. Machine guns busy at night causing annoyance to Ration Parties etc.	WCN
	3/5/16.		Quiet.	WCN
	4/5/16		Quiet.	WCN
	5/5/16		Quiet.	WCN
	6/5/16		Quiet Relieved by 13th Middlesex Regt. Battalion moved to RED LODGE.	WCN
RED LODGE	7/5/16		Working parties.	WCN
	8/5/16.		Enemy shelled top of Hill 63 but did not get down to us. Working Parties.	WCN
	9/5/16		Quiet. Working Parties.	WCN
	10/5/16		Quiet. "	WCN
	11/5/16		Quiet "	WCN
TRENCHES	12/5/16		Relieved 13th Middlesex Regt in the trenches.	WCN
	13/5/16		Quiet.	WCN
	14/5/16		STINKING FARM shelled again. A few casualties through a day. not being knocked in.	WCN
	15/5/16		Quiet	WCN
	16/5/16		Another day. not knocked out at STINKING FARM. One platoon was moved to FLETCHERS FIELD	WCN
	17/5/16		Quiet.	WCN

1875 Wt. W593/826 1,000,000 4/15 J.B.C. & A. A.D.S.S./Forms/C. 2118.

Army Form C. 2118

WAR DIARY

or

~~INTELLIGENCE SUMMARY~~

(Erase heading not required.)

Instructions regarding War Diaries and Intelligence Summaries are contained in F. S. Regs., Part II. and the Staff Manual respectively. Title Pages will be prepared in manuscript.

Place	Date	Hour	Summary of Events and Information	Remarks and references to Appendices
KORTEPYP.	18/5/16		Quiet. Relieved by 13th Middlesex. Battalion moved to KORTEPYP.	WCN
	19/5/16		Working parties by night.	WCN.
			Tour in Trenches changed from 6 days to 8.	WCN.
	20/5/16		Beautiful weather. Working parties by night.	WCN.
	21/5/16		Nothing to report	WCN.
	22/5/16		" "	WCN.
	23/5/16			
	24/5/16		Holiday granted by G.O.C. Two games of football in the morning. A v B (won) Officers (won) v Sergeants. Afternoon was devoted to Sports. The G.O.C. and Brigadier both came and had tea afterwards. In the evening there was a concert which was unfortunately stopped by rain.	WCN.
	25/5/16		Large working parties.	WCN.
TRENCHES	26/5/16		Relieved 13th Middlesex in the trenches.	WCN.
	27/5/16		Cpl Pink + Drummer Gardner awarded Military Medal.	WCN.
	28/5/16		Quiet. PLOS DOUCE FARM shelled every half hour in the evening.	WCN
	29/5/16		Quiet	WCN.
	30/5/16		Quiet.	WCN
	31/5/16		Quiet.	WCN.

73rd Brigade.
24th Division

9th BATTALION.

ROYAL SUSSEX REGIMENT.

June 1 9 1 6.

9th Sussex

Vol 10

June

XXIV

CONFIDENTIEL.

WAR DIARY

OF

9th Bn ROYAL SUSSEX REGT.

From 1.6.16. To 30.6.16

John Langdon Lt Col

Comdg 9th Bn Royal Sussex Regt.

2.7.16

10.F

4 sheets

Instructions regarding War Diaries and Intelligence Summaries are contained in F. S. Regs., Part II. and the Staff Manual respectively. Title Pages will be prepared in manuscript.

WAR DIARY
or
INTELLIGENCE SUMMARY
(Erase heading not required.)

Army Form C. 2118

Place	Date	Hour	Summary of Events and Information	Remarks and references to Appendices
TRENCHES.	1.6.16.		Quiet.	WCN.
	2.6.16		Quiet.	WCN.
	3.6.16		Relieved by 13th Bn Middlesex Regt. Battalion moved back to Brigade Reserve at RED LODGE.	WCN.
RED LODGE.	4.6.16.		Quiet. We had to find large working Parties.	WCN
	5.6.16.		Quiet. ——— ditto. ———	WCN.
	6.6.16.		Quiet.	WCN.
	7.6.16.		Quiet.	WCN.
	8.6.16.		Quiet.	WCN.
	9.6.16.		Quiet. Capt F.E. CERELY struck off the strength. Sick to England.	WCN.
	10.6.16		Quiet.	WCN.
	11.6.16		Quiet. Relieved 13th Bn Middlesex Regt in the Trenches.	WCN.
TRENCHES.	12.6.16.		Quiet. Draft of 43 O.R arrived.	WCN.
	13.6.16		Quiet.	WCN.
	14.6.16		Quiet	WCN.
	15.6.16		Quiet.	WCN.

1875 Wt. W593/826 1,000,000 4/15 J.B.C. & A. A.D.S.S./Forms/C. 2118.

Army Form C. 2118

Instructions regarding War Diaries and Intelligence Summaries are contained in F. S. Regs., Part II. and the Staff Manual respectively. Title Pages will be prepared in manuscript.

WAR DIARY
or
~~INTELLIGENCE SUMMARY~~
(Erase heading not required.)

Place	Date	Hour	Summary of Events and Information	Remarks and references to Appendices
TRENCHES.	16.6.16		Quiet by day. Germans made a gas attack at about 12.30 am on 17th.	WCN.
	17.6.16		There was no infantry attack. Gas lasted about 40 minutes in 3 continuous waves. Men wore their gas helmets for 1 hour and twenty minutes. A heavy bombardment went on during the gas also heavy Machine gun fire. A large number of men were gassed. Relieved by the 26th Bn 7th Australian Brigade. Battalion moved back in motor lorries to ST JANS CAPPEL. ~~Capt~~ ROGERSON, 2nd Lt BANHAM, 2nd Lt BERRY slightly gassed.	WCN.
ST. JANS CAPPEL.	18.6.16.		Quiet.	WCN.
	19.6.16		Quiet. Draft of 42 O.R arrived.	WCN.
	20.6.16.		Quiet. Battalion moved from ST JANS CAPPEL to WAKEFIELD HUTS near LOCRE. Divisional Reserve.	WCN.
WAKEFIELD HUTS.	21.6.16.		Capt ROGERSON returned from Hospital. Draft of 13 O.R arrived.	WCN.
	22.6.16.		200 All ranks from 9th Bn Royal Sussex Regt, 7th Bn Northamptonshire Regt and 400 from 72nd Bde inspected by G.O.C 2nd Army.	WCN.
	23.6.16.		Quiet.	WCN.
	24.6.16.		Quiet.	WCN.
	25.6.16		Church Parade at Y.M.CA. hut LOCRE.	WCN.
	26.6.16		2nd LT FOSTER posted to C Coy.	WCN.

1875 Wt. W593/826 1,000,000 4/15 J.B.C. & A. A.D.S.S./Forms/C. 2118.

Instructions regarding War Diaries and Intelligence Summaries are contained in F. S. Regs., Part II. and the Staff Manual respectively. Title Pages will be prepared in manuscript.

WAR DIARY
or
~~INTELLIGENCE SUMMARY~~
(Erase heading not required.)

Army Form C. 2118

Place	Date	Hour	Summary of Events and Information	Remarks and references to Appendices
	27.6.16.		Relieved 13th Bn Middlesex Regt in Trenches.	WCN.
TRENCHES.	28.6.16.		Several raids took place on our right. Enemy retaliated heavily all along our line, with Trenchmortars, minenwerfers & shelling.	WCN.
	29.6.16.		Enemy very restless and bombarded our line 3 times during the night.	WCN.
	30.6.16.		Quiet.	WCN.

1875 Wt. W593/826 1,000,000 4/15 J.B.C. & A. A.D.S.S./Forms/C. 2118.

73rd Inf.Bde.
24th Div.

WAR DIARY

~~7th~~ 9th BATTN. THE ROYAL SUSSEX REGIMENT.

J U L Y

1 9 1 6

CONFIDENTIAL.

13

24 July

Vol 11

WAR DIARY

9th Bn ROYAL SUSSEX REGT

FROM. 1. 7. 16. TO. 31. 7. 16.

John Langdon
Lt. Col
Comdg 9th Bn Royal Sussex Regt.

31.7.16.

11 I
3 sheets

Instructions regarding War Diaries and Intelligence Summaries are contained in F. S. Regs., Part II. and the Staff Manual respectively. Title Pages will be prepared in manuscript.

WAR DIARY
or
INTELLIGENCE SUMMARY
(Erase heading not required.)

Army Form C. 2118

Place	Date	Hour	Summary of Events and Information	Remarks and references to Appendices
TRENCHES.	1/7/16.		Quiet day in the Trenches. Battalion relieved by 13th Middlesex Regt. Battalion moved to WAKEFIELD Huts as Divisional Reserve.	WCN
WAKEFIELD HUTS. KEMMEL SHELTERS	2/7/16. to 6/7/16.		Working Parties in the morning and evening. Nothing of importance occurred. Major Stokes returned off leave. On 6th Battalion moved to KEMMEL SHELTERS, half the Battalion being in Bivouacs and half in huts.	WCN.
	7/7/16.		Nothing of importance to report. Capt McIvor went to Hospital Sick.	WCN.
DRANOUTRE.	8/7/16.		Battalion moved to DRANOUTRE in barns and huts, relieving the 12th Royal Fusiliers.	WCN
	9/7/16.		Nothing of importance occurred.	WCN
	10/7/16		— — —	WCN
TRENCHES.	11/7/16		Battalion moved to Trenches C4 - D4. HQ at ST QUENTIN'S CABARET. 3 Companies in front line, 1 in Support. Relieved 12th Royal Fusiliers.	WCN
	12/7/16 to 14/7/16		Quiet. Nothing to report. 2nd Lt. G.W. PRINCE wounded.	WCN.
	15/7/16 16/7/16		Quiet. Gas Cylinders were installed on Battalion Front.	WCN
	17/7/16		Quiet. Gas was going to be let off but cancelled.	WCN.

1875 Wt. W593/826 1,000,000 4/15 J.B.C. & A. A.D.S.S./Forms/C. 2118.

Instructions regarding War Diaries and Intelligence Summaries are contained in F. S. Regs., Part II. and the Staff Manual respectively. Title Pages will be prepared in manuscript.

WAR DIARY
or
~~INTELLIGENCE SUMMARY~~
(Erase heading not required.)

Army Form C. 2118

Place	Date	Hour	Summary of Events and Information	Remarks and references to Appendices
TRENCHES.	18/7/16.		Quiet. No for relieved	WCN.
	19/7/16.		Quiet. No for relieved	WCN.
	20/7/16		Quiet Moved to Fletre Relieved by 7th D.C.L.I. Battalion in Billets over a scattered area. Taken from BULFORD Camp to FLETRE by Lorries and Busses.	WCN.
FLETRE (COQ de PAILLE)	21/7/16 22/7/16 23/7/16		Battalion Training Commenced	WCN.
	24/7/16.		Battalion marched to GODEWAERSVELDE to entrain. Train left at 8.30 pm.	WCN.
MONTAGNE.	25/7/16.		Train arrived at SALEUX about 6 miles S.S.E of AMIENS at about 5.30 am. Battalion marched to MONTAGNE where they were billeted. Billets Good and fairly central.	WCN.
	26/7/16. to 30/7/16.		Battalion Training carried on Open order fighting, wood fighting practises etc. Special attention paid to Bayonet Training.	WCN.
	31/7/16		Battalion marched away from MONTAGNE.	

1875 Wt. W593/826 1,000,000 4/15 J.B.C. & A. A.D.S.S./Forms/C. 2118.

73rd Brigade.
24th Division

9th BATTALION.

ROYAL SUSSEX REGIMENT.

August 1 9 1 6.

73/24

Vol 12

Instructions regarding War Diaries and Intelligence Summaries are contained in F. S. Regs., Part II. and the Staff Manual respectively. Title pages will be prepared in manuscript.

WAR DIARY
or
INTELLIGENCE SUMMARY.
(Erase heading not required.)

Army Form C. 2118.

Place	Date	Hour	Summary of Events and Information	Remarks and references to Appendices
Confidential				
			War Diary of 9th Royal Sussex Regt For month of August 1916	12 I 6 sheets

8353 Wt. W2544/1454 700,000 5/15 D. D. & L. A.D.S.S./Forms/C. 2118.

Instructions regarding War Diaries and Intelligence Summaries are contained in F. S. Regs., Part II. and the Staff Manual respectively. Title Pages will be prepared in manuscript.

WAR DIARY

or

~~INTELLIGENCE SUMMARY~~

(Erase heading not required.)

Army Form C. 2118

Place	Date	Hour	Summary of Events and Information	Remarks and references to Appendices
Corbie-sur-Somme	1-8-16		Battalion at Bayonet Fighting. A & B Coys in morning. C & D Coys in afternoon	HCC
Sailly-le-Sec	2-8-16		Battalion fell in 4-45 am. marched 4-55 am for Sailly-le-Sec, reaching here about 7-30 am. Rested until 5.30 pm then marched to Happy Valley arriving about 9 pm	HCC
Happy Valley	3-8-16		Battalion in training. In Bivouac	
" "	4-8-16		" " " Two O.R accidentally wounded by hand grenade while visiting original German lines. One afterwards died of his wounds (Pte F. B. Fuller)	HCC
" "	5-8-16		Battalion in training. ~~Particularly~~ attention paid to advancing behind barrage	HCC
" "	6-8-16		Battalion in training. Large working party for work in forward area found, 7/8/16. This party shelled by enemy. 6 OR wounded.	HCC
" "	7-8-16			H.C.C
The Citadel	8-8-16		Moved from Happy Valley forward to near the Citadel in Corps Reserve.	
" "	9-8-16		Battalion in training. Attacking trenches	HCC
" "	10-8-16		In afternoon A & B Coys moved to Montauban defences. 2/Lt W.S. Mansell transferred to R.F.C & struck off.	H.C.C
The Craters	11-8-16		C and D Coys moved to the "Craters" just through Carnoy. In Bivouac. Capt Horton to hosp.	H.C.C.
" "	12-8-16		~~Salvage~~ Work in forward area.	H.C.C
" "	13-8-16		The Craters. A few heavy shells dropped near. Cpl Wynne killed, & another OR wd. 2/Lt Treacher to hospital.	H.C.C
" "	14-8-16		2/Lt Hawkridge to hospital ~~Salvage~~ Work in forward area. Moved back to Mansell Copse	H.C.C
~~Mansell Copse~~ The Citadel	15-8-16		Battalion training in attack.	H.C.C
" "	16-8-16		" " " " Moved at 5-30 pm to relieve 9th E. Surrey's in trenches before Guillemont. Stopped at Carnoy & sent back to Mansell Copse arriving about midnight.	H.C.C HCC

1875 Wt. W593/826 1,000,000 4/15 J.B.C. & A. A.D.S.S./Forms/C. 2118.

Instructions regarding War Diaries and Intelligence Summaries are contained in F. S. Regs., Part II. and the Staff Manual respectively. Title Pages will be prepared in manuscript.

WAR DIARY
or
INTELLIGENCE SUMMARY
(Erase heading not required.)

Army Form C. 2118

Place	Date	Hour	Summary of Events and Information	Remarks and references to Appendices
~~[illegible]~~ Citadel	17·8·16	8·30pm	Moved to Briqueterie preparatory to attack.	H.C.C
			Attack on Guillemont	
	18·8·16.		Officers in Action. Lt-Col. J. F. P. Langdon (C.O.) Lt. H.C. Coleman (Adj.)	
			A Coy. Capt. McIvor, Lt Shackel, 2/Lt. E Best.	
Attack on			B " " McNair V.C. 2/Lt. C M Prince, 2/Lt K.E Bright.	
Outskirts			C " " Rogerson, 2/Lt B Kidler, 2/Lt G. C. Mole.	
of			D " " Austin, Lt. H. L'Estrange, Lt Hemming	
Guillemont			Intelligence Officer. 2/Lt H Treacher, 2/Lt P. J Surridge.	
			M. G. O. 2/Lt Dudeney. Bombing Officer 2/Lt L. E. Baker	
			Sig. Officer 2/Lt Attwood, Medical Off. Lt. A A E Newth RAMC,	
			Plan of Attack 7th Northamptonshire Regt. to attack at 2.45 pm & take German Front Line & the Quarries. 9th Royal Sussex Regt. to attack at 5 am on the 19th & advance half way through fortified village of GUILLEMONT.	
			Moved to Support Trenches in front of Guillemont; A + B Coys at 12 noon C+D Coys at 3 pm.	
	18·8·16		At 2.45 pm. 7 Northants attacked successfully. A + B Coys moved to front line Trenches. 7th Northants lost heavily in hand to hand fighting & at 4-30 pm were reinforced by part of A & B Coys. Capt A. R. McIvor & Capt. E. A. McNair V.C. were wounded in trying to find a route across No Mans Land.	H.C.C

1875 Wt. W593/826 1,000,000 4/15 J.B.C. & A. A.D.S.S./Forms/C. 2118.

Instructions regarding War Diaries and Intelligence Summaries are contained in F. S. Regs., Part II. and the Staff Manual respectively. Title Pages will be prepared in manuscript.

WAR DIARY
or
INTELLIGENCE SUMMARY
(Erase heading not required.)

Army Form C. 2118

Place	Date	Hour	Summary of Events and Information	Remarks and references to Appendices
	18/8/16.		2/Lt. C. M. Prince was killed during bombardment & 2/Lt Baker wounded. 2/Lt. K. C. Bright was killed by Machine Gun fire leading his men across to reinforce.	A.C.C
	19/8/16		At 7.45 am C. Coy was sent to reinforce and took up position on right of the line held by 7th Northants & a few men of A & B Coys of 9th R. Sussex under Major Murphy acting C.O. 7th Northants. This position was held through the night. Rations were taken up by D. Coy who also built a strong point on the right flank (which was in the air). During the early morning Capt. E. S. Rogerson was killed and Capt W. J. T. Austin wounded by rifle fire. The 8th R. W. Kents relieved 7th Northants & 9th R. Sussex during the night of 19th–20th. Total casualties. Officers – Killed 3. Wounded 4. Other Ranks. Killed 23. Wounded 133. Missing 23.	A.C.C
	20/8/16		The Battalion moved to the Craters on relief	A.C.C.

1875 · Wt. W593/826 1,000,000 4/15 J.B.C. & A. A.D.S.S./Forms/C. 2118.

Instructions regarding War Diaries and Intelligence Summaries are contained in F. S. Regs., Part II. and the Staff Manual respectively. Title Pages will be prepared in manuscript.

WAR DIARY
or
INTELLIGENCE SUMMARY
(Erase heading not required.)

Army Form C. 2118

Place	Date	Hour	Summary of Events and Information	Remarks and references to Appendices
The Craters	20/8/16		Draft of 18 OR arrived from 5th R. Sussex. The Bn ~~found~~ found a working party. There were 11 OR wounded during the day.	H.C.C
	21/8/16		Quiet.	H.C.C.
	22/8/16		Bn moved to Bivouacs at Sandpits.	H.C.C.
	23/8/16		Quiet.	H.C.C
	24/8/16		Quiet	H.C.C
	25/8/16		Moved to Bivouacs near Dernancourt. Very showery weather (21st to 29th Reorganization & training were proceeded with)	H.C.C
	30/8/16		Battalion moved to trenches on left of DELVILLE Wood Officers in Action Lt-Col J. F. P. Langdon (C.O.) Lt. H.C. Coleman (Adj.) A. Coy. Capt. M. Campbell Johnston 2/Lt E. Best, 2/Lt J. A. Flowers. B " Lt. G. M. Shackel 2/Lt C. V. Newton, 2/Lt G. M. W. Prowse. C " 2/Lt T. Foster, 2/Lt P. J. Surridge, 2/Lt G. C. Mole. D " Lt. H. N. L'Estrange 2/Lt J. A. Paul, 2/Lt J. P. Mostyn Intelligence Officer 2/Lt H. Treacher M. G. O. 2/Lt C.H. Dudeney Medical Officer Lt. A. A. E. Newth R.A.M.C.	H.C.C

1875 Wt. W593/826 1,000,000 4/15 J.B.C. & A. A.D.S.S./Forms/C. 2118.

Instructions regarding War Diaries and Intelligence Summaries are contained in F. S. Regs., Part II. and the Staff Manual respectively. Title Pages will be prepared in manuscript.

WAR DIARY
or
INTELLIGENCE SUMMARY
(Erase heading not required.)

Army Form C. 2118

Place	Date	Hour	Summary of Events and Information	Remarks and references to Appendices
	31/8/16.		Germans attacked at 2pm after a heavy bombardment & broke through line held by Battalion on our left. A & D Coys in front line & held on to their trench & were reinforced by two platoons of C. Coy. The remaining two platoons under Lt-Col Langdon & 2/Lt Foster of C Coy opposed the enemy bombing party who were endeavouring to cut in on our left rear & held them till the arrival of a Coy of 2nd Leinsters about 5 pm. These two platoons of C. Coy then strengthened the front line 2/Lt J. A. FLOWERS was killed by sniper on afternoon of 31st.	H.C.C.

1875 Wt. W593/826 1,000,000 4/15 J.B.C. & A. A.D.S.S./Forms/C. 2118.

73rd Brigade.
24th Division

9th BATTALION.

ROYAL SUSSEX REGIMENT.

September 1 9 1 6.

Instructions regarding War Diaries and Intelligence Summaries are contained in F. S. Regs., Part II. and the Staff Manual respectively. Title pages will be prepared in manuscript.

WAR DIARY
or
INTELLIGENCE SUMMARY.
(Erase heading not required.)

Army Form C. 2118.

24 73/34

Place	Date	Hour	Summary of Events and Information	Remarks and references to Appendices
Confidential			4th Royal Sussex	vol 13
			War Diary	
			for month of September 1916	

18. I
4 sheets

2353 Wt. W2544/1454 700,000 5/15 D. D. & L. A.D.S.S./Forms/C. 2118.

Instructions regarding War Diaries and Intelligence Summaries are contained in F. S. Regs., Part II. and the Staff Manual respectively. Title Pages will be prepared in manuscript.

WAR DIARY
or
INTELLIGENCE SUMMARY
(Erase heading not required.)

Army Form C. 2118

Place	Date	Hour	Summary of Events and Information	Remarks and references to Appendices
	1/9/16		In front line trenches to left of DELVILLE WOOD, with 2 platoons of "B" Co in immediate support. The line was held through the night 31st/1st against several German attacks, and the men suffered severely from want of rations. During the morning while attempting to get up with a ration party R.S.M. OWEN WILLIAMS was wounded. In the afternoon the Germans on our left rear were driven back by another Bn + the situation cleared considerably.	H.C.C.
	2/9/16		A quieter day. Occasional bombardment only.	H.C.C.
	3/9/16		2nd LIEUT. G.M.W. PROWSE wounded by shrapnel early in the morning. The Bn was relieved by the 7th NORTHAMPTONS + became Bn in support.	H.C.C.
	4/9/16		2nd LIEUT J.P. MOSTYN wounded early in the morning by shrapnel. In the afternoon Bn moved to Reserve Area.	H.C.C.
			Total Casualties from 30/8/16 to 4/9/16 inclusive.	
			Officers — Killed 1, Wounded 2	
			O.R. — Killed 27, Wounded 82, Missing 6	
			2Lt. J.J. BANHAM took command of "C" Coy + 2Lt. T. FOSTER of "D" Co.	

1875 Wt. W593/826 1,000,000 4/15 J.B.C. & A. A.D.S.S./Forms/C. 2118.

Instructions regarding War Diaries and Intelligence Summaries are contained in F. S. Regs., Part II. and the Staff Manual respectively. Title Pages will be prepared in manuscript.

WAR DIARY
or
INTELLIGENCE SUMMARY
(Erase heading not required.)

Army Form C. 2118

Place	Date	Hour	Summary of Events and Information	Remarks and references to Appendices
	5/9/16		Bn moved to billets in DERNENCOURT.	H.C.C.
	6/9/16		Bn entrained + moved to BRUCAMPS, where they were in billets.	H.C.C
	7/9/16 to 20/9/16		Training and re-organisation.	H.C.C
	11/9/16		2nd Lt. H. TREACHER to Hospital	H.C.C
			2nd Lt. W.D. CHEPMELL joined from 10th Bn. Royal Sussex Regt + posted to "A" Co.	
	14/9/16		Lt. + Quartermaster C.A. PITMAN struck off strength, sick to England.	H.C.C
	15/9/16		Draft of 28 O.R. arrived.	H.C.C
	17/9/16		Draft of 8 O.R. arrived.	H.C.C
	19/9/16		Draft of 5 officers + 13 O.R arrived	H.C.C
			2nd Lt. V.F.F. WARD posted to "A" Co.	
			2nd Lt. W.F. HARTT " " "D" Co.	
			2nd Lt. E. PHIPPS " " "B" Co.	
			2nd Lt. R. BORNIER " " "C" Co.	
			2nd Lt. H. SAXON " " "C" Co.	
	20/9/16		Bn entrained + moved to MARLES-LES-MINES, where they were in billets.	H.C.C
	22/9/16		Bn marched to HAILLICOURT + were billeted.	H.C.C
	23/9/16		21 O.R. re-inforcements arrived	
			Bn marched from HAILLICOURT to CAMBLAIN L'ABBE + relieved 10th Argyle + Sutherland Highlanders in billets.	H.C.C.

1875 Wt. W593/826 1,000,000 4/15 J.B.C. & A. A.D.S.S./Forms/C. 2118.

Instructions regarding War Diaries and Intelligence Summaries are contained in F. S. Regs., Part II. and the Staff Manual respectively. Title Pages will be prepared in manuscript.

WAR DIARY
or
INTELLIGENCE SUMMARY
(Erase heading not required.)

Army Form C. 2118

Place	Date	Hour	Summary of Events and Information	Remarks and references to Appendices
~~24/~~	24/9/16		Bn marched to VILLERS-AU-BOIS + relieved 3rd Bn. South African Brigade in Brigade Reserve.	
			49 O.R. Reinforcements arrived.	
	26/9/16		6 O.R. do. do.	
	28/9/16		2 Officer Reinforcements.	
			2nd Lt. J.C. WIGGS, posted to "D" Co	
			2nd Lt. R.W. RAMSBY, do. do.	
	30/9/16		95 O.R. Reinforcements arrived.	

1875 Wt. W593/826 1,000,000 4/15 J.B.C. & A. A.D.S.S./Forms/C. 2118.

73rd Brigade.
24th Division.

9th BATTALION

ROYAL SUSSEX REGIMENT.

October 1916.

Instructions regarding War Diaries and Intelligence Summaries are contained in F. S. Regs., Part II. and the Staff Manual respectively. Title Pages will be prepared in manuscript.

WAR DIARY or INTELLIGENCE SUMMARY of 9 R Sussex Regt

(Erase heading not required.)

Army Form C. 2118

Vol 14

Place	Date	Hour	Summary of Events and Information	Remarks and references to Appendices
	1/10/16		Bn. relieved 13th Middlesex in front line in front of SOUCHEZ	HCC
	3/10/16		3 O.R. Reinforcements arrived.	HCC
	7/10/16		2/Lt. T.E. BOURDILLON returned from 2nd Army Grenade School,	HCC
	10/10/16		Bn relieved by 12th ROYAL FUSILIERS & marched into billets at CAMBLAIN L'ABBE, with A & B Coys at VILLER au BOIS. The nine days in the line were quiet except for considerable trench artillery activity. Casualties – Officers 2/Lt R. BURNIER wounded O.R. 1 killed, 1 died of wounds, 7 wounded. Major R.H. WAITHMAN joined the Battn.	HCC
	10/10/16 to 18/10/16		Bn. training.	HCC
	12/10/16		19 O.R. Reinforcements arrived	HCC
	16/10/16		4 O.R. Reinforcements arrived	HCC
	18/10/16		Bn. moved into support at CABARET ROUGE behind VIMY RIDGE.	HCC
	18/10/16 to 27/10/16		Casualties: 1 O.R wounded.	HCC
	27/10/16		Bn. marched to ESTREE CAUCHIE, being relieved by 15th Bn. Canadian Infantry.	HCC
			2/Lt J.A. HAWKRIDGE returned to duty from Hospital	
	28/10/16		Bn. marched to billets at MAZINGARBE	HCC

14 I
2 sheets

1875 Wt. W593/826 1,000,000 4/15 J.B.C. & A. A.D.S.S./Forms/C. 2118.

Instructions regarding War Diaries and Intelligence Summaries are contained in F. S. Regs., Part II. and the Staff Manual respectively. Title Pages will be prepared in manuscript.

WAR DIARY
or
INTELLIGENCE SUMMARY
(Erase heading not required.)

Army Form C. 2118

Place	Date	Hour	Summary of Events and Information	Remarks and references to Appendices
	29/4/16		Bn moved into line in Loos area, relieving 12th Bn South Wales Borderers.	WC
	30/4/16		Capt. W. J. F. AUSTIN reported for duty from England	WC

1875 Wt. W593/826 1,000,000 4/15 J.B.C. & A. A.D.S.S./Forms/C. 2118.

73rd Brigade.
24th Division.

9th BATTALION

ROYAL SUSSEX REGIMENT.

November 1916.

Instructions regarding War Diaries and Intelligence Summaries are contained in F. S. Regs., Part II. and the Staff Manual respectively. Title pages will be prepared in manuscript.

WAR DIARY
or
INTELLIGENCE SUMMARY.

(Erase heading not required.)

Army Form C. 2118.

Vol 15

Place	Date	Hour	Summary of Events and Information	Remarks and references to Appendices
			9th Royal Sussex Regt War Diary for month of November 1916	15.I 2 sheets

2353 Wt. W2544/1454 700,000 5/15 D. D. & L. A.D.S.S./Forms/C. 2118.

Instructions regarding War Diaries and Intelligence Summaries are contained in F. S. Regs., Part II. and the Staff Manual respectively. Title Pages will be prepared in manuscript.

WAR DIARY
or
INTELLIGENCE SUMMARY
(Erase heading not required.)

Army Form C. 2118

~~Place~~ Date	~~Date~~	Hour	Summary of Events and Information	Remarks and references to Appendices
1/11/16 to 6/11/16			Bn. in Line at LOOS. Casualties 1 Officer died of wounds, 4 O.R. wounded.	H.C.C
1/11/16			2/Lt R. BURNIER returned to duty Major J.L. STOKES appointed Town Major of HAILLICOURT.	H.C.C.
5/11/16			2/Lt J.A. HAWKRIDGE wounded on wiring party, & died on 6th.	H.C.C.
6/11/16			Bn moved to Reserve in N. MAROC.	H.C.C.
7/11/16			Draft of 7 O.R. arrived	H.C.C.
8/11/16			Draft of 4 O.R arrived – Capt. CAMPBELL-JOHNSON appointed 2nd-in-command Major R.H. WAITHMAN appointed to command 1st Bn. E. YORKS REGT.	H.C.C. H.C.C.
12/11/16			Bn. moved into Line at LOOS.	H.C.C.
13/11/16			Capt. T FOSTER to Hospital.	H.C.C.
14/11/16			2/Lt. A.F. BEST joined Bn. from England	H.C.C.
18/11/16			Bn. moved to Support in MAROC. Lt. H.H. L'ESTRANGE transferred to T.M. Battery & struck off.	H.C.C.
23/11/16			Lt. Col J.F.P. LANGDON vacated command of Bn. Major M.V.B. HILL, 1st Royal Fusiliers took command of Bn.	H.C.C.
24/11/16			Bn moved into line – LOOS.	H.C.C.
26/11/16			Capt. W.J.F. AUSTIN wounded. Bn. moved to Reserve. H.Q. & 2 Coys at LES BREBIS & 2 Coys at MAROC	H.C.C.
30/11/16			2/Lt C.V. NEWTON took command of D Coy.	H.C.C.

1875 Wt. W593/826 1,000,000 4/15 J.B.C. & A. A.D.S.S./Forms/C. 2118.

73rd Brigade.
24th Division.

9th BATTALION

ROYAL SUSSEX REGIMENT.

December 1916.

Instructions regarding War Diaries and Intelligence Summaries are contained in F. S. Regs., Part II. and the Staff Manual respectively. Title pages will be prepared in manuscript.

WAR DIARY
or
INTELLIGENCE SUMMARY.
(Erase heading not required.)

Army Form C. 2118.

T332

16.I
2 sheets

Place	Date	Hour	Summary of Events and Information	Remarks and references to Appendices
			Vol 16	
			Confidential	
			War Diary of 9th Royal Sussex Regt for month of December 1916.	

2353 Wt. W2544/1454 700,000 5/15 D. D. & L. A.D.S.S./Forms/C. 2118.

Instructions regarding War Diaries and Intelligence Summaries are contained in F. S. Regs., Part II. and the Staff Manual respectively. Title Pages will be prepared in manuscript.

WAR DIARY
or
INTELLIGENCE SUMMARY
(Erase heading not required.)

Army Form C. 2118

Place	Date Dec	Hour	Summary of Events and Information	Remarks and references to Appendices
	1st		A & B Coys at LES BREBIS started training, C & D Coys at Maroc aid fatigues.	
	2nd		ditto & Baths for A & B Coys.	
	3rd		Inter Coy relief. 2/Lt Attwood returned from short leave.	
	4th		A & B Coys at Maroc C & D Baths at LES BREBIS.	
	5th		C & D training A & B fatigues.	
	6th		Btn relieved 12th MX in Loos sector 3 casualties, 1 killed.	
	7th		Usual working parties & trench routine.	
	8		ditto	
	9th		as above, Bosh quite quiet.	
	10th		weather cold enemys attitude nervous	
	11th		Three casualties	
	12th		2 casualties, Moved to Maroc 2 coys MAROC 1. DUKE ST 1. TRAVERS & ST JAMES KEEP	
	13th		Working parties,	
	14		Working parties,	
	15		Nothing of interest usual carrying parties & inter Coy relief.	
	16		C & D Coys in MAROC A & B in close support	
	17		usual fatigues.	
	18		Btn relieved 13 MX in Loos Trenches.	
	19		C & D Coys in front line A & B in Enclosure.	
	20		All quiet, work as usual	
	21		No casualties, bosch very quiet, meggie & lulu very reticent. 2/Lt Attwood act adj.	
	22		Bosh got wind up & sent a few whiz bangs over, soon calmed down, when 11 pairs spend	
	23		All quiet usual work.	
	24		Three casualties, accomplished more by good luck than good shooting. Btn went to Les Brebis	
	25		Xmas day, dinner for two coys	
	26		Baths, & working parties, & refitting	
	27		Inter Coy relief.	
	28		Fatigues etc. & 2 coy Xmas dinner.	
	29		Baths & refitting for 2 Coys	
	30		Btn relieved 13 MX in Loos trenches, bosch quite lively 3 casualties.	
	31st		2 Casualties,	

G Attwood
2/Lt & act adj
9th Royal Sussex Regt

1875 Wt. W593/826 1,000,000 4/15 J.B.C. & A. A.D.S.S./Forms/C. 2118.

Army Form C. 2118.

Vol 17

Instructions regarding War Diaries and Intelligence Summaries are contained in F. S. Regs., Part II. and the Staff Manual respectively. Title pages will be prepared in manuscript.

WAR DIARY
or
INTELLIGENCE SUMMARY.
(Erase heading not required.)

Place	Date	Hour	Summary of Events and Information	Remarks and references to Appendices
			Confidential War Diary of 9th Royal Sussex Regiment for the month of January 1917.	17 I 2 sheet

2353 Wt. W2541/1454 700,000 5/15 D. D. & L. A.D.S.S./Forms/C. 2118.

January 1917

Instructions regarding War Diaries and Intelligence Summaries are contained in F. S. Regs., Part II. and the Staff Manual respectively. Title Pages will be prepared in manuscript.

9th BN. ROYAL SUSSEX REGT. No. IX/1. Date.........

WAR DIARY
or
INTELLIGENCE SUMMARY

(Erase heading not required.)

Army Form C. 2118.

9th Royal Sussex Regt

Place	Date 1917	Hour	Summary of Events and Information	Remarks and references to Appendices
	1/1/17 to 5/1/17		Bn. in the Line at LOOS. Bombardment with Gas Shells on 1st.	HCC
	2/1/17		2/Lt E.R. HOLDEN joined Bn + posted to "A" Co.	HCC
			2/Lt. A. JACKSON joined Bn + posted to "D" Co.	HCC
	5/1/17		Bn relieved by 13th Middlesex Regt.	HCC
	5/1/17 to 11/1/17		Bn in Brigade Reserve at MAROC, with 2 companies forward. All men employed on Working Parties.	HCC HCC
	11/1/17 to 17/1/17		Bn. relieved 13th Middlesex in the Line on 11th. Fairly quiet period.	HCC
	17/1/17 to 23/1/17		Bn relieved by 13th Middlesex + became Divisional Reserve, with H.Q. + two Companies at LES BREBIS + two companies at MAROC. Companies at MAROC employed on working parties. Companies at LES BREBIS – re-fitting + training.	HCC HCC
	18/1/17		Captain L. D. CHRISTIE joined from 1st Bn – + posted to "B" Company	HCC
			2/Lt. V. E. BOURDILLON joined Bn + posted to "C" Coy.	
	19/1/17		2/Lt. H. M. GEARY joined Bn + posted to "D" Coy.	HCC
			2/Lt. H. G. WILHAM joined Bn. + proceeded to Training Bn.	
	23/1/17 to 29/1/17		Bn. relieved 13th Middlesex Regt in the Line. On early morning of 24th, Germans attempted raid on Bn. on our right. He did not reach our trenches. We captured one wounded German.	HCC
	28/1/17		2/Lt. E. PHIPPS wounded in action.	HCC
	29/1/17 to 31/1/17		Bn. relieved by 13th Middlesex Regt. + became Bn in Brigade Reserve with three Coys at MAROC + 1 Coy forward. All men on Working Parties.	HCC

H.C. Coleman Lt + Adjt for O.C.
9th Royal Sussex Regt

1875 Wt. W593/826 1,000,000 4/15 J.B.C. & A. A.D.S.S./Forms/C. 2118.

Army Form C. 2118.

WAR DIARY
or
INTELLIGENCE SUMMARY.
(*Erase heading not required.*)

Instructions regarding War Diaries and Intelligence Summaries are contained in F. S. Regs., Part II. and the Staff Manual respectively. Title pages will be prepared in manuscript.

Vol 18

18 I
2 sheets

Place	Date	Hour	Summary of Events and Information	Remarks and references to Appendices
Confidential			9th Bn. The Royal Sussex Regiment. War Diary for the month of February 1917.	

Instructions regarding War Diaries and Intelligence Summaries are contained in F. S. Regs., Part II. and the Staff Manual respectively. Title Pages will be prepared in manuscript.

WAR DIARY
or
INTELLIGENCE SUMMARY
(Erase heading not required.)

Army Form C. 2118

Place	Date	Hour	Summary of Events and Information	Remarks and references to Appendices
	1/2/17		Bn in Brigade Reserve at MAROC.	HCC
	4/2/17		Bn. relieved 13th Middlesex in the Line.	HCC
	4/2/17 to 11/2/17		Fairly quiet tour in the line	HCC
	11/2/17		Bn relieved by 10th Bn, Loyal North Lancs. Regiment, & moved to LES BREBIS.	HCC
	12/2/17		Bn moved to Rest Area & were billeted at HESDIGNEUL. Inspected by Field Marshal Commanding-in-Chief on the line of march.	HCC
	13/2/17 to 15/2/17		Spent in cleaning up, re-organization, kit inspections, etc.	H.C.C.
	16/2/17		73rd Infantry Brigade & units from other arms inspected by GEN. NIVELLE, Commanding-in-Chief French Army. Inspection held at HESDIGNEUL. Bn. marched past after inspection. G.O.C. 1st Army expressed his satisfaction "that so creditable a sample of the British Army was forthcoming".	H.C.C.
	17/2/17 to 28/2/17		Progressive scheme of training carried out.	H.C.C
	24/2/17		2/Lt W.R. CHITTENDEN joined Bn.	H.C.C

1875 Wt. W593/826 1,000,000 4/15 J.B.C. & A. A.D.S.S./Forms/C. 2118.

Army Form C. 2118.

Instructions regarding War Diaries and Intelligence Summaries are contained in F. S. Regs., Part II. and the Staff Manual respectively. Title pages will be prepared in manuscript.

WAR DIARY
or
INTELLIGENCE SUMMARY.
(Erase heading not required.)

Vol 19

Place	Date	Hour	Summary of Events and Information	Remarks and references to Appendices
Secret			War Diary for the month of March 1917. of 9th Battalion The Royal Sussex Regiment.	

19 I
2 sheets

2353 Wt. W2544/1454 700,000 5/15 D. D. & L. A.D.S.S./Forms/C. 2118.

9/Royal Sussex Regt

Instructions regarding War Diaries and Intelligence Summaries are contained in F. S. Regs., Part II. and the Staff Manual respectively. Title Pages will be prepared in manuscript.

WAR DIARY
or
INTELLIGENCE SUMMARY
(Erase heading not required.)

Army Form C. 2118

Place	Date	Hour	Summary of Events and Information	Remarks and references to Appendices
	1/3/17 3/3/17		Bn in Rest Area at HESDIGNEUL. Training proceeded with & final preparations made for return to the Line.	HCC
	4/3/17		Bn moved to BOUVIGNY HUTS, in support for defence of LORETTE SPUR. Two days spent in training & reconnoitring the new area.	HCC
	6/3/17		Bn Moved to Divisional Reserve at SAINS-EN-GOHELLE. Training continued.	HCC
	9/3/17		Capt L. D. CHRISTIE took command of "C" Coy. Capt. T. FOSTER appointed acting 2nd-in-C. of Bn.	HCC
	10/3/17		Bn. relieved 13th Middlesex in the Line - Left sub-section - SOUCHEZ - S. 2. b., M. 32 a & b. Sheet 36 C. - Germans attempted raid under cover of bombardment about 3 hours after relief. This was nipped in the bud by rifle & L.G. fire. Fairly quiet after that.	HCC
	16/3/17		Bn. relieved by 13th Middlesex Regt & took over defences of LORETTE SPUR with H.Q. at ABLAIN St. NAZAIRE.	HCC
	22/3/17		Bn relieved 13th Middlesex in the Line.	HCC
	31/3/17		On 26th, 27th, & 28th Germans bombarded our front heavily at intervals. Our retaliation was very heavy. There was no infantry action. Lt. Col. M.V.B. Hill, M.C. went on leave to England 23/3/17 - Capt. T. FOSTER took temporary command of Bn.	HCC

1875 Wt. W593/826 1,000,000 4/15 J.B.C. & A. A.D.S.S./Forms/C. 2118.

9th ROYAL SUSSEX REGIMENT

73rd INFANTRY BRIGADE

24th DIVISION

APRIL 1917

Instructions regarding War Diaries and Intelligence Summaries are contained in F. S. Regs., Part II. and the Staff Manual respectively. Title pages will be prepared in manuscript.

WAR DIARY
or
~~INTELLIGENCE~~ SUMMARY.
(Erase heading not required.)

Army Form C. 2118.

Vol 20

Place	Date	Hour	Summary of Events and Information	Remarks and references to Appendices
Secret			9th Royal Sussex Regiment for the month of April 1917	20 I 5 sheets +21 I

2353 Wt. W2544/1454 700,000 5/15 D. D. & L. A.D.S.S./Forms/C. 2118.

Instructions regarding War Diaries and Intelligence Summaries are contained in F. S. Regs., Part II. and the Staff Manual respectively. Title Pages will be prepared in manuscript.

WAR DIARY
or
INTELLIGENCE SUMMARY
(Erase heading not required.)

Army Form C. 2118.

Place	Date	Hour	Summary of Events and Information	Remarks and references to Appendices
	1/4/17		Bn in Line in Left Sub-section – SOUCHEZ. Relieved on night 1st/2nd by 2 Coys 8th Bn. the BUFFS. Bn. moved to Divisional Reserve in billets at FOSSE 10.	HCC
	2/4/17		Major M. CAMPBELL-JOHNSTON struck off strength + attached to H.Q. 3rd Army.	HCC
	2/4/17 to 10/4/17		Bn. trained under Capt T FOSTER for attack ordered for 10th. Lt. Col Hill, M.C returned from leave – 10/4/17. Attack postponed till 12/4/17	HCC
	11/4/17		Bn. took over portion of front from 8th Buffs on evening of 11th	HCC
	12/4/17		Attack on BOIS-EN-HACHE – (S2b + M32d – Sheet 36c)	

The attack was carried out in conjunction with the 2nd Leinsters on our right, + in co-operation with an attack by the Canadian Corps. The objectives were the German 1st + 2nd line, which meant the capture of his commanding position in the Bois-en-HACHE. "A" Coy on the left + "B" Coy on the right were detailed to take the 2nd line, + hold it as a line of observation. "C" Coy was detailed to "mop up", consolidate + hold as line of resistance the enemy front line. "D" Coy was held in reserve. The attack was timed for 5 a.m on the 12th, just before dawn. All Companies moved into position of assembly without delay or casualty by 1 a.m. + Tea + Rum were issued to the men. The difficult operation of forming up on the proper alignment was carried out under cover of a blizzard 5 mins before zero. HCC

Instructions regarding War Diaries and Intelligence Summaries are contained in F. S. Regs., Part II. and the Staff Manual respectively. Title Pages will be prepared in manuscript.

WAR DIARY
or
INTELLIGENCE SUMMARY
(Erase heading not required.)

Army Form C. 2118

Place	Date	Hour	Summary of Events and Information	Remarks and references to Appendices
	12/4/17		In the attack heavy casualties were at once sustained from M.G. fire. The first objective was at once captured with about 60 casualties, including 3 officers of "B" Coy, 1 of "A" Coy, + 1 of "C" Coy. About 6 Germans who fought were bayonetted, the remainder were captured or ran away. At 5.10 a.m. the advance continued. "A" Coy reached all their objectives + established a line of posts 80 yds in advance of German front line. In this advance "A" + "B" + "C" Coys each lost an officer. Three attempts at a [illegible] attack were made but were driven off. A counter-attack against the last one resulted in the capture of 2 prisoners. "B" Coy, in spite of the loss of all their officers reached their objective in small parties, one in touch with "A" Coy + 1 in touch with the 2nd Leinsters. 12 men were found killed 20 yds in front of the objective. The dug-outs in the front line were picquetted, 150 yds of the line was wired by Lt. Lloyd Davis + a party of 129 Field Co. R.E. with 15 men of D Coy. A Vickers Gun was successfully got into position in the centre of this line, + a Stokes Gun with 140 rounds was carried to a position on the left of the enemy front line. The ammunition was carried by men of D Coy. During the day "A" Coy got considerable shelling, but the casualties were very few.	H.C.C.

1875 Wt. W593/826 1,000,000 4/15 J.B.C. & A. A.D.S.S./Forms/C. 2118.

Army Form C. 2118

Instructions regarding War Diaries and Intelligence Summaries are contained in F. S. Regs., Part II. and the Staff Manual respectively. Title Pages will be prepared in manuscript.

WAR DIARY
or
INTELLIGENCE SUMMARY
(Erase heading not required.)

Place	Date	Hour	Summary of Events and Information	Remarks and references to Appendices
	12/4/17		The attack took place in a blinding snow-storm + over ground full of large shell-holes + churned into a sea of mud by bad weather + heavy shelling.	HCC
	13/4/17.		The night 12th/13th was comparatively quiet, but the unusual darkness + heaviness of the ground made communication difficult. The morning of the 13th was quiet except for shelling by single guns. At 1 p.m. it was seen that the enemy was shelling his own line + the village of ANGRES. Consequently at 1.45 p.m. patrols were sent out under 2/Lt P. ATTWOOD + 2/Lt H. SAXON 500 yds from the German 2nd line + reported that enemy had withdrawn except for a M.G. + two snipers who were firing. Bn. H.Q. was established in the German front line by 4 o'clock. By this time our patrol had bombed the enemy out of FOSSE 6. An outpost line was established by D Coy on the SOUCHEZ River + before dark a patrol under 2/Lt R. BURNIER reached CALVERY Trench in S.3.a + BUQUET MILL at S 3 a. 55.90. The outpost line was held through the night + by 7 a.m. the Bn was relieved by 12th Bn. Royal Fusiliers	HCC

1875 Wt. W593/826 1,000,000 4/15 J.B.C. & A. A.D.S.S./Forms/C. 2118.

Instructions regarding War Diaries and Intelligence Summaries are contained in F. S. Regs., Part II. and the Staff Manual respectively. Title Pages will be prepared in manuscript.

WAR DIARY
or
INTELLIGENCE SUMMARY
(Erase heading not required.)

Army Form C. 2118

Place	Date	Hour	Summary of Events and Information	Remarks and references to Appendices
	13/4/17		19 Prisoners were captured + a large number of German dead were found in the captured trenches. Our Casualties were Officers 5 killed — 4 wounded. O.R. Killed 40 Wounded 63 Died of wounds — O.R. 4 Total — all ranks 116.	HCC
			Officers in action	
			C.O. Lt Col. M.V.B. HILL, M.C. 2nd-in-C. Capt T. FOSTER. Adjt. Lt H.C. COLEMAN	
			Sigs. Off. 2/Lt P. ATTWOOD Int. Officer 2/Lt. R. BURNIER Bomb Off. 2/Lt G.C. MOLE	
			"A" Co: Capt. C.E. GOAD; Lt W.D. CHEPMELL (killed); 2/Lt V.F.F. WARD (wounded); 2/Lt E.R. HOLDEN (wounded)	
			"B" Co: Capt. G.M. SHACKEL (wounded); Lt W.B. SHAW (killed); 2/Lt G.M.W. PROWSE (killed); 2/Lt A. CARTER (killed)	
			"C" Co: 2/Lt B.H. VIDLER (killed); 2/Lt H. SAXON; 2/Lt H.G. WELHAM; 2/Lt W.R. CHITTENDEN (wounded)	
			"D" Co: 2/Lt J.E. PAUL; 2/Lt R.W. RUMSBY; 2/Lt H.M. GEARY; 2/Lt A. JACKSON	
			C.S.M. BARNARD, "A" Co. was killed.	
	14/4/17		Bn. moved on relief to MARQUEFFLES FARM. Weather was still bad.	HCC

Instructions regarding War Diaries and Intelligence Summaries are contained in F. S. Regs., Part II. and the Staff Manual respectively. Title Pages will be prepared in manuscript.

WAR DIARY
or
INTELLIGENCE SUMMARY
(Erase heading not required.)

Army Form C. 2118

Place	Date	Hour	Summary of Events and Information	Remarks and references to Appendices
	17/4/17		Bn. marched to HESDIGNEUL into billets.	HCC
	18/4/17		Bn marched to AUCHEL + were billeted	HCC
	19/4/17		Bn marched to Training Area + were billetted at ESTREE BLANCHE	HCC
	20/4/17 to 25/4/17		Bn. rested + re-organised. Capt. L.D. CHRISTIE took command of B Co. 2/LTS RUMSBY + GEARY were transferred to "B" Co. 2/LT T.J. SURRIDGE took command of "C" Coy temporarily.	HCC
			2/LTS C.O. O'BEIRNE ("A" Co) N.M. ADAMS ("B" Co) W.E. PRICE ("C" Co) + C.H. KNIGHT ("D" Co) joined 20/4/17.	
			2/LT W.F. HARTT – sick to England 13-4-17.	
	21/4/17		CAPT A.A.E. NEWTH, R.A.M.C. (attd) struck off strength. CAPT. CHESTER HARRIS, R.A.M.C. attd to Bn	HCC
	26/4/17		Bn. marched to RAIMBERT	HCC
	27/4/17		Bn marched into camp at HOUCHIN – Bde in support to 1st Corps.	HCC
	28/4/17 to 30/4/17		Training carried on.	HCC
	29/4/17		Extract from London Gazette – 2/LT C.E. GOAD to be LIEUT – 12-2-17. 2/LT A.V. BURD joined + posted to "B" Co.	HCC
			Football Matches 29th 9th Royal Sussex 4 goals 73 Bde H.Q. 1 goal	
			30th 9th Royal Sussex 2 goals 2nd Leinsters nil.	

21
I
[illegible]

Instructions regarding War Diaries and Intelligence Summaries are contained in F. S. Regs., Part II. and the Staff Manual respectively. Title pages will be prepared in manuscript.

WAR DIARY
or
INTELLIGENCE SUMMARY.
(Erase heading not required.)

Army Form C. 2118.

Vol 21

Place	Date	Hour	Summary of Events and Information	Remarks and references to Appendices
			Confidential War Diary of 9th Battalion Royal Sussex Regt for the month of May 1917	22 I 2 sheets

Instructions regarding War Diaries and Intelligence Summaries are contained in F. S. Regs., Part II. and the Staff Manual respectively. Title Pages will be prepared in manuscript.

9th BN. ROYAL SUSSEX REGT. No. Bn. 353 Date ......

WAR DIARY
or
INTELLIGENCE SUMMARY
(Erase heading not required.)

9th Royal Sussex Regt.

Army Form C. 2118

Place	Date	Hour	Summary of Events and Information	Remarks and references to Appendices
	May 1917			
	1st. to 8th.		Bn. in Camp at HOUCHIN. Training + re-organization carried out. Several Brigade + Bn. Field days in the BOIS-des-DAMES near BRUAY were arranged. The weather was good + much useful work was done.	H.C.C.
	2nd		2/Lt G. DAVIS joined Bn. from Artists Rifles.	H.C.C.
	7th		2/Lt E.O.R. BYWORTH joined from England	H.C.C.
	9th		Bn. left HOUCHIN at 9.30 a.m. + marched into billets at Mt BERNENCHON at 2 p.m.	H.C.C.
	10th		Bn left Mt BERNENCHON at 10.30 a.m. + arrived at THIENNES at 2 p.m, where they were billeted.	H.C.C.
	11th.		Inspection + farewell address on leaving Divn by G.O.C. 24th Divn Maj. Gen. J. E. CAPPER.	H.C.C.
	12th.		Marched from THIENNES to billets near STEENVOORDE.	H.C.C.
	14th		Marched to Camp at HEKSKEN, near RENINGHELST.	H.C.C.
	15th to 28th.		Bn. was detailed for working parties, for which every available man was used.	H.C.C.
	26th		2/Lt A.H. LATTER joined Bn. from England	H.C.C.
	29th + 30th		Training + organisation of new drafts.	H.C.C.
	31st.		Bn. moved to Corps Training Area at STEENVOORDE	H.C.C.

1875 Wt. W593/826 1,000,000 4/15 J.B.C. & A. A.D.S.S./Forms/C. 2118.

Army Form C. 2118.

Instructions regarding War Diaries and Intelligence Summaries are contained in F. S. Regs., Part II. and the Staff Manual respectively. Title pages will be prepared in manuscript.

WAR DIARY
or
INTELLIGENCE SUMMARY.
(Erase heading not required.)

73/24

Vol 22

Place	Date	Hour	Summary of Events and Information	Remarks and references to Appendices
Confidential			War Diary of 9th Battalion The Royal Sussex Regt for month of June 1917	23 I 5 sheets

2353 Wt. W2544/1454 700,000 5/15 D. D. & L. A.D.S.S. Forms/C 2118.

Instructions regarding War Diaries and Intelligence Summaries are contained in F. S. Regs., Part II. and the Staff Manual respectively. Title Pages will be prepared in manuscript.

11/331

WAR DIARY
or
INTELLIGENCE SUMMARY
(Erase heading not required.)

9th Royal Sussex 8/9

Army Form C. 2118

Place	Date	Hour	Summary of Events and Information	Remarks and references to Appendices
1/6/17 to 3/6/17			Bn at STEENVOORDE, training for attack. A practice ground was flagged out to show the various objectives, & the operations were practised thoroughly in conjunction with other Battalions of the Division.	H.C.C.
4/6/17			Bn. moved to Camp at LYSSENHOEK. The following officers joined the Bn from England:- "A" Co. 2/Lt S.T. TREW; "B" Co. 2/Lt. D.W.G. MAY, 2/Lt A.G.G. PYE; "C" Co. 2/Lt R. HUDSON; "D" Co. 2/Lt A.D. WATSON, 2/Lt G.D. ROBERTS.	H.C.C
5/6/17			Bn. moved to OTTAWA Camp near OUDERDOM.	
			<u>Battle of Messines Ridge.</u>	
			<u>Task of Battalion</u> - To capture part of the final objective - S.W. of HOLLEBEKE on a front of 600 yds northward from the ROOZEBEEK - (Map Ref - Sheet 28 - O.16.a.90.50 to O.10.d.45.60) A line running N.E. & S.W. at a distance of from 500 to 750 yds in front of this was captured previously by other troops. The Bn. was supported by 7th Northamptonshire Regt. On the right were the 1st Royal Fusiliers & on the left the 13th Middlesex.	
6/6/17			Bn. left Camp at 11.30 p.m & marched to assembly trenches at CHATEAU SEGARD, near DICKEBUSCH. On arrival the assembly trenches were heavily shelled with gas shells. Casualties were slight (1 O.R. killed & 3 gassed) & the troops were got into position satisfactorily.	HCC
7/6/17			3.10 a.m. was the time for the first attack. The shelling of back areas at once ceased & the work of issuing Bombs, Tools, etc. was carried on without interruption. At 11.30 a.m. Bn. moved in artillery formation to old British front line. Here a halt of about an hour was made. At 2 p.m. Bn again moved forward slowly over [illegible] very broken ground.	H.C.C

1875 Wt. W593/826 1,000,000 4/15 J.B.C. & A. A.D.S.S./Forms/C. 2118.

Army Form C. 2118

Instructions regarding War Diaries and Intelligence Summaries are contained in F. S. Regs., Part II. and the Staff Manual respectively. Title Pages will be prepared in manuscript.

WAR DIARY
or
INTELLIGENCE SUMMARY
(Erase heading not required.)

Place	Date	Hour	Summary of Events and Information	Remarks and references to Appendices
7/6/17.			The advance continued over the ground captured by the 41st Division + by ZERO Time, 3.10 p.m., troops had deployed under our barrage. The advance under the barrage took 20 minutes. The objective was taken without much opposition + contact was established with the flank Battalions. The total casualties up to the evening of the 7th were under 40 of all ranks.	H.C.C.
8/6/17 to 11/6/17			Bn. held the line + consolidated the position. Strong points were constructed + communication trenches cleared. Enemy shelling increased each day + the final casualties were :- Officers. 6 wounded - Lt. A.V. REWELL, 2/Lt P.J. SURRIDGE, 2/Lt J.C. WIGGS, 2/Lt A.V. BURD, 2/Lt C.O. O'BEIRNE, 2/Lt. W.E. PRICE, Other ranks. 31 killed, 134 wounded, 3 missing.	H.C.C.
11/6/17			Bn. relieved by 10th Bn. The QUEENS + moved to OUDERDOM.	H.C.C.
12/6/17			The following officers arrived :- "A" Coy 2/Lt J.P. STEPHENSON. "C" C. 2/Lt H. BOTTING.	H.C.C.
13/6/17			Bn. moved to MICMAC CAMP, near OUDERDOM. Major T. FOSTER detailed to command temporarily 7th Northamptonshire Regt.	H.C.C.
15/6/17			Bn. relieved 1st Royal Fusiliers as Bn in support in Hill 60 Sector, + carried on work of consolidation of strong points + support trenches.	H.C.C.
16/6/17			Major. J.C.D. BIRTWHISTLE joined from 8th Bn. Royal Sussex Regt. Rev. R.P. DODD, C.F. wounded at duty.	H.C.C.
18/6/17			R.S.M. COLES, H.A. wounded. C.S.M. STANDEN appointed A/R.S.M.	H.C.C.
19/6/17			Bn. relieved 7th Northamptons in the front line. During this tour there was no infantry action, but hostile artillery fire was very heavy.	H.C.C.

1875 Wt. W593/826 1,000,000 4/15 J.B.C. & A. A.D.S.S./Forms/C. 2118.

Instructions regarding War Diaries and Intelligence Summaries are contained in F. S. Regs., Part II. and the Staff Manual respectively. Title Pages will be prepared in manuscript.

WAR DIARY
or
INTELLIGENCE SUMMARY
(Erase heading not required.)

Army Form C. 2118

Place	Date	Hour	Summary of Events and Information	Remarks and references to Appendices
19/6/17 to 23/6/17			Work of consolidation was carried on steadily, but under considerable difficulties. Casualties for 5 days were:- 1 Officer wounded 2/Lt E.O.R. BYWORTH – Other ranks 19 killed – 51 wounded.	H.C.C.
23/6/17			Bn. relieved by 8th Bn, The QUEENS, + moved to MICMAC CAMP, near OUDERDOM.	H.C.C.
26/6/17			Major T. FOSTER rejoined from 7th NORTHAMPTONS.	H.C.C.
27/6/17			Bn. moved by train to billets in Rest Area at NIELLES-LES-BLEQUIN.	
			Lt. N.E. YOUNG rejoined Bn from 73rd Inf. Bde H.Q. + posted to "A" Coy.	H.C.C.
28/6/17 to 30/6/17			Bn. rested + re-organized.	H.C.C.
			During the month the following HONOURS were awarded:-	
			MILITARY CROSS — CAPT. C.V. NEWTON	
			2/Lt. H.G. WELHAM	
			2/Lt R.W. RUMSBY	
			DISTINGUISHED CONDUCT MEDAL No 10537 Pte A.J. DELL.	H.C.C.
			MILITARY MEDAL No 2946 Cpl H.G. SILVER	
			No 3125 Sgt. W.G. TICKNER	
			No 16763 Pte E. ISARD	
			No 5786 Sgt C. FULLER	
			MEDAILLE MILITAIRE No 1381 Sgt J. CHILLMAN.	

1875 Wt. W593/826 1,000,000 4/15 J.B.C. & A. A.D.S.S./Forms/C. 2118.

Instructions regarding War Diaries and Intelligence Summaries are contained in F. S. Regs., Part II. and the Staff Manual respectively. Title pages will be prepared in manuscript.

WAR DIARY
or
INTELLIGENCE SUMMARY.
(Erase heading not required.)

Army Form C. 2118.

24

Vol 23

Place	Date	Hour	Summary of Events and Information	Remarks and references to Appendices
Confidential			War Diary of 9th Battalion Royal Sussex Regiment for month of July 1917	24-I

July 1917 — WAR DIARY or INTELLIGENCE SUMMARY. (Erase heading not required.) — 9th Royal Sussex Regt. — Army Form C. 2118.

Instructions regarding War Diaries and Intelligence Summaries are contained in F. S. Regs., Part II. and the Staff Manual respectively. Title pages will be prepared in manuscript.

Place	Date	Hour	Summary of Events and Information	Remarks and references to Appendices
In the Field	1st to 8th July		Battalion in Rest Area at VIELLES by BLEQUIN. One week's good training for individuals but in. A Platoon of "C" Coy gave a good display of Fire control and musketry under a Musketry Instructor from II Army School. On 6th July a draft of 150 OR. joined the Battalion, the best we have ever received, all young men with previous experience in France. On 7th July Capt. C.V. NEWTON, M.C. gave a good demonstration of Guard mounting in the Village Square which was much appreciated by the N.C.O's. The following Officers joined during the week - Lieut. G. COMPTON (D.C.M. and Military Medal) Lieut S. HORSCROFT and were posted to A and B Coys - Lieut. A.W. GOLDEN to "C" Coy. Lieuts W.E. ARICE and A.V. BURD to "C" and "B" Coys from Hospital. both wounded on 7th June.	H.C.C.
	9th to 15th July		Training continued. Lieut. V.F.F. WARD joined "A" Coy. from 11th Battn. He was wounded with the Battalion at BOIS en HACHE on 12th April. Lieut. H.C. LISSIMAN joined on 10th and posted to "B" Coy. 11th July the Battalion had a field day's training in the Divisional Training Area. The ground which was covered by standing corn was not very suitable, but some very good Company exercises were carried out, in which the Rifle Grenade was made good use of.	H.C.C.
	17th		The Battalion left VIELLES at 2.15am and marched 16 miles to RENESCURE. In spite	

Sheet II

9th Royal Sussex Regt

Army Form C. 2118.

WAR DIARY
or
INTELLIGENCE SUMMARY.
(Erase heading not required.)

Instructions regarding War Diaries and Intelligence Summaries are contained in F. S. Regs., Part II. and the Staff Manual respectively. Title pages will be prepared in manuscript.

Place	Date	Hour	Summary of Events and Information	Remarks and references to Appendices
	July			
In the			of the heat at 10am only one man was behind the Transport at the end of the march	H.C.C.
Field	18th		Marched to CAESTRE under 72nd Inf Bde.	H.C.C.
	19		Marched to EECKE by Companies (about 1 mile)	H.C.C.
	20		Marched to LISSENHOEK - 9 miles without a man falling out of the ranks	H.C.C.
	21		Marched to MICMAC Camp near RENINGHELST - "A" and "C" Coys. went on to CANADA Tunnels to relieve the 23rd Division	H.C.C.
	22		"B" and "D" Coys. and HQ marched to CANADA Tunnels and "A" and "C" Coy. took over Front line Mt. SORREL Sector from 9th YORKS. This sector was the left hand pivot of the MESSINES Battle on 7th June.	H.C.C.
	23		Handed over part of our left Company front to 8th BUFFS, so that the 17th I.B. could hold the front from which they were going to attack. The move cost no some casualties as it was an night night. HQ moved from HEDGE STREET Tunnels to CANADA Tunnels which being originally a Mining system do not make very comfortable quarters for Infantry to live in. The trouble of keeping them dry is very great. Lieut. A.F. BEST Wounded and went to Transport lines.	H.C.C.
	24th to 29th		The Battalion remained in the line, making preparations for the Brigade's	H.C.C.

D. D. & L., London, E.C. (A7893) Wt. W809/M1672 350,000 1/17 Sch. 52a Forms/C.2118/14

Sheet III

Instructions regarding War Diaries and Intelligence Summaries are contained in F. S. Regs., Part II, and the Staff Manual respectively. Title pages will be prepared in manuscript.

WAR DIARY ~~or~~ INTELLIGENCE SUMMARY.

(Erase heading not required.)

9th Royal Sussex Regt.

Army Form C. 2118.

Place	Date	Hour	Summary of Events and Information	Remarks and references to Appendices
In the Field	July 24th to 29th 30th		attack on the 31st. Rain considerably impeded the work and the darkness and shelling at dusk and dawn made it hard for parties to reconnoitre the line.	H.C.C.
			By 8am the Battalion was back in MCMAHC Camp "A" Coy suffered some casualties from Gas shells which brought out huge blisters on their backs and necks. 2/Lt J.F. STEVENSON and C.S.M. STURT were both casualties. Lieuts R. HUDSON and W.E. PRICE were both gassed. 2/Lieut G. COMPTON killed on 26th.	H.C.C.
	31st		At 5am Battalion "stood to" preparatory to moving at 15 minutes notice. Orders to move came at 10.45am and Battalion moved up to OLD FRENCH Trench and ECLUSE Trench. The labour of getting 2 Cookers and 2 Water Carts through VOORMEZEELE on which a 11" gun was steadily firing was amply repaid by the hot food that could be given to the men.	
			At 7.30pm "B" and "D" Coys moved to LARCH WOOD and CANADA Street Tunnels respectively and H.Q. to the same place.	H.C.C.

D. D. & L., London, E.C. (A7833) Wt. W803/M1672 350,000 4/17 Sch. 52a Forms C/2118/14

Army Form C. 2118.

Instructions regarding War Diaries and Intelligence Summaries are contained in F. S. Regs., Part II. and the Staff Manual respectively. Title pages will be prepared in manuscript.

WAR DIARY

~~or~~

~~INTELLIGENCE SUMMARY.~~

(Erase heading not required.)

Vol 2

Place	Date	Hour	Summary of Events and Information	Remarks and references to Appendices
Secret.			9th. Battalion Royal Sussex Regiment. for the month of August 1917.	

25 I
5 sheets

2353 Wt. W2544/1454 700,000 5/15 D. D. & L. A.D.S.S. Forms/C. 2118.

9th Royal Sussex Regt.

Instructions regarding War Diaries and Intelligence Summaries are contained in F. S. Regs., Part II. and the Staff Manual respectively. Title pages will be prepared in manuscript.

WAR DIARY
or
~~INTELLIGENCE SUMMARY.~~
(Erase heading not required.)

Army Form C. 2118.

Place	Date	Hour	Summary of Events and Information	Remarks and references to Appendices
	1st		Bn. had moved up into Support after the attack on July 31st. H.Q. + B Coy. in Larch Wood Tunnels. D Coy in Canada St. Tunnels, A + C Coys in Ecluse Trench + Convent Lane, near Vormezeele.	H.C.C.
	3rd		Bn. took over front held by 17th Inf Bde. D Coy in front line W. of HET PAPPOTJE Fm, B Coy in support, A + C Coys in HEDGE St.	H.C.C.
	6/7th		C Coy relieved D, + A Coy relieved B, in order to facilitate Bn relief the next night.	H.C.C.
	1st to 7th		During this period the weather was extremely bad. Consolidation and re-organising the line was carried out under great difficulties.	H.C.C.
	8th		Bn. was relieved in early morning by 1st Royal Fusiliers. On relief Bn moved to "Z" Camp, DICKEBUSCH, 800 yds N.N.W. of Dickebusch Church.	H.C.C.
	8th/11th		This time was occupied by resting and re-organising.	H.C.C.
	11th		Bn relieved 1st Royal Fusiliers on same front. B Coy right front, A Coy centre front, D Coy right support, C Coy Hedge St Tunnels. The left was held by D Coy. 12th Sherwood Foresters.	H.C.C.
	11th-15th		Weather was better than in previous tour + casualties were slight. Considerable	

D. D. & L., London, E.C. (A7883) Wt. W803/M1672 350,000 4/17 Sch. 52a Forms C/2118/14

Instructions regarding War Diaries and Intelligence Summaries are contained in F. S. Regs., Part II, and the Staff Manual respectively. Title pages will be prepared in manuscript.

WAR DIARY
or
~~INTELLIGENCE SUMMARY.~~
(Erase heading not required.)

Army Form C. 2118.

Place	Date	Hour	Summary of Events and Information	Remarks and references to Appendices
			progress was made in work on the line. A system of naming dug-outs, etc. was put into force with excellent results. Guides, runners, + working parties found their way much more easily. Three German bombing attacks were driven off, + a party organized + led by Lt N.E. YOUNG raided a German post. It was found to be occupied only by a single sentry. He was taken prisoner.	H.C.C.
	15th		2/Lt L.J. FORD wounded.	H.C.C.
	15th/16th		Bn. was relieved by 1st N. STAFFS. + moved to MICMAC CAMP.	H.C.C.
	16th		2/Lt W.E. PALING + 2/Lt H.A. GOODACRE joined from England + posted to A + C Coys respectively.	H.C.C.
	18th		2/Lt E.C. REGAN + 2/Lt S.W. HALE joined from England + posted to B + D Coys respectively.	H.C.C.
	19th		2/Lt E.L. HALL joined from England + posted to "A" Coy. R.S.Major H.A.Coles rejoined Bn. Lt Col M.V.B. HILL D.S.O., M.C. proceeded on leave. Major T. FOSTER took command of Bn.	
			Bn moved to "L" Camp, Dickebusch.	H.C.C.
	16/22nd		Weather was fairly fine + this was taken advantage of by enemy aeroplanes for night bombing raids. An anti-aircraft Lewis gun was mounted in Camp to engage any enemy aeroplanes, who came within range.	H.C.C.

D. D. & L., London, E.C.
(A7853) Wt. W803/M1672 350,000 4/17 Sch. 52a Forms/C/2118/14

Army Form C. 2118.

Instructions regarding War Diaries and Intelligence Summaries are contained in F. S. Regs., Part II. and the Staff Manual respectively. Title pages will be prepared in manuscript.

~~WAR DIARY~~ or INTELLIGENCE SUMMARY.

(Erase heading not required.)

Place	Date	Hour	Summary of Events and Information	Remarks and references to Appendices
			Only small working parties were required during this period + consequently valuable training was carried out.	H.C.C.
	23rd		Bn. relieved the 8th BUFFS as Bn in Bde Support – B Coy in HEDGE ST TUNNELS – D Coy in CANADA ST. TUNNELS, C. Coy in METROPOLITAN LEFT, H.Q. + A Coy in LARCH WOOD TUNNELS.	H.C.C.
	24/27th		Bn. was engaged in wiring support line + carrying parties for M.G. Coy, Tunnelling Coy, Field Coy, R.E., 13th Middlesex + 2nd Leinsters. The shelling of back areas was much less than in previous tours + casualties were slight.	H.C.C.
	27th		Bn. was relieved by 1st N. STAFFS + 1 Coy 9th E. SURREYS + moved to MICMAC CAMP. Relief was carried out under very unpleasant weather conditions	H.C.C.
	28/30th		The Camp was drained + a start was made in building sandbag walls between tents + shelters to localise the effect of the horizontal burst of aeroplane bombs.	H.C.C.
	31st		Bn. moved to H Camp. 500 yds N.N.W. of DICKEBUSCH Church. A large flight of GOTHA Aeroplanes came over in the afternoon. This was the first time we had seen this type of German aeroplane	H.C.C.

D. D. & L., London, E. (A7893) Wt. W809/M1672 350,000 1/17 Sch. 52a Forms C/2118/14

S P E C I A L O R D E R.

****

9th. BATTALION ROYAL SUSSEX REGIMENT.

I would like the Officers and men to be told how very much the Brigade appreciates the work done by your Battalion in the trenches during the preparations for the recent operations. A great deal of hard work had to be done in a very short time, stores had to be carried up and dumps made.

During this period the Battalion was exposed to heavy shell fire night and day, but in spite of this all arrangements were complete and up to time. Difficulties were overcome with cheerfulness and everything was carried out with that thoroughness and soldierly spirit which is a special feature of the Battalion.

H.Q. 73 I.B.
7. 8. 17.

Brigadier General,
Commanding 73rd. Infantry Brigade.

Instructions regarding War Diaries and Intelligence Summaries are contained in F. S. Regs., Part II. and the Staff Manual respectively. Title pages will be prepared in manuscript.

WAR DIARY

or

~~INTELLIGENCE SUMMARY.~~

(*Erase heading not required.*)

Army Form C. 2118.

Vol 25

267
4 sheets

Place	Date	Hour	Summary of Events and Information	Remarks and references to Appendices
Secret			9th Battalion Royal Sussex Regiment for the month of September 1917.	

9th ROYAL SUSSEX Regiment.

WAR DIARY or INTELLIGENCE SUMMARY.

(Erase heading not required.)

Instructions regarding War Diaries and Intelligence Summaries are contained in F. S. Regs., Part II. and the Staff Manual respectively. Title pages will be prepared in manuscript.

Army Form C. 2118.

Place	Date	Hour	Summary of Events and Information	Remarks and references to Appendices
In the Field	-	1917 Sept. 1st - 3rd	Battalion in Camp at DICKEBUSCH. Brigade in Support. Enemy aeroplanes very active during this period dropping bombs on back areas.	H.C.C.
		3rd/4th	Battalion relieved 3rd RIFLE BRIGADE in the line (CLONMEL COPSE and BODMIN COPSE) "C" Coy Right front - "D" Coy left front - "A" Coy Right support - "B" Coy left support - H.Q. in HEDGE STREET Tunnels.	H.C.C.
		4th to 7th	This tour was rather quieter than previous tours, but at times enemy shelling was heavy and a number of gas shells were used. Officers of the 41st and 23rd Divisions were busy reconnoitring the line for the intended attack, and work was being pushed ahead making dumps, tracks, light railways, Dressing Stations, burying cable &c.	H.C.C.
		7/8th	Battalion relieved by 8th QUEENS and moved to "D" Camp, MICMAC. This Camp had been moved to a new site and was greatly improved. Training was carried on in the mornings.	H.C.C.
		11th	Battalion moved to "L" Camp DICKEBUSCH. Working parties were found to make Dug-outs near ZILLEBEKE.	H.C.C.
		13th	Battalion moved to Camp at H.33 c. 5.8 (28) near HALLEBAST.	H.C.C.
		14th	Battalion marched to HEKSKEN. An easy march at a slow pace owing to	H.C.C.

I

D. D. & L., London, E.C. (A7853) Wt. W803/M1672 350,000 4/17 Sch. 52a Forms C/2118/14

Instructions regarding War Diaries and Intelligence Summaries are contained in F. S. Regs., Part II, and the Staff Manual respectively. Title pages will be prepared in manuscript.

WAR DIARY or INTELLIGENCE SUMMARY.

(Erase heading not required.)

Army Form C. 2118.

Place	Date	Hour	Summary of Events and Information	Remarks and references to Appendices
Continued		1917 14/9/17	heavy traffic. In the afternoon a football match was played against a Siege Battery in Camp. Result 1 – 1.	H.C.
		15th	Battalion moved by Busses to Billets near STEENWERCKE. Move entailed march of about 8 miles.	H.C.
		15th to 21st	Billets were good though scattered. Training was carried on with a view to resuming Trench Warfare. Mornings were occupied by training of Platoons and Specialists with Company Commanders. Afternoons were devoted to football, cricket, running, tug of war &c. Each Company held a Sports meeting in anticipation of Battalion Sports later. These 6 days were spent pleasantly. Some good training was carried out.	H.C.
		21st	Battalion moved by train from BAILLEUL to BAPAUME. Journey was very interesting, especially going "over the top" at ARRAS. Battalion marched from BAPAUME to Camp at BARASTE.	H.C.
		23rd	Battalion Sports were held. A very successful day. The tug of war (won by H.Qs) was a great success, and a new bomb throwing contest also aroused much interest. The success of the representatives of Headquarters in this, and other events, was very striking. A Concert was held in the evening with the help of outside	

D. D. & L., London, E.C. (A7833) Wt. W803/M1672 350,000 4/17 Sch. 52a Forms C/2118/14

Instructions regarding War Diaries and Intelligence Summaries are contained in F. S. Regs., Part II. and the Staff Manual respectively. Title pages will be prepared in manuscript.

WAR DIARY or INTELLIGENCE SUMMARY.

(Erase heading not required.)

8th BN. ROYAL SUSSEX REGT. No. III

Army Form C. 2118.

Place	Date	Hour	Summary of Events and Information	Remarks and references to Appendices
Continued		1917 23/9/17	talent, and was an unusually good one.	H.C.C.
		24th	Battalion marched to HAUT ALLAINES. Battalion marched past G.O.C. en route. The hot day and hilly country made it a trying march. Bathing in the afternoon was very welcome.	H.C.C.
		25th	Battalion moved by buses to HERVILLY.	H.C.C.
		26th	Battalion relieved 23rd NORTHUMBERLAND FUSILIERS (4th TYNESIDE SCOTTISH) in the line at HARGICOURT. "A" Coy left front - "B" Coy Right front - "D" Coy. Support - "C" Coy Reserve.	H.C.C.
		26th to 30th	This part of the line was a pleasant change from YPRES. Trenches were in very good order considering that the line had only been established about 3 weeks. Enemy activity on our front was limited to sniping (which was met by counter measures) and fairly heavy bursts of shelling on the line and on HARGICOURT. Work was taken in hand to put the trenches in a state to withstand the Winter.	H.C.C.
			The following Officers joined Battalion during the month: - 2/Lieut. E. DAWSON on 4/9/17 and posted to "A" Coy. Capt. A.V. REWELL "A" Coy. rejoined from England (wounded) 8/9/17. 2/Lieut. J. MANN on 9/9/17 posted to "B" Coy. 2/Lieut. G.R. DUFFIELD on 19/9/17 posted to "A" Coy.	H.C.C.

D. D. & L., London, E.C. (A7833) Wt. W593/M1672 350,000 4/17 Sch. 52a Forms/C/2118/14

Instructions regarding War Diaries and Intelligence Summaries are contained in F. S. Regs., Part II. and the Staff Manual respectively. Title pages will be prepared in manuscript.

WAR DIARY

or

~~INTELLIGENCE SUMMARY~~.

(Erase heading not required.)

Army Form C. 2118.

Vol 26

Confidential.

Place	Date	Hour	Summary of Events and Information	Remarks and references to Appendices
			9th Battalion The Royal Sussex Regiment for the month of October 1917.	

27 I
4 sheets

2353 Wt. W2544/1454 700,000 5/15 D. D. & L. A.D.S.S. Forms/C. 2118.

October 1917.

Instructions regarding War Diaries and Intelligence Summaries are contained in F. S. Regs., Part II. and the Staff Manual respectively. Title pages will be prepared in manuscript.

9th Royal Sussex Regiment

WAR DIARY

~~or~~

~~INTELLIGENCE SUMMARY.~~

(Erase heading not required.)

9th Bn. ROYAL SUSSEX REGT.
No. Ax 38
Date..................

Army Form C. 2118.

Place	Date	Hour	Summary of Events and Information	Remarks and references to Appendices
Field	1st to 4th Oct.		Battalion in the line at MALAKOFF FARM. "C" Coy Right Front – "D" Coy Left Front. "A" & "B" Coys in Support. Work was chiefly devoted to clearing Front line, which was very muddy, and increasing accommodation for Support Companies.	MCC
	4th		Battalion moved to Brigade Reserve being relieved by 3 Coys. 13th MIDDLESEX Regt and 1 Coy 2nd LEINSTER Regt. Disposition of Coys – "A" Coy in Support to 13th Middlesex at HARDY BANK. "B" Coy in support to 2nd LEINSTERS at ENGINE SUPPORT. Headquarters and "C" & "D" Coys at HARGICOURT QUARRY.	MCC
	4th to 8th		Working parties took all available men. Owing to bad weather, the trenches required much work to maintain them in good condition.	MCC
	8th		Battalion relieved 13th MIDDLESEX in Front line, holding RIFLEMAN POST, BENJAMIN POST and LITTLE BENJAMIN. "B" Coy Right Front. "A" Coy Left Front. "C" Coy in Support in HUSSAR ROAD and "D" Coy in Reserve at HARDY BANK.	MCC
	11th		Inter-Company Relief.	MCC
	8th to 14th		A very quiet 6 days. No casualties. A considerable amount of wire was put out during this tour and Bomb proof shelters were constructed. During this tour the left Coy. (100 men) held 1500 Yards of Front line. Such a thing would not have	

D. D. & L., London, E.C. (A7833) Wt. W803/M1672 350,000 4/17 Sch. 52a. Forms C/2118/14

SHEET II

9th ROYAL SUSSEX Regt.

October 1917

Army Form C. 2118.

WAR DIARY or INTELLIGENCE SUMMARY.

(Erase heading not required.)

Instructions regarding War Diaries and Intelligence Summaries are contained in F. S. Regs., Part II. and the Staff Manual respectively. Title pages will be prepared in manuscript.

Place	Date	Hour	Summary of Events and Information	Remarks and references to Appendices
	8th – 14th		been believed 2 years ago, when Company Commanders were checked for not having a man in every fire-bay.	H.C.C.
	14th		Battalion relieved by 13th MIDDLESEX and moved to Divisional Reserve at HERVILLY. Only 1 days training was possible owing to Working parties.	H.C.C.
	17th		Battalion exercise was carried out – Divisional Commander and B.G.C. being present. An attack in open country against an enemy rear-guard was practised.	H.C.C.
	18th		A Football match was played – Officers – v – NCOs and Men. The latter won by 2 goals to 1. The Divisional Band played during the match.	H.C.C.
	20th		Battalion relieved 13th MIDDLESEX in the line previously held by the 6th Coy. "A" and "B" Coys. Left + Right Fronts respectively – "C" Coy. Reserve + "D" Coy. Support.	H.C.C.
	23rd		Inter-Company Relief.	H.C.C.
	27th – 30th		Battalion relieved by 13th MIDDLESEX and moved to Brigade Reserve – H.Q. "C" and "D" Coys. in TEMPLEUX QUARRIES. "A" and "B" in HARGICOURT QUARRY. Over 200 men daily were employed on Brigade Working parties.	H.C.C.
			On the 12th Major T. FOSTER was granted 6 months light duty in England. Major J. J. BANHAM became Acting Second-in-Command; and Lieut. H. SAXON MC took command	

D. D. & L., London, E.C.
(A7883) Wt. W807/M1672 350,000 4/17 Sch. 52a Forms C/2118/14

Sheet III

9th Royal Sussex Regiment

WAR DIARY
or
INTELLIGENCE SUMMARY.
(Erase heading not required.)

October 1917

Army Form C. 2118.

Instructions regarding War Diaries and Intelligence Summaries are contained in F. S. Regs., Part II. and the Staff Manual respectively. Title pages will be prepared in manuscript.

Place	Date	Hour	Summary of Events and Information	Remarks and references to Appendices
			L. C. Cox	ACC
			Casualties during the month were 3 OR Killed and 5 OR Wounded. These	
			casualties are the lowest experienced by the Battalion in one month's tour in the trenches	
			& which 6 days only were spent out of the shelled area.	ACC

D. D. & L., London, E.C.
(A7883) Wt. W803/M1672 350,000 4/17 Sch. 52a Forms/C/2118/14

Instructions regarding War Diaries and Intelligence Summaries are contained in F. S. Regs., Part II. and the Staff Manual respectively. Title pages will be prepared in manuscript.

73/74

WAR DIARY

~~INTELLIGENCE SUMMARY.~~

(Erase heading not required.)

Army Form C. 2118.

Vol 27

Place	Date	Hour	Summary of Events and Information	Remarks and references to Appendices
Confidential			9th Battalion Royal Sussex Regiment.	
			for the month of	
			November 1917	
			—	

28. 4 sheets

A6945 Wt. W11422/M1160 350,000 12/16 D. D. & L. Forms/C./2118/14.

November 1917 — 9th Royal Sussex Regiment

WAR DIARY
or
INTELLIGENCE SUMMARY.
(Erase heading not required.)

9th BN. ROYAL SUSSEX REGT. No. 5x27 Date 2.12.17

Army Form C. 2118.

Instructions regarding War Diaries and Intelligence Summaries are contained in F. S. Regs., Part II. and the Staff Manual respectively. Title pages will be prepared in manuscript.

Place	Date	Hour	Summary of Events and Information	Remarks and references to Appendices
Field	1st to 3rd		Battalion in Brigade Reserve. H.Q. + C + D Coys in TEMPLEUX QUARRIES. A + B Coys in HARGICOURT QUARRIES. Over 200 men were found daily for Working Parties.	GSP
	3rd		Battalion relieved 13th MIDDLESEX REGT. in front line holding RIFLEMAN POST to LITTLE BENJAMIN. D Coy Right Front. C Coy Left Front. B Coy Support. A Coy Reserve.	GSP GSP
	5th		Battalion took over line to the right as far as MALAKOFF FARM. This increased Battalion front to a mile as the crow flies. Right Front Coy. MALAKOFF SUPPORT CARBINE + part of RIFLE PIT TRENCH. RIFLEMAN, BENJAMIN and LITTLE BENJAMIN POSTS. B Coy relieved D Coy and 1 Coy of NORTHANTS. Lieut. Paul R Carruthers U.S.A. attached for 4 days instruction in trench warfare.	GSP
	6th		A Coy relieved C Coy	GSP
	3rd–9th		Work during this tour consisted chiefly in wiring and improving trenches	
	9th		Battalion relieved by 19th MIDDLESEX REGT. and moved to Divisional Reserve at HERVILLY.	GSP
	11th		Divisional Band played in Recreation Room.	GSP
	14th		Football Match against 12th SHERWOODS at ROISEL. Lost 2 goals to 1 after a good game.	GSP
	9th–15th		Only one days training was possible owing to Working Parties.	GSP
	15th		Battalion relieved 13th MIDDLESEX REGT. in the line. MALAKOFF FARM to LITTLE	GSP

D. D. & L., London, E.C. (A7853) Wt. W803/M1672 350,000 4/17 Sch. 52a Forms/C/2118/14

Instructions regarding War Diaries and Intelligence Summaries are contained in F. S. Regs., Part II, and the Staff Manual respectively. Title pages will be prepared in manuscript.

WAR DIARY
or
INTELLIGENCE SUMMARY.
(Erase heading not required.)

9th BN. ROYAL SUSSEX REGT.
No. Sx27
Date 2.12.17

Army Form C. 2118.

Place	Date	Hour	Summary of Events and Information	Remarks and references to Appendices
Field	15th		BENJAMIN POST. D Coy Right Front C Coy Left Front. B Coy Right Support A Coy Left Support	[illegible]
	18th		5.30am. Heavy shelling commenced on Brigade on our Left and on our Front. followed by raid against the Brigade on our Left. Bosche made a demonstration with Flammenwerfer against our Right Coy. opposite MALAKOFF FARM. Our Casualties 2 men gassed. Inter-Coy. Relief took place.	[illegible]
	20th		In order to assist attack of 55th Division on our left - ZERO 6.20 am. we made a demonstration with dummy figures opposite RIFLEMAN POST and BENJAMIN POST which drew some retaliation. Casualties 1 died of wounds. 3 wounded	[illegible]
	21st		Another demonstration was made by A & B Coys with "P" (Smoke) bombs. this drew considerable retaliation. Casualties. 2 killed. The Battalion was relieved by 13th MIDDLESEX REGT and moved to BRIGADE RESERVE. H.Q. B & D Coys at HARGICOURT QUARRIES. A & C Coys at TEMPLEUX QUARRIES.	[illegible]
	23rd to 26th incl.		Battalion found over 200 men per day for Working Parties	[illegible]
	27th		Battalion relieved 13th MIDDLESEX REGT. in the line. MALAKOFF FARM to LITTLE BENJAMIN POST. D Coy Right Front. C Coy Left Front. B Coy Right Support. A Coy Left Support	[illegible]

D. D. & L., London, E.C. (A7833) Wt. W803/M1672 350,000 4/17 Sch. 52a. Forms C/2118/14

Instructions regarding War Diaries and Intelligence Summaries are contained in F. S. Regs., Part II. and the Staff Manual respectively. Title pages will be prepared in manuscript.

WAR DIARY or INTELLIGENCE SUMMARY.

(Erase heading not required.)

Army Form C. 2118.

Place	Date	Hour	Summary of Events and Information	Remarks and references to Appendices
Field	30th		Heavy shelling all day on and in rear of Left Bay Front, especially HUSSAR ROAD and along Valley South of LEMPIRE and RONSSOY, the latter being chiefly gas shell. Enemy attacked 55th Division on our Left.	[illegible]

D. D. & L., London, E.C.
(A7833) Wt. W609/M1672 350,000 4/17 Sch. 52a Forms/C2118/14

Army Form C. 2118.

Instructions regarding War Diaries and Intelligence Summaries are contained in F. S. Regs., Part II. and the Staff Manual respectively. Title pages will be prepared in manuscript.

WAR DIARY

~~or~~

~~INTELLIGENCE SUMMARY.~~

(Erase heading not required.)

Vol 28

Place	Date	Hour	Summary of Events and Information	Remarks and references to Appendices
~~Confidential~~			9th Battalion Royal Sussex Regiment	
			for the month of	
			December 1917	
				29 I 6 sheet

A6945 Wt. W11422/M1160 350,000 12/16 D. D. & L. Forms/C./2118/14.

Instructions regarding War Diaries and Intelligence Summaries are contained in F. S. Regs., Part II, and the Staff Manual respectively. Title pages will be prepared in manuscript.

9th Royal Sussex Regiment

WAR DIARY
or
INTELLIGENCE SUMMARY.
(Erase heading not required.)

9th BN. ROYAL SUSSEX REGT.
No. 5x51
Date 4.1.18

Army Form C. 2118.

Place	Date	Hour	Summary of Events and Information	Remarks and references to Appendices
FIELD	1917 Dec 1-4th		Battalion in the line. MALAKOFF FARM to LITTLE BENJAMIN. Enemy Gas shell activity. Much wiring was done.	H.C.C.
	4th		Battalion relieved in the line by 13th MIDDLESEX REGT and moved to Reserve at HERVILLY.	H.C.C.
	5th-10th		Battalion training by Corps. One Coy each day absorbed by Working Parties. Raiding Party of 42 men under 2/LT. D.W.G. MAY, 2/LT. E.L. HALL & 2/LT. J. MANN carried out two days special training	H.C.C.
	10th		Battalion relieved 13th MIDDLESEX REGT. in the line.	H.C.C.
	12th		Raid carried out by Battalion. ZERO 2.30 am. Enemy withdrew his posts and no enemy were encountered. His trenches were found to be in fairly good condition, being duckboarded but not revetted. Practically no retaliation. For further details see O. Os. attached	
	10th-16th		Fairly quiet tour. Some enemy gas shelling. Battalion concentrated on wiring	H.C.C.
	16th		Battalion relieved in the line by 13th MIDDLESEX REGT and moved to Brigade Support at TEMPLEUX QUARRIES.	H.C.C.

D. D. & L., London, E.C.
(A7883) Wt. W803/M1672 350,000 4/17 Sch. 52a Forms C/2118/14

Instructions regarding War Diaries and Intelligence Summaries are contained in F. S. Regs., Part II. and the Staff Manual respectively. Title pages will be prepared in manuscript.

9th Royal Sussex Regiment

WAR DIARY or INTELLIGENCE SUMMARY.

(Erase heading not required.)

9th BN. ROYAL SUSSEX REGT.
No. Sx51
Date 4.1.18

Army Form C. 2118.

Place	Date	Hour	Summary of Events and Information	Remarks and references to Appendices
FIELD	DEC. 17th		Snow fell during night 16th/17th. 80 men found for Working Parties.	
	18th		Battalion relieved in Brigade Support by 12th ROYAL FUSILIERS. and moved to VENDELLES (Brigade in Support).	H.C.C.
	18th-27th		Two Coys. employed on Working Parties each day. Remainder cleared the roads of snow.	H.C.C.
	23rd		The following Officers joined the Battn. from England. Lt. D.C. HESTALL. 2/Lt. R.F. BULLETT, " F.H. BRAY.	H.C.C.
	25th		Christmas Day was celebrated by a Dinner for the men at mid-day which was a great success. The W.Os and Sergeants dined in the evening and a Battalion Dinner was arranged for the Officers. Unfortunately no hall was available for a concert.	H.C.C.
	26th		The whole Battalion was employed on carrying wire for the JEANCOURT Switch line.	H.C.C.
	27th		Battalion relieved 12th ROYAL FUSILIERS. as Support Battalion. H.Q. 'B' & 'C' Coys at TEMPLEUX QUARRIES. 'D' Coy at HARGICOURT and 'A' Coy. attached to 7th NORTHANTS. in the line.	H.C.C.
	27th-31st		These few days were a much appreciated rest.	H.C.C.

D. D. & L., London, E.C. (A7883) Wt. W803/M1672 350,000 4/17 Sch. 52a Forms C/2118/14

9th Royal Sussex Regiment

Instructions regarding War Diaries and Intelligence Summaries are contained in F. S. Regs., Part II. and the Staff Manual respectively. Title pages will be prepared in manuscript.

WAR DIARY
or
INTELLIGENCE SUMMARY.
(Erase heading not required.)

9th BN. ROYAL SUSSEX REGT.
No. Sx 51
Date 4.1.18

Army Form C. 2118.

Place	Date	Hour	Summary of Events and Information	Remarks and references to Appendices
FIELD.	DEC. 31st		Battalion relieved 7th NORTHANTS in the line at HARGICOURT. Dispositions as follows:- RIGHT COY. 'C' Coy. CENTRE COY. 'D' Coy. LEFT COY. 'B' Coy. SUPPORT COY. 'A' Coy. RESERVE COY. 'D' COY. 7th NORTHANTS.	N.C.C.
			HONOURS	
			The following Officers and N.C.Os were mentioned in FIELD-MARSHAL SIR DOUGLAS HAIG'S Despatch dated 7th November 1917:-	
			LIEUT. COL. M.V.B. HILL D.S.O. M.C. MAJOR T. FOSTER. 560. SGT. E. CUTTING. & 8590 SGT. A.J. NEWNHAM	H.C.C.

D. D. & L., London, E.C.
(A7883) Wt. W807/M1672 350,000 4/17 Sch. 52a Forms/C/2118/4

S E C R E T.

Ref. Maps
Trench Sheet
[illegible]
1/10,000.

Copy. No. [illegible]

9th Royal Sussex Regiment

O P E R A T I O N   O R D E R
No. 180.

1. The 9th Royal Sussex Regiment will raid the Enemy Trenches on the night of 11th/12th December, 1917. to secure prisoners.

2. The jumping-off positions from our line will be :-
   (1) 15 yards south of Left Sap F.30.c.95.15.
   (2) 25 yards north of Left Sap.
   (3) 60 yards north of Left Sap.

3. The 73rd LIGHT TRENCH MORTAR BATTERY will co-operate by cutting the wire previously, taking care as much as possible to deceive the enemy by shooting well over the Front Line with some rounds while cutting the wire with others.
   At ZERO the Battery will fire one round from three guns; as soon as these burst, they will fire one more round per gun. The bursting of the second rounds will be the signal to rush. The second rounds will be closely followed by two 'dud' shells fired on Enemy Front Line. Fire will then be maintained at a slow rate of fire on Enemy Support Line A.25.d.22.22. The rate of fire will be quickened at ZERO plus 10, and kept up until two minutes after the rocket signal for withdrawal is sent up.

4. The 7th NORTHANTS will arrange to fire a salvo of Mills Rifle Grenades from the Right Sap into the Enemy Lines at A.25.d.[illegible]., and will maintain a slow rate of fire on this target until they hear the signal for withdrawal, when they will fire a quick succession of salvoes for two minutes, and then cease fire ; or, if this signal is not heard for two minutes after the rocket goes up.

5. The signal for withdrawal will be given by O.C. Raiding Party by blowing a Hunter's Horn, or a succession of two 'longs' and a 'short' (Morse G) on the whistle.
   When this is heard 2/LIEUT. J. MANN will send up from the Left Sap a rocket bursting into many colours.

6. At ZERO plus 2 the Artillery will open on targets as arranged.

7. WITHDRAWAL. The two sections of "A" Coy. and right hand section of "D" Coy. will withdraw to Coy. Headqrs. in SUGAR TRENCH. The remainder to Coy. Headqrs. in MALAKOFF TRENCH, unless there is a heavy barrage to prevent them doing so, in which case they will come to SUGAR TRENCH.
   PRISONERS. Prisoners will be sent to either of these dug-outs and kept there until all is quiet.

8. Battalion H.Q. will be established at the Right Battalion Coy. Headqrs. in SUGAR TRENCH from two hours before ZERO, until the 'ALL CLEAR' signal is given, which will be the code word "RED".

9. MEDICAL ARRANGEMENTS. The M.O. will establish a Dressing Station at Headqrs. SUGAR TRENCH, also an auxiliary one at Coy. Headqrs. MALAKOFF TRENCH.

Continued.

10. The Signal Officer will arrange :-
i. To synchronise watches at Right Battalion H.Q. L.S.I.S.C. at 3-0pm and 6-0pm.
ii. To put out a wire from SUGAR TRENCH to MALAKOFF TRENCH Coy. H.Q. for use in case of emergency.
O.C. "D" Coy. will also send a watch to be synchronised at 6-0pm as in (i).

P L E A S E   A C K N O W L E D G E.

Issued at 4-30pm.
Dec. 9th. 1917.

J Ward
Lieut & A/Adjt.
for O.C. 9th Royal Sussex Regiment.

Distribution.

Copy No.
1. File.
2. War Diary.
3. Commanding Officer.
4. Second in Command.
5. Intelligence Officer.
6. Signalling Officer.
7. Medical Officer.
8. O.C. "A" Coy.
9. O.C. "B" Coy.
10. O.C. "C" Coy.
11. O.C. "D" Coy.
12. 2/LIEUT. D.W.G. MAY.
13. 2/LIEUT. R.L. HALL.
14. 2/LIEUT. J. MANN.
15. 73rd INFANTRY BRIGADE.
16. 7th NORTHANTS.
17. 13th MIDDLESEX REGT.
18. 2nd LEINSTER REGT.
19. 73rd MACHINE GUN COY.
20. 73rd LIGHT TRENCH MORTAR BATTERY.
21. A.P.M. 24th DIVISION.

Army Form C. 2118.

Instructions regarding War Diaries and Intelligence Summaries are contained in F. S. Regs., Part II. and the Staff Manual respectively. Title pages will be prepared in manuscript.

WAR DIARY

~~or~~

~~INTELLIGENCE SUMMARY.~~

(Erase heading not required.)

Vol 29

Place	Date	Hour	Summary of Events and Information	Remarks and references to Appendices
Confidential			9th Battalion Royal Sussex Regiment	
			for the month of	
			January 1918	
				a.H.
				30 I 5 sheets

A6945 Wt. W11422/M1160 350,000 12/16 D. D. & L. Forms/C./2118/14.

7th Royal Sussex Regt.

WAR DIARY or INTELLIGENCE SUMMARY.

(Erase heading not required.)

Instructions regarding War Diaries and Intelligence Summaries are contained in F. S. Regs., Part II. and the Staff Manual respectively. Title pages will be prepared in manuscript.

Army Form C. 2118.

Place	Date	Hour	Summary of Events and Information	Remarks and references to Appendices
FIELD	1918. Jan. 1st		Battalion in the line at HARGICOURT. LIEUT. COL. M.V.B. HILL D.S.O. M.C. proceeded on leave and Major J.J. BANHAM took over command of Battalion.	H.C.C.
	1st–4th		A very quiet tour in the line. The snow lasted throughout the whole tour and condition of the trenches was good. No Casualties during this tour.	H.C.C.
	4th		Battalion relieved by 1st NORTH STAFFS and moved to Camp at MONTIGNY FARM.	H.C.C.
	5th–7th		Battalion provided Working Parties for the Intermediate Line - JEANCOURT - HESBECOURT. Concert Party of 7th NORTHANTS. gave a much appreciated performance on 6th	H.C.C.
	8th		Battalion moved to VRAIGNES CAMP exchanging Billets with 8th Battn THE BUFFS. Rather a trying march owing to the bad state of roads and a heavy snow storm.	H.C.C.
	8th–20th		Battalion was engaged chiefly on Working Parties, but a fair amount of training was possible, notably musketry and Classes for N.C.O.	H.C.C.

D. D. & L., London, E.C. (A7883) Wt. W803/M1672 350,000 4/17 Sch. 52a Forms/C2118/14

9th Royal Sussex Regt.

Army Form C. 2118.

Instructions regarding War Diaries and Intelligence Summaries are contained in F. S. Regs., Part II. and the Staff Manual respectively. Title pages will be prepared in manuscript.

WAR DIARY or INTELLIGENCE SUMMARY.

(Erase heading not required.)

Place	Date	Hour	Summary of Events and Information	Remarks and references to Appendices
FIELD	Jan 17th		2/LT. A.V. BURD left Battalion for TANK CORPS.	H.C.C.
	8th-20th		A considerable amount of work was put in making protection around Huts against aeroplane bombs and also in draining the Camp which was very muddy when the thaw came.	
			Two debates were held and were very popular. There was unfortunately no hut large enough for a concert.	H.C.C.
	13th		2/LT. A.V. FULLINGER joined Battalion and posted to B Company.	
			An inter-Company Football Cup Competition was started and also an Inter-Battalion League Competition. The first round of the Cup Competition was played. A Coy beat B Coy 2nd LEINSTERS 5 goals against 2. B Coy lost to H.Q. 73rd INFANTRY BRIGADE 3 goals to nil. C Coy lost to C Coy 2nd LEINSTERS by 4 goals against 2. D Coy lost to D Coy 7th NORTHANTS 4 - 2.	H.C.C.
	20th		Battalion relieved 3rd RIFLE BRIGADE as Battalion in Brigade Reserve at TEMPLEUX QUARRIES. Capt. C.E. GOAD M.C. appointed Zone Commander of the HARGICOURT TRENCH Area and detached from the Battalion.	H.C.C.
	20th-26th		A quiet period in which the Battalion was engaged on Working Parties.	H.C.C.

D. D. & L., London, E.C.
(A7833) Wt. W803/M1672 350,000 4/17 Sch. 52a Forms C/2118/14

9th Royal Sussex Regt.

Instructions regarding War Diaries and Intelligence Summaries are contained in F. S. Regs., Part II, and the Staff Manual respectively. Title pages will be prepared in manuscript.

WAR DIARY
or
INTELLIGENCE SUMMARY.
(Erase heading not required.)

9th BN. ROYAL SUSSEX REGT.
No. Sx 68
Date 4/2/18

Army Form C. 2118.

Place	Date	Hour	Summary of Events and Information	Remarks and references to Appendices
FIELD	Jan 26th		Battalion relieved 7th NORTHANTS in front line.	H.C.C.
	26th-29		A quiet tour. Casualties 1 O.R. killed. The trenches were in a bad state and much work had to be done to put them in good order again.	H.C.C.
	29th		Battalion relieved by 8th Battn. THE QUEENS & moved to Brigade in Support at VENDELLES.	H.C.C.
	30th		LT. R.W. RUMSBY M.C. transferred to R.F.C.	H.C.C.
	30th-31st		Battalion employed on Working Parties, Baths & Inspections.	H.C.C.
			The noteworthy features of the month were:- 1. The amount of good work done in constructing new defensive lines. 2. The making of a Defence Scheme for the defence in an emergency of each village occupied by troops, including the construction of a Strong point to be manned by an Inlying Picquet and having a permanent look out post towards the front line. 3. The construction of splinter proof protection to huts as a precaution against enemy bombing raids. 4. The systematic improvement of accommodation and comfort of Officers' and men's billets. 5. The large increase in the leave allotment. During this month	

D. D. & L., London, E.C. (A7833) Wt. W593/M1672 350,000 4/17 Sch. 52a. Forms C/2118/14

Instructions regarding War Diaries and Intelligence Summaries are contained in F. S. Regs., Part II. and the Staff Manual respectively. Title pages will be prepared in manuscript.

9th Royal Sussex Regt.

WAR DIARY

or

INTELLIGENCE SUMMARY.

(Erase heading not required.)

9th BN. ROYAL SUSSEX REGT.
No. SX68
Date 4/2/18.

Army Form C. 2118.

Place	Date	Hour	Summary of Events and Information	Remarks and references to Appendices
FIELD	Jan		10 Officers and 101 men were granted leave to England	H.C.C.
			HONOURS	
			Major R. F. DODD and A/Captain H. C. COLEMAN awarded the MILITARY CROSS.	
			No 9841. CSM. J. BARTLETT awarded the DISTINGUISHED CONDUCT MEDAL.	
			No. 7248. Sgt. F. WOOD awarded the Belgian CROIX DE GUERRE.	H.C.C.

D. D. & L., London, E.C.
(A;883) Wt. W593/M1672 350,000 1/17 Sch. 52a Forms/C/2118/14

Instructions regarding War Diaries and Intelligence Summaries are contained in F. S. Regs., Par. II, and the Staff Manual respectively. Title pages will be prepared in manuscript.

WAR DIARY
or
~~INTELLIGENCE SUMMARY~~.
(Erase heading not required.)

Army Form C. 2118.

Vol 30

Place	Date	Hour	Summary of Events and Information	Remarks and references to Appendices
Confidential			9th Bn Royal Sussex Regiment for the month of February 1918	L.A. 31.F 5 sheets

A6945 Wt. W11422/M1160 350,000 12/16 D. D. & L. Forms/C./2118/14.

Instructions regarding War Diaries and Intelligence Summaries are contained in F. S. Regs., Part II. and the Staff Manual respectively. Title Pages will be prepared in manuscript.

WAR DIARY
or
INTELLIGENCE SUMMARY
(Erase heading not required.)

Army Form C. 2118

Place	Date Feb:	Hour	Summary of Events and Information	Remarks and references to Appendices
	1st to 14th.		Battalion at VENDELLES, accommodated in NISSEN + ADRIAN Huts, + forming part of Brigade in Support. 200 to 250 men were found for working parties daily. All other available men were employed on work to improve the Camp. Ovens and brick paths, were built. Splinter-proof walls were built round the huts as protection against Bombs. Time was found for a little gardening to improve the appearance of the Camp. Football Matches were arranged on most afternoons; the Batt: team did not meet with much success. The following games were played besides inter-company games. Association Football. v. Household Cavalry. lost 1-3; v. 13th Middlesex, lost 0-5; v. H.Q. 73rd Inf. Bde. lost 1-2. Rugby Football, 73rd Inf Bde v. 24th Div. Train, won 6pts - 5pts. Hockey. v. 24th Div. H.Q. Drawn 2-2. A good Y.M.C.A. Hut was available + several excellent concerts were arranged, notably one given by the 17th Inf. Bde Concert Party. Two or three evenings were also devoted to Boxing. Training was limited to two Refresher Lewis Gun Classes per Coy + a Senior N.C.O.s Class taken each day by an officer who was an expert in the particular subject.	H.C.C
	6th		A Lecture was given by Major JOYCE, M.C on "The British Soldiers War Aims"	H.C.C
	9th		Five officers attended a demonstration of the co-operation of Tanks + Infantry in attack.	
			A meeting of officers was addressed by A.C.G., Fifth Army, the Rev. Neville TALBOT, M.C.	H.C.C

Instructions regarding War Diaries and Intelligence Summaries are contained in F. S. Regs., Part II. and the Staff Manual respectively. Title Pages will be prepared in manuscript.

WAR DIARY
or
INTELLIGENCE SUMMARY
(Erase heading not required.)

8th B[illegible] [illegible]AL SUSSEX REGT.

Army Form C. 2118

Place	Date	Hour	Summary of Events and Information	Remarks and references to Appendices
	10th		A draft of 1 Officer & 94 O.R. joined from 12th Bn. Royal Sussex Regt which has been disbanded.	H.C.C.
	14th		Bn relieved 3rd Rifle Brigade in the Line, as Centre Bn, holding from FISH LANE to CARBINE TRENCH. Two Companies held the line in depth & 2 Coys & Bn H.Q. were at TEMPLEUX QUARRIES.	H.C.C.
	17th		A silent raid was successfully carried out by a party of 16 O.R. under 2/Lt D.W.G. MAY & 2/Lt H.C. LISSIMAN. The Senior N.C.O's of the party were Sgt TODMAN, M.M. of B Coy & L/Sgt FARRANT of D Coy. The party left our lines at 10.30p.m. & proceeded to TROLLOPE TRENCH. The enemy wire had been reconnoitred the previous evening & found to be weak. 2 officers & 10 O.R. crawled through enemy wire to parapet of the trench. At this moment two of the enemy patrolled above trench behind the parados. They were allowed to pass as the raiding party was not in position. Two officers & 2 N.C.O's then crossed the trench & lay out in a semi-circle 15 yds behind the trench. The enemy patrol of 2 men returned & when they were in the centre of the party, the signal (by string) was given to rush. There was a short struggle & the enemy were then over-powered & taken back without any casualties, not a shot having been fired. The success of the raid was due to the excellent leadership & the courage of the whole party, but was made possible by good observation & study of aeroplane photos, by which the route of patrol was discovered.	H.C.C.

1875 Wt. W593/826 1,000,000 4/15 J.B.C. & A. A.D.S.S./Forms/C. 2118.

Instructions regarding War Diaries and Intelligence Summaries are contained in F. S. Regs., Part II. and the Staff Manual respectively. Title Pages will be prepared in manuscript.

WAR DIARY
or
INTELLIGENCE SUMMARY
(Erase heading not required.)

9th BN. SUSSEX REGT.
No. ....
Date... ....

Army Form C. 2118

Place	Date	Hour	Summary of Events and Information	Remarks and references to Appendices
	14th to 22nd.		A very quiet time, except for a shoot on RUBY WOOD which provoked a certain amount of retaliation. An attempted enemy raid on BOWER LANE on the 19th was broken up by Lewis Gun + Rifle fire.	HCC
	22nd		Bn. took over front from RUBY LANE to LITTLE BEN, relieving 13th Middlesex on left + handing over a few posts on right to the 8th QUEENS. The defence of the line was now well organized in depth. All three Brigades were in the line, each having one Bn in the Outpost Zone, one Bn in the Battle Zone + one Bn in billets in Reserve	HCC
	25th		Bn. was relieved by 13th MIDDLESEX + became Support Bn of the Brigade, holding the Battle Zone, with H.Q. at TEMPLEUX QUARRIES. From 25th to the end of the month the line livened up considerably. Each night there was a considerable bombardment on fronts to our flank. On the 28th the enemy raided a Bn of the 66th Division which had that day taken over the line in front of us from the 13th Middlesex. The raid was very creditably repulsed with casualties to the enemy including 2 unwounded prisoners.	HCC
			Casualties during the month. Lt. R. BURNIER was wounded while acting as Brigade Intelligence Officer on 19th February + died at C.C.S. at TINCOURT on 21st February. He had been with the Bn since Sept. '16 + as Intelligence Officer had done very valuable work	HCC

1875 Wt. W593/826 1,000,000 4/15 J.B.C. & A. A.D.S.S./Forms/C. 2118.

Instructions regarding War Diaries and Intelligence Summaries are contained in F. S. Regs., Part II. and the Staff Manual respectively. Title Pages will be prepared in manuscript.

WAR DIARY
or
INTELLIGENCE SUMMARY
(Erase heading not required.)

9th BN. R[illegible]L SUSSEX REGT.
No. ....
Date ....

Army Form C. 2118

Place	Date	Hour	Summary of Events and Information	Remarks and references to Appendices
			Casualties. Other ranks – 1 killed – 2 died of wounds.	HCC
			Honours. Military Cross – 2/Lt D.W.G. MAY – B Coy	
			Bar to Military Medal – No 13042 L/Cpl W.T. BALL – A Coy.	
			Military Medal – No 305 L/Sgt A.A. FARRANT – D Coy.	
			No 6697 Pte F. GRIFFIN – B Coy	
			No 14942 L/Cpl T.W. DICKERSON – C Coy	HCC

1875 Wt. W593/826 1,000,000 4/15 J.B.C. & A. A.D.S.S./Forms/C. 2118.

73rd Brigade.

24th Division.

9th BATTALION

ROYAL SUSSEX REGIMENT

M A R C H 1 9 1 8

Appendix :-

Report on Operations 21 - 27.3.18.

(24 Div) 73/24

Army Form C. 2118.

Instructions regarding War Diaries and Intelligence Summaries are contained in F. S. Regs., Part II, and the Staff Manual respectively. Title pages will be prepared in manuscript.

WAR DIARY
or
~~INTELLIGENCE SUMMARY.~~
(Erase heading not required.)

Vol 31

Place	Date	Hour	Summary of Events and Information	Remarks and references to Appendices
~~Confidential~~			9th Bn. Royal Sussex Regiment for the month of March 1918	32.I 20 mut

A6945 Wt. W11422/M1160 350,000 12/16 D. D. & L. Forms/C./2118/14.

MARCH 1918. 9 ROYAL SUSSEX Regiment

WAR DIARY
or
INTELLIGENCE SUMMARY.
(Erase heading not required.)

Instructions regarding War Diaries and Intelligence Summaries are contained in F. S. Regs., Part II. and the Staff Manual respectively. Title pages will be prepared in manuscript.

9th BN. ROYAL SUSSEX REGT. No. RS/145 Date ....

Army Form C. 2118.

Place	Date	Hour	Summary of Events and Information	Remarks and references to Appendices
Field	1st		Battalion situated in TEMPLEUX Quarry and HARDY BANKS. 11pm heavy bombardment of Front line and Battalion "Stood to" during enemy raid on EAST posts at CARBINE Trench	H.C.C.
	2nd		Battalion relieved by 6th LANCASHIRE FUS and marched to HANCOURT in a blizzard	H.C.C.
	3rd to 20th		Battalion in training at HANCOURT, concentrated chiefly on Musketry and Platoon exercises. Brigade All-round efficiency competition was competed for but was unfinished. Battalion found a few Working parties	H.C.C.
	15th		B Coy moved to VENDELLES for attachment to 258th Tunnelling Coy. REs	H.C.C.
	20		Battle positions at HESBECOURT reconnoitred by CO OC Coys Signalling Officer and 1 additional Officer per Company	H.C.C.
	21st		Battalion Stood to at 5am and went up to Battle positions at HESBECOURT through rather a heavy gas barrage and took up dispositions as under in the Redoubt line	

Instructions regarding War Diaries and Intelligence Summaries are contained in F. S. Regs., Part II. and the Staff Manual respectively. Title pages will be prepared in manuscript.

WAR DIARY
or
INTELLIGENCE SUMMARY.
(Erase heading not required.)

Army Form C. 2118.

Place	Date	Hour	Summary of Events and Information	Remarks and references to Appendices
Continued	21st		The Bosche first appeared in front of TRINITY at about 3pm but failed to make any headway. The line was reinforced by stragglers coming back from the front. HESBECOURT was heavily shelled up to about 2pm also TRIFLE, but the forward line was not heavily shelled until about 2.30pm when enemy dropped 5'9s into wire at TRINKET	H.C.
			The night was quiet. "D" Coy was relieved by Cavalry and took up position in WHITE CHALK TRENCH between WASTART and TRIFLE	H.C.
	22nd		The enemy attacked TRINKET at 6am under cover of a thick mist but did not take it until it was entirely surrounded at about 11am. TRINITY was also heavily engaged and were almost cut off but were able to withdraw down a Shallow trench to TRIFLE	H.C.
			Enemy also attacked WASTART in the mist and forced Cavalry to withdraw thus exposing "D" Coys right flank and forcing them to retire on to HESBECOURT line. The Bosche worked round their right flank until he got on to the high ground in the region of HERVILLY Wood forcing "D" Coy back into line with Battalion HQ who had taken up a position along the light railway running from HESBECOURT to HERVILLY.	
			A party was sent round and took up a position on the high ground in rear of HERVILLY Wood preventing a further outflanking movement on the part of the enemy.	
			At about 2pm the position in front of HESBECOURT became untenable and the Battalion was withdrawn on to the ROISEL–MONTIGNY Road where a rear-guard action was fought by about 30 men on the high ground to the S.W of HERVILLY temporarily checking large numbers of the enemy.	H.C.

A5834 Wt. W4973/M687 750,000 8/16 D. D. & L. Ltd. Forms/C2118/13.

Instructions regarding War Diaries and Intelligence Summaries are contained in F. S. Regs., Part II. and the Staff Manual respectively. Title pages will be prepared in manuscript.

WAR DIARY
or
INTELLIGENCE SUMMARY.
(Erase heading not required.)

9th BN. ROYAL SUSSEX REGT.
No.......................
Date.......................

Army Form C. 2118.

Place	Date	Hour	Summary of Events and Information	Remarks and references to Appendices
Continued	22nd		advancing through HERVILLY and HERVILLY Wood. This party then retired fighting through the Green line at BERNES (held by 24th Divisional Depot Battalion) and concentrated at MERAUCOURT. The strength of the Battalion was found to be about 120 rifles.	H.C.
	23rd		The Battalion marched off at 5am and took up a position in a thick mist at GUISANCOURT (arriving about 6am). At 8am orders were received to withdraw, which order was carried out, without engaging the enemy. The 73rd F.A. Battery was attached to the Battalion.	H.C.
			The withdrawal was continued to the River SOMME at FALVY where the Battalion took up a position forward of the bridge head. This was only held for about an hour when the Battalion was relieved by the 72nd Inf. Bde, and retired across the SOMME and marched to MARCHELEPOT, but returned in the afternoon to ?ICOURT.	H.C.
	24th		Battalion marched off at 6am to CHAULNES arriving about 7.30 and remained until 1pm when it was ordered to take up a position in front of PUSEAUX which was reached at 3pm and well consolidated. Patrols went forward to PUNCHY and remained till dusk but touch was not obtained with enemy.	H.C.
	25		The Battalion was ordered forward to counter-attack at BRESLINCOURT and advanced at 8am and encountered heavy machine gun fire just outside BRESLINCOURT and was unable to advance further, but held the ground until 2pm when position became untenable, and orders were given to withdraw to original line taken up in the morning. Owing to heavy casualties in	

A5834 Wt. W4973/M687 750,000 8/16 D. D. & L. Ltd. Forms/C.2118/13.

II

Instructions regarding War Diaries and Intelligence Summaries are contained in F. S. Regs., Part II. and the Staff Manual respectively. Title pages will be prepared in manuscript.

WAR DIARY
or
INTELLIGENCE SUMMARY.
(Erase heading not required.)

9th BN. ROYAL SUSSEX REGT.
No.........................
Date.......................

Army Form C. 2118.

Place	Date	Hour	Summary of Events and Information	Remarks and references to Appendices
Continued	25		Officers it was found impossible to reorganise on this line so the Battalion was withdrawn behind PUSEAUX where it was reorganised and went forward again to original morning's line. This however soon became untenable owing to bodies of the enemy working round the flanks and the Battalion withdrew fighting and formed a defensive flank behind PUSEAUX.	
			At dusk Battalion withdrew to a prepared line about 400 yards in rear.	M.C.
	26.		At 12.30 am a further withdrawal was ordered on to HALLU - CHAULNES line which was successfully accomplished. 200 reinforcements arrived from a Composite Battalion.	
			At dawn Battalion was again ordered to withdraw which order was carried out successfully without casualties to an old Trench line about 700 yards in front of VRELY - ROUVROY Road on a ridge overlooking MEHARICOURT. The enemy were seen advancing in force to MEHARICOURT but on coming under fire he withdrew to the Woods in rear.	
			A patrol was pushed out to MEHARICOURT and found no enemy in the village. The night was quiet.	M.C.
	27.		The enemy attacked at about 10 am and succeeded in entering a system of trenches on our right and bombed down the trenches held by "A" Coy and 3rd L.T.M.B. He was repeatedly driven back by bayonet charges down the Trench but we were unable to eject him entirely as there were no bombs available. Finally a block was formed and some very good work was done by "A" Coy's Lewis Guns in holding this block. Bombs arrived about 5 pm after which there was	

A5834 Wt. W4973/M687 750,000 8/16 D. D. & L. Ltd. Forms/C.2118/13.

IY

Instructions regarding War Diaries and Intelligence Summaries are contained in F. S. Regs., Part II. and the Staff Manual respectively. Title pages will be prepared in manuscript.

WAR DIARY
or
INTELLIGENCE SUMMARY.
(Erase heading not required.)

9th BN. ROYAL SUSSEX REGT.
No. ....
Date ....

Army Form C. 2118.

Place	Date	Hour	Summary of Events and Information	Remarks and references to Appendices
Continued	27.		little difficulty in holding the enemy.	H.C.
	28.		Orders were received to withdraw to Brigade Support to the Valley down which Railway runs behind VRELY and WARVILLERS which operation was carried out about 3am. At about noon orders were received to withdraw further on to the CAIX - le QUESNEL line which was completed by 1.30pm. At 5pm it was noticed that the Battalions on both flanks were withdrawing so an Officer immediately went to Brigade H.Q. to ascertain the situation and found that orders to withdraw had been issued but had failed to reach the Battalion. Accordingly an immediate withdrawal was carried out to VILLERS-aux-ERABLES where the Brigade concentrated. At about 7.30pm the Brigade formed up and proceeded by march route to CASTEL where Battalion bivouacked in the Bois de SENECAT arriving there about 2am.	H.C.
	29.		Battalion marched off at about 2.30pm and took up an outpost line in front of Wood on the high ground overlooking the River between CASTEL and MOREUIL. At 6pm outposts were withdrawn and Battalion marched to Billets in THEZY-GLIMONT passing West of Bois de SENECAT and thence through HAILLES.	H.C.
	30.		At 5am Battalion took up a position holding Bridge-heads at BERTEAUCOURT and THENNES which were relieved by 7th NORTHAMPTONS at 5pm.	H.C.

A5834 Wt. W4973/M687 750,000 8/16 D. D. & L. Ltd. Forms/C.2118/13.

Instructions regarding War Diaries and Intelligence Summaries are contained in F. S. Regs., Part II. and the Staff Manual respectively. Title pages will be prepared in manuscript.

WAR DIARY
or
INTELLIGENCE SUMMARY.
(Erase heading not required.)

Army Form C. 2118.

Place	Date	Hour	Summary of Events and Information	Remarks and references to Appendices
	31.		1 Section was sent to watch Bridge at HAILLES at 10am but was relieved at 3pm. At 5pm Battalion relieved 7th NORTHANTS in the position held previous day. A statement of the Casualties sustained by the Battalion during operations is attached. A Narrative of the Operations carried out by the 73rd Infantry Brigade from 21st March to 8th April 1918 is attached.	H.R.C.

VI

A5834 Wt. W4973/M687 750,000 8/16 D. D. & L. Ltd. Forms/C2118/13.

Diary of Lt.-Col. M.V.B. Hill

March 21st - 27th 1918.

x - x - x - x - x - x

Commanding A Battn.
No. 3 Bde. Z. Div.
9th Royal Sussex Regt.
73rd Infantry Bde.
24th Division.
XIX Corps. Fifth Army.

1 9 1 8.

March 2-20th — The Battalion spent 18 days of glorious weather in a camp at Hancourt. The number of working parties taking the period as a whole were not very great so that the greater part of the time was devoted to training in which all ranks shewed exceptional enthusiasm. This enthusiam could be attributed to the spirit of platoon competition and the prospect of competing in the all round efficiency competition that was being got up in the Brigade. The range which was close to our Camp was in constant use and seemed to give more pleasure to the men than a game of football.

21st. 4.40 a.m. — Was awakened by a heavy bombardment and at once came to the conclusion that it was the beginning of the long expected German attack. The Battalion stood to and cookers were not going.

6 a.m. — Received orders to "Man Battle Positions". These were 4 redoubts about 1 mile behind the Front line of Y Division. They had been dug the night before last and had been fitted up with rations and S.A.A. at Midnight 20-21st. The trenches in places were however only 1 foot deep.

6.30. — All Companies were clear of the village and on their way to their redoubts - about 2 hours march.

9.30. — Dispositions. Trinket. Redoubt. C.Company.

Capt. H. Saxon. M.C.

Lts. Wilson, 2nd.-Lts. Chichester & Clerihew.

Trinity Redoubt A.Company. Capt. A.V.Rewell.

2nd.-Lts. Hall, Davison & Chapman.

These 2 redoubts were situated on the high ground running from Fervaque Farm, behind L.10.A. and Templeur. They were well wired, on reverse slope (the greater part) and about 600 yds. apart. The fact that they were on reverse slope naturally spoilt their field of fire but must have saved them casualties from artillery fire. The enemy however could not be prevented from getting to the wire in daylight.

21st March. — Upstart Redoubt on high ground between Jeancourt & Hesbecourt. — D. Company. 2nd.-Lt. Bishop (O.C.) Paling Hally & Fraser.

Triple Redoubt just in front of Hesbecourt. — B. Company. Lt. Surridge, 2nd.-Lts. Lissiman, Regen, Pullinger.

21st March.	Hesbecourt.	Head Qtrs.	Lt.-Col. M.V.B.Hill Capt. A.F. Best. Lt.Paul actg/adjt. 2nd.-Lt. May & Capt.C. Harris. R.A.M.C.

About 40 casualties were suffered when moving up chiefly by B and D Companies on Hesbe - & Jean - Court Road. Gas shelling was considerable round Hervilly and Hervilly Wood and Hesbecourt. Regan killed and Surridge wounded by 1 shell. A Company got to their redoubt with only 1 casualty. They kept to high ground north of Hesbecourt, Scouts sent forward to study barrage would have saved casualties. Lewis Gun Limbers were too heavily loaded and could not go across country with their companies. They might have been unloaded sooner.

1 p.m. Shelling round H.Q. was heavy. A mule in a mess cart standing outside our Nissen Hut was hit direct by a 5.9 - casualties considerable including 2 valuable runners. The placidity of the mule before it was hit was remarkable. It (the mule) undoubtedly broke the shock of the shell and saved many casualties. We changed our Headquarters.

C.Company reported "Enemy in L. 10a. Troops withdrawing. C. Company stands". C. Company at 2 p.m. were firing to right rear besides to their front.

4 p.m. "A" Company reported enemy all round Trinket (C. Coy.) and in Capeza Copse. Trinket apparently fallen. Other people reported this too, but it did not fall for another 21 hours. Afternoon much quieter. Rations all got up to H.Qrs. Sent details of Y Div. under a Major to protect A company's left flank and watch the north from the high ground south of Roisel - Templeux Road.

8 p.m. Visited A and C Companies. The line between them was filled with details of Y Division also the sunken road on left of A Company leading to Templeux. Got some details of Y Division to dig in on right of C Company and Cavalry were going to patrol from them to Capeza Copse which was held by Y Division.

Officers surviving:	A.Coy.	Rewell, Davison, Hall and Chapman.
	B. "	Mann (O.C.)& Pullinger (reinforcement)
	C. "	Saxon & (?) Clerihew.
	D. "	Bishop, Fraser, Hally and Paling.

22nd.
2 a.m. A and C Company's each captured a couple of prisoners in our wire during the night. Cavalry relieved D. Company who then occupied trench between Upstart Redoubt and Hesbecourt. Entrenching Battalion came up and dug in in front of B. Company. I heard they fought like devils next day. Received appreciation from B.G.C. of the effect we had had on other troops in neighbourhood. All companies fetched their rations and water during the night.

Got a little food and rest during the early morning.

8.18 a.m. D Company found that Upstart Redoubt was in the hands of the enemy.

8.30 a.m. Captain Best reported that enemy Machine Guns active from E end of Hervilly Wood - accordingly turned out H.Q. and manned Light Railway from Hesbecourt to Hervilly. Machine Gun bullets swept all this ground. We could hear for the next 3 or 4 hours B Company's Lewis Gunners being very active. During morning many troops (Y Div. and Cavalry) came through Hesbecourt. These were rallied and got to take up line on North of us, but our barrage came down in the midst of them which was intended to be defending Hervilly which was thought to have fallen in enemy's hands at 10 a.m. Sent my orderly to inform artillery that Trinket 1 mile further on was still held by C Company. Went on trying to rally troops who were quite 200 in number, but there being no line to take up just there I found it difficult. Tried to do the same

11.30 a.m. thing at Roisel where I found a Colonel and 300 men and plenty of Officers and told them to hold Roisel and I would try and do the same to Hervilly and high grounds south of it. (A Squadron of cavalry came up at 10.30 to retake Hervilly!!).

On my way back I looked in at our old Transport Officers Mess which was deserted and contained no sign of a drink.

12.45 Found Paul and his H.Q. Platoon holding High ground on Montigny Road. Withdrew May and his details from Light Railway behind Hesbecourt. My servant who I engaged on the Quays of St. Nazaire on 21st September 1914 was wounded in the arm. I had long looked on him as my mascot as up to this day neither of us had been wounded.

1.30 About this time A and C Companies had the Germans all round them and nobody on their flanks. D Company - 1000 yards further behind had been attacked from the South opposite. A Company saw the relics of C Company surrendering* after having fired every round. Not a single man of either these Companies had come back so far. A Company having some dead ground behind them and a long belt of wire on their left were able to withdraw although the Germans had Machine Guns within 50 yards of them. The Germans followed them the other side of the wire all the way back to Hesbecourt inflicting about 30% casualties including Capt. Rewell (wounded). This withdrawal must have taken place about 1.30.

*not true, but see Capt. Saxons account.

The defence of Trinket and Trinity Redoubts delayed the enemy nearly 24 hours. Unsupported by artillery and with their right flank most hopelessly exposed by the fall of Fervaque Farm they just stuck it until further resistance was useless. "C Company Stands", will I hope for many years to come recall one of the most glorious incidents inthe history of the Royal Sussex Regiment.

B Company withdrew after this but not until the Germans were West of Hesbecourt - Roisel Road.

1.50 p.m. Enemy came through Hesbecourt in very large numbers with artillery close behind him.

2.15 To return to the story of H.Q. which was all I knew anything about at this time. About 20 rifles, 2nd.-Lieut. May, Paul and myself took up position on Montiguey Road and carried out a nice little rearguard action, concentrating our fire first on Hervilly Wood where enemy scouts were seen, then on to enemy advancing over Hervilly Football Ground then on to an enemy Machine Gun which was pushed across the Hervilly Road. We drew its fire alright! and so saved it being turned on to a mass of troops going in direction of Details Camp. Casualties - Drum Sergt., Signalling Sergt. and Corporal and D Company's Sergt. and Lance.-Corporal. We claimed a dozen victims. Tanks and a squadron of cavalry dismounted were on the scene, but did not do much. One Tank had at 11 o'clock got to near (sic) Upstart Redoubt and undoubtedly held up the enemy for some time.

3.15 Started for Bernes and then Montecourt where about 100 men, all told, turned up. On our way to Bernes, British Hotchkiss guns opened on us, but by waving our caps and maps we got them to stop.

It took us about 2½ hours going very slowly to get from Hervilly to Montecourt via Bernes. "W"* Division had just arrived and were digging in on the green line. Tried to get some Cavalry with Hotchkiss Guns to stay on the crest 200 yards in front of this line and engage the enemy as he gave such a very good target coming away from Hervilly but met with no success. Went through Hancourt where all our blankets and haversacks had to be left. There was also an enormous heavy ammunition dump which had to be abandoned.

* (50th)

5.30 p.m. Plenty of food and tea for the men, found some blankets for them so had hopes of getting some rest in the tents. Some men of B and A Companies under Mann and Hall got to Hamel where they again engaged the enemy. They joined us at Chaulnes on 24th very tired and hungry.

7.0 p.m. Transport had to move off, Some shells burst within 50 yards of our tents so we evacuated them and spent the night in a sunken road nearby.

23rd.4. a.m. Moved off to Geuzacourt via Flez. Map reading in the mist rather difficult as so many roads on the Map could not be found to exist.

Dispositions:			
	A. Company.	On Right.	Capt.Collingbourne 2nd.-Lieuts.Duffield and Davis.
	B and C (details)	On Left.	2nd.-Lts. Golden and(?) Pullinger.
	D. Company.	Support.	(?) Fraser and Halley.

C Battalion on our left and B Battalion in support.

8.30 Sent May on a horse to look for troops on our right - he rode for 1½ miles and found no one.

Recieved orders to withdraw to Falvy on the Somme.

11.30 On arrival at Somme (about 5 miles) about this time the Battn. stood to guard the Bridgehead while C Battn. and No. 1 Brigade 2 Battns. crossed over. "B" Battn. and another Battn. were still a long way back fighting a rear-guard action. No. 2 Brigade turned up and disposed themselves also to protect the Bridgehead - so I got permission to withdraw over the river. Today was very like a field day as we had not yet seen an enemy and everyone seemed very happy

3.0 p.m. Passed through Licourt (2 miles) but had to come back and support "T" Division who were holding the river. Saw a lot of cavalry moving forward on x west side of river. They were a very fine sight. Did not see them come back again. Before I reached Licourt the enemy was shelling the cross-roads E of it and forced some Ambulances to withdraw.

5.0 p.m. Majors Barnham and Young joined us with the details with whom they had been holding the line on the previous night in front of ~~the~~ Montecourt, Cookers turned up and men were well fed. A Battn. Commander of "T" Division was asking for very strong reinforcements to his front line on the river, but nobody seemed to decide who should do it. Brigade H.Q. spent the night with us in a cellar - there were wire-netting beds for all - but too cold to be of much use. Lieutenant Ward had ^a^ heart-burn very badly, made enormous creakings of his bed every time he turned over, and was always mumbling in his sleep about S.A.A.

6.0 p.m. Reconnoitred the ridge behind the Front line with Collingbourne to decide action in case of attack. Saw Germans in very large numbers moving on East side of the river towards Peronne.

24th. 7 a.m. Moved off to Chaulnes - about 4 miles off - men singing the whole way - having marched or covered during the previous day at least 14 miles and having had no breakfast. At first halt met cookers which just had sufficient tea for all.

10 a.m. Breakfast. Kidneys and champagne. Had a good wash and change and 2 hours sleep. Put on my best tunic to be destroyed 3 days later by a gun-shot wound.

1. p.m. Went to Brigade H.Q. and received orders to go to Puiseux 2 miles S.E. of us. Moved off at 2 p.m.

4. p.m. The positions east of village were good - plenty of wire in front of us. "B" Battn. on right and the old Corps on left.

Dispositions:

Right.	C.Company.	Holden and Hall.
Left.	D.Company.	Capt. Young, 2nd-Lts. Halley and Fraser.
Rt. Support.	A.Company.	Capt. Collingbourne, 2nd.-Lt. Duffield.
Lt. Support.	B.Company.	2nd.-Lts. Mann and Pullinger.
Reserve.		L.T.M. Battery. Lts. L'Estrange & Smith

7. p.m. Had a long walk in search of Colonel Hancock, dined with him and Colonel Whitty and discussed position of Machine Guns and advisability of getting everybody behind the wire. Companies did a lot of good digging and made a good position. Plenty of food for the men. Very cold night - very little sleep.

25th. 7. a.m. Orders received to advance to Dreslincourt to co-operate with French counter-attack. C and D Companies were to make good the ground up to Dreslincourt and then A and B to go through them and counter-attack with the French. (B Battalion was on our right). D Company found enemy in Dreslincourt so occupied trenches 600 yards from them in a good position - so long as their flanks were all right. C Company (on right at level crossing in touch with B Battalion) seemed to have a lot of rough ground in front of them over which the enemy subsequently advanced. B and A in support on the Railway 100 yards behind. The gutter on side of Railway 18" deep was all the cover they had - the same with H.Q. Railway was absolutely taped with Machine Gun Fire and by Whizzbang battery. Captain Collingbourne badly hit in lung. Troops on our left withdrew for no apparent good reason - enemy crept round C and D Companies all the morning.

12.30 p.m. Received orders that French were counter-attacking at 11 a.m. and we were to "co-operate as much as possible"

There was not the slightest sign of the French.

2.0. Received orders to withdraw as nobody was on our left. A and B got back with only a few casualties, but only about 15 of D and C got away - as these were in a salient and almost entirely surrounded. 2nd.-Lt. Golden was shot at close range and also Capt.Young* who insisted on being the last of his Company to leave the trench. Thus (I thought) ended the career of an idealist and enthusiast who inspired his Company to reach the highest state of efficiency. In fact he never rested in content with what he had done, but always tried to go one better. As I was going down the Railway back to the morning's positions one of our Scout aeroplanes crashed to earth near us. Something shot out from the seat, in 1/10th of a second the whole plane was a sheet of flame and 3 minutes afterwards one wondered whether a plane really did come down. 2nd.-Lieut. Mann was then hit in the leg close to me and I speedily got him 50 yards away before the next shell came which it soon did. Held his main artery which was pumping away like a fire hose while the Doctor put on a torniquet and bound up his shattered foot. Got him on to a stretcher shook him by the hand and assured him,in response to his anxious enquiry whether he had given satisfaction, that he had more than done so. A heavy ammunition dump was then blown up by a Boche shell, and we had to walk through a hail of fragments.

*reported prisoner and wounded on 9th May.

Men were with difficulty reformed at old positions on account of 5.9's falling amongst us. No. 1. I.B. reported to have withdrawn so gave orders to reform other side of village and after consultation with Officer Commanding C Battalion to withdraw to Hally. On arrival we were ordered to return as other Brigades had done not so. (sic) The men about-turned in very good style - appearing to have quite recovered from what they had just been through. A and B Companies had both lost during the day 25% o.r's and their Company Commanders (it was the Fourth B had lost in the five days and the second A had lost). C Company was for the second time in 5 days non-existant and D Company, 1 Sergeant and 15 men. H.Q. 1 now used as a fighting platoon.

Having returned a horse I borrowed from Machine Gun Company - which incidently jumped a trench remarkably well - I hurried back into the village into which a few 5.9's were dropping and reached the East end of it. Could locate no Germans in our area but saw quite a number near the railway. ~~Baxix~~ Detailed May, Paul and Pullinger and Duffield each with a platoon (20 strong) to advance in extended order and make good our old positions. They did this on the right but on the left of the copse where our H.Q. had been - they did not get so far as they engaged the enemy at about 200 yards range. Got C Company, C Battalion to advance on North side of village which prevented our flank being turned. They put up a very good fight until compelled to withdraw by the enemy in large numbers getting round them. This was about 5 p.m. when I withdrew all our fellows to West side of the village and conformed with another Company of C Battalion who were in line with B Battn. Shortly after received orders to withdraw another 500 yards to conform with No. 1 Brigade whose right was at Chaulnes Station. Our line was very extended as the railway which ran E.N.E. continued to be our boundary and we were withdrawing slightly South of West. Had a gap of 400 yards with no wire or trench. Got into touch myself with C Battn. No. 1 Brigade but nobody after that succeeded in finding them.

26th 2 a.m. Brigade withdrew to Hallu line. There was a full moon and we were lucky in not being spotted - though sniping did increase a bit - Lost my Compass - £7. 7. 0. Major Barnham made a splendid dump of rations and 5 Dixies of tea for us. I believe we were the only unit to get it, though it cost us the dixies. Were reinforced by 3 Nondscript platoons with 3 new Cadet Officers. Their appearence was very different to that of our men. They had pale faces and brand new khaki - our fellows had weather beaten faces and very weather beaten khaki. Had 3 hours rest and some good food in a comfortable dugout - felt quite certain that next morning would be the end of all things and we decided to fight to the last round and then withdraw if there was any chance.

9.15. But at 9.15 we were again withdrawing under Brigade orders - we could do this without being seen - Merciful Providence - I gave orders to Companies to withdraw in a due West direction keeping the Railway on their right which ran slightly N of W. I ommitted to mention that there was a branch Railway which ran due South. After going a mile I saw troops keeping this Railway on their right so I came back over ½ mile and put them right just in time. A signaller I sent to do this was much to slow in attracting their attention.

Marched through Chilly - the ground here was a mass of shell holes and trenches - being an old Battlefield - and arrived in nice compact Artillery formation which enabled us to go straight into position on the Bouvicy - Roisers line. Had time to fill every man's waterbottle in village Menaricourt ¼ mile in front of our line.

1. p.m. Saw a lot of Lorries in their innocence going towards Bouvrey, they were soon spotted and shelled so they beat a hasty retreat. Enemy must have been well forward on our right.

3. p.m. Enemy appeared in large numbers through Chilly and South of it but at 5 p.m. they appeared to withdraw hurriedly and our patrols shortly after reported village in front of us clear of the enemy. We could hear a lot of Machine Guns and Artillery fire the other side of Chilly but could not make out what it was.

6. p.m. Took over more line from No. 2 Brigade and our right became the apex of a dangerous salient on account of the line the trench took. Gave urgent orders to Companies to dig slits so as to get protection from the flanks.

My Command now consisted of 2 Companies.

No. 1. under 2nd.-Lt. Duffield.

A. Company.	1 Platoon.	
B. Company.	2 Platoons.	Pullinger and Hally.
C.and D.	1 Platoon.	Fraser.

No. 2. under Lieut. L'Estrange.

L.T.M. (20 men)	1.Platoon.	Lieut. Smith.
2 platoons of Reinforcements.	-	2 Officers.

27th. Again Tea and Rations were successfully brought up during the night. My heels were now so sore and my tenden Achilles so stiff that I could only walk about 1 mile an hour - so I rested nearly the whole night - though I did not get much sleep, my feet next morning were much better.

9. a.m. Heard once again that barking of enemy Machine Guns which now only meant one thing - "our men withdrawing" - I rushed out of the gun pit which had been our H.Q. for the night - and saw troops withdrawing in large numbers about $\frac{3}{4}$ mile on our left and also small units past our very door. O.C. "B" Battn. and myself - tho' we thought for a moment we would have to do the same thing - got to our men in Front line and told them we were all going to stay whoever went. There appeared to be no infantry attack on our left and the situation was soon restored.

(At Stand-to this morning, Pullinger scattered an enemy patrol - killing 2 and capturing 2 including a German Doctor. The Maps this Officer had on him were very good - all the valleys were marked green and the contours brown. The higher the contour the browner. The most in-experienced Map-reader could see at a glance which was a hill and which a valley).

10.15. Boche got into trench held by details of "V" Div. on L'Estrange's right and started bombing him. They also got a Machine Gun into a position from which it could enfilade his trench. After spending a great deal of S.A.A., and putting up a very good fight he was compelled to withdraw to the left having suffered a large number of casualties from the Machine Gun which got bullets right into the trench. They accordingly withdrew across the Road which ran through the middle of our line. Lt. Smith established a block which

I saw him guarding with his section. I got Coy. Sergt. Maj. Head to make another Block further back and put B Coy. into the trench running at rt. L's (sic) to Front Line. Then went to C Bn. and explained position to them and told Capt. Stratton – who with another Coy. was in close support to me – the situation and showed him some landmarks to guide him in case he should have to counter-attack. On our way to an O.P. some long range Machine Gun fire was only just going over our heads – so by walking (or rather running) 30 yards nearer the Machine Gun we put ourselves in greater xx safety. I then heard once again the Machine Guns barking and saw the troops all moving left handed some of them out of the trench. I immediately got the other Company of C Bn. to advance at the "High Porte" towards them – with the result that the troops rallied at once. All thanks to this Coy. of C Bn. Then rushed on to First Line and along top of trench to get our men to charge the Boche in the trench who had not advanced so far as I thought – when I stopped a bullet from the left. Fell down about 10 yards behind the parapet where Coy. Sergt. Maj. Head tied my arm up very well so that it did not have to be touched until I got almost to Abbeville. I noticed B Coy. were still in their trench and am curious to know what happened after.

- - - - - - - - - - - - - - - -

Written by Captain H.A.SAXON. M.C.

commanding C. Company of 9th Royal Sussex Regiment

after his return from Germany, in December 1918.

- - - - - - - - - - - - - - - - - -

"C" Company. March 21 - 22.

On March 21st C Coy. left Hancourt about 6.20 a.m. - slightly over 80 strong. The C.O. watched us march out. I stopped with him for a minute or two, when he particularly impressed on me the fact that there was no necessity to hurry, and that the men should be allowed to take the march up at an easy pace. We were moving by platoons and during my short halt No. 9, the leading platoon took the Bernes road and a platoon of the Northamptons got in between that platoon and No. 10. We got into touch with No. 9 again before we reached our battle position. The only effect of this loss of connection was to prevent us striking as far north as we might have done - we could not afford to let the Coy. separate, all the Officers were new to the district and the Coy., Johnstone - Wilson - who was in charge of No. 9 on that day, - and I had reconnoitred the position the day before and were the only men who had seen it on the ground. As we neared Hervilly we again saw the C.O. who told us that the village was then fairly free from gas. We were then moving by sections and passed safely through Hervilly. As we passed along the sunken portion of the road between that village and Hesbécourt shells began to fall round us, a few men in about the centre of the Coy., on their Section Commanders order, got up on the top and 2 or 3 were slightly wounded, they could be brought down again - not a shell fell in the road. We passed Triple Redoubt just as Pullinger's platoon reached it. I made a short detour to avoid the howitzer battery in front of Hesbecourt which was being shelled - in trying to get on to the track again I led the Coy. right over it - it was so badly cut up by shell fire that I failed to recognize the small portion I could see in the mist.

We took shelter in a trench,- from the sound we judged that the Boche were putting a barrage down about 200 yards in front. I went forward with Sergt. Fuller and found No. 9 platoon also taking shelter. During the time I was away shells began to fall round the Coy. and Chichester very promptly moved their position. Johnstone - Wilson had gone forward to reconnoitre, he did this regardless of the way the shells were falling all round him and found out how the barrage was placed, and that there was no pressing need to push on. I have learnt since that his coolness then and his behaviour later made a very great impression on the men. The barrage, which was more or less along the line of which our position formed part, lifted and we reached Trinket Redoubt about 9.15. The Redoubt had been made from part of an existing partly dug trench line. It lay across a small road leading from Hesbecourt to Hargicourt, just on the reverse slope of the highest ground which this road crosses before it drops down to L.10.a. It allowed a field of fire to the immediate front of about a dozen yards beyond the wire, I have noticed that the men always strongly disliked such positions. It was very strongly wired in front, which was undoubtedly all that had been considered when the original trench was marked out. There was a partly completed "single apron" on the right front but no wire on the remainder of the right or on the rear or left flank. Only in one small portion was the trench so much as a yard deep. There was a supply of S.A.A., bombs, rifle grenades, iron rations and water. We had nearly two hours digging before we had any news from the front. The mist began to clear before 11 a.m. and the sun to shine through.

We saw no sigh of anything unusual in front, it was a beautiful morning, an R.F.A. Sergt. Major had told us that everything was known, the boche fire would cease at 2 p.m. and that they were not coming over that day!.

Shortly after the mist lifted Sergt. Greenfield, was on the look-out, came back waving his rifle cheering, and calling "Johnny's coming".

Sergt. Greenwood (sic) was always a fighting man.

Just after we reached the Redoubt two shells fell just at the back of the trench, it seemed almost as if the guns being about to move forward, the boche "emptied guns", no shells came immediately before or after.

These shells hit Cpl. Hyder and two other men, the two men were killed almost at once. Hyder was terribly smashed about the lower part of the body and legs, when he saw me getting near him he pushed himself up on one arm and said "Is the Company alright sir" when I told him it was, he went on "then Im all right" and fell back, he was even then growing grey in the face and though we got him down, I heard he died almost at once. Hyder was a splendid fellow, a few days before he had been third - the first man to finish - in the battalion cross-country trial. He had developed to an extraordinary extent with promotion, the very character of his face seemed to change and strengthen with added responsibility. I dont think those of us who were within hearing, will forget Hyder easily. I think the spirit of these two N.C.O's was typical of the Company.

Several times during the winter, when we were in reserve, I had gone into the huts in the evening to inspect stove, there were certain of the men who would start a conversation and we would discuss the past doings of the Coy. and battalion - this had happened several times and I had expressed the opinion that a push by the Boche - which would be smashed- was about the only chance of finishing the war and many of the men agreed with me, it was rather in this light that many of them looked at the boche advance.

Soon after Greenfield's warning men of the 2/6 Manchesters began to fall back through us, these men were not in touch with the enemy, two platoons under their company commander Captain Collier afterwards came forward again and joined us, holding the right front of the redoubt - they fought splendidly to the end, staying with us when the rest of their battalion retired from Carpeza Copse.

Before noon we could see the Boche advancing in large numbers from the direction of Cote Wood. There was no sound of Machine Gun or rifle fire being used against them and as they advanced there was no sign of resistance. I was informed by an Officer of the 66th Div. that the main line of the defence in Hargicourt had not been manned - this was later confirmed by another officer. The only artillery fire directed against the enemy visible to us, came from a Field battery a short distance to our right rear (this battery or at first two and later one gun remained firing at the Boche whilst they advanced along Fervague Farm ridge).

It was at the appearance of the Boche that the spirit of the men seemed to break properly through their Sussex reserve + a spirit that remained in evidence throughout the next 24 hours.

They were in the best of spirits and seemed delighted that they hadnt marched up there without cause. I was continually greeted with the remark that 'my' push seemed to have come!. Within half an hour of our first sight of the Boche we heard a Lewis firing and later saw two men retiring and occasionally stopping to fire, this gun belonged to the Manchesters and was the only form of resistance which we saw offered forward of our position, they retired to our left, shouting a cheery message that it was 'all right'. We heard the sound of Boche M.G's from Fervaque Farm and for about ten minutes L.G's and bombs- then silence from the Farm. About the same time the enemy began to appear on our right front - No. 11 platoon was on the right. 10 in the centre and 9 on the left. We opened fire - a considerable number of the shots were effective as I saw a number of bodies in front of the wire, during the night, this was pretty good snap shooting. We had not much difficulty on the right and centre but the pressure on No.9 was strong and they suffered a number of casualties. We were under pretty considerable rifle and M.G. fire. Johnstone-Wilson had posted some of his platoon in a small trench in front of the wire, these men he visited continually - when the attack became stronger, finding he could not get these men back by signal, he went out to bring them in (I knew nothing of this at the time) and was hit on the way back with them, he lay out for a long time in a shell hole, unable to get in owing to the ~~enemy~~ heavy fire.

There is no doubt that Wilson's wound was very unfortunate for us, I feel convinced, that had he been in charge on the left at the end, we should not have been caught as we were, his pluck, resource, and knowledge of "the game" made a great impression on all of us. After rather a stiff time on the left, for a few minutes, the Boche ceased to press and worked right and left, on the right he went out of view but on the left, although our fire kept him some distance off there seemed a chance that he would get in between ourselves and A Coy., but a Vickers gun and a line of men could be seen advancing and the Boche cleared off. We had lost one L.G. from shell fire and after this I asked the C.O. for another which he sent us. The men had shouted and jeered at the Boche calling "Come on Johnny" - "this the way to Paris" or "to Sussex" or " its only poor old C. Coy." or "the Swedes". We could see them working along the ridge behind Fervaque Farm and a few of the better shots tried "collecting Johnny" as they called it, but the range was too great and I dont think we did more than delay them. The machine gun-fire from this ridge became very much hotter, and although all except the sentries got well down, and more "slits" were made, the bullets seemed to fall right into the trench, Chichester and a number of men were hit. We could see the Boche carrying their M.G's - two men to a gun. A few days before the C.O. had criticised the way one platoon of the Coy. had brought their L.G. into action, men in the other platoons reminded them of this when they saw how the boche carried their guns.

Field guns began to enfilade us from the right - as we had plenty of room we did not suffer much, but lost a splendid man in Corpl. Humfries, I had been told by the men that he was afraid of nothing, he was certainly always cheerful however bad things were.

Our own guns began to fire but either put their shells in our trench or behind it. Shortly before 4 p.m. the sentries on the right reported that the boche were bringing up T.M's in front of them - it was now most difficult to move about, bullets from M.G's and rifles were cutting the top of the trench, but we managed to get rifle grenades ready where the T.M's were reported.

There was much dead and broken ground on the right and rear and the boche were obviously getting much closer and were now firing heavily from our right rear and were in much greater numbers. They made several little rushes, but from the shouting they didnt seem to be getting on very well with each other - they couldnt time the rushes so that they all came together and our shooting was very good, the men again called to "Johnny" to come on. The C.O. had sent us a message that he looked to us to uphold the reputation of the Battalion, and I think that it was at this time that some of them asked me whether he would consider that we were doing so, if he were there and whether he wouldnt like to be there. Most of the men seemed to think the Boche wernt playing the game in going round us and we all agreed in wishing that the whole battalion were in line and they were forced to come straight at us - one man wanted something like a picture he had seen of the second battle of Ypres and a few "decent targets". I thought they didnt appreciate the significance of the way the enemy were working steadily along on our right without any opposition, until I heard a section regretting the fact that the rest of the battalion would never know that we hadn't gone down at the first rush. At this time we seemed all that was left of the army in France! we heard no other firing. The M.G. fire which had been heavy for some hours began to die down and we were able to have a look round and count up our casualties - We had then lost 2 Officers and 35 men. As it grew dark the boche fire ceased and they seemed to be withdrawing, Capt. Collier of the Manchesters decided that he aught to join up with his own battalion in Carpeza Copse and withdrew his men, to form a line of posts between us and the Copse. I went out along the line he was forming to try and find him and was astonished to find the C.O. walking up the road. He told us that there were rations for us in Hesbecourt and that he had arranged with the artillery to lengthen 200 yards as we had complained that they were dropping on us, he seemed to find nothing wrong with life except that there was "too much retiring going on ", he apparently paid things up with the Manchesters who returned to their original position. The Boche retired to about 50 yards in front of the Redoubt but they must have been much further forward on our right - we took two prisoners in our rear during the night, We feared that the C.O. might have walked into some of them until we heard later that he was back at H.Q. The first part of the night was rather anxious work, it seemed likely that the enemy would just walk over us from the rear. We could hear tanks or tractors moving in front during the night. Between 1 and 2 a.m. I went out in front of the wire to see if there were any signs of trench mortars, the mist was thick but I could see a party who seemed to be putting up wire on low pickets, they may have been moving their dead but they halted and stooped down at very regular intervals, the bodies of the men whom we had shot put the wind up me ! I didnt realize at first that they were dead.

March 22nd. Mist again very thick. A patrol shortly after 7 a.m. reported Carpeza Copse in the hands of the enemy and no sign of the Manchesters, we never saw anything of the Cavalry which we understood were between us and the Copse. We had heard no sounds of fireing from Carpeza Copse, the first few hours of the morning were quiet - the Boche evidently worked round us under cover of the mist, though we couldnt see them we could hear them all round. The silence except for them was extraordinary - if it been anyone but the battalion behind us we should have thought they had cleared and left us. Soon after 7 rifle shots at the Redoubt in ever increasing numbers and within about half an hour the M.G's began again. Our Field guns began - this time they made excellent shooting - a shell in front or behind must have hit Boche but they put them right along the trench - some of the men were convinced that they were boche guns - but they were ours firing at pretty nearly extreme range, they caused a number of casualties - particularly amongst the Manchesters - by this time we had no stretcher bearers - a runner failed to get through and many walking wounded who went down must have been taken, the shelling went on and we tried a runner round by A Coy. - he never came back but a message came from Rewell that he was cut off. Wev heard Lewis Guns going hard in the rear - the men cheered and shouted " "good old B Company", I think part of it - for a time - was"D" - it certainly was a most cheering sound.

Boche trench mortars opened fire from the front - at the same time their M.G.fire from the right increased greatly and more guns opened from the rear, the mist was still fairly thick. Corpl. Anderson and his R.G. squad tackled the trench mortars - only one gun of which was landing them in the trench. We heard orders shouted from the rear and the M.G's in the rear ceased fire. We started firing steadily to the rear. Eitherthe Boche had'nt put their T.M's under cover or else the rifle grenade shooting at a target that couldnt be seen was very good - the mortar's fire began to slaken and stopped. The boche in the rear seemed to just lack the pluck to do the last few yards. The men's blood was up and it certainly would have cost them more than our numbers to have got into the trench, but if they had made a rush enough must have got in to finish us, but as soon as they got into view from the dead ground and a few went down the others funked it. After this effort I served out the last of the S.A.A. from the store we found in the trench, the Manchesters were using a great deal. "Whizz-bangs" came from our right rear - the M.G's went on all the time with rifle fire - there was obviously more men round us and their M.G's were much nearer. We always felt that, if we had to go, we could deal with these close in with R.G. and bombs. Some of the wounded still tried to get away by working North-west.

We had of course no news, no idea of the size of the front on which the Boche attack had been made - the front to the north of us seemed to be firm enough - we could hear firing further east than we were. Rewell had not been attacked or even approached a few hours before- the open ground to our left rear, as the mist cleared, could be seen to be free from the enemy - we knew that at last half the battalion was behind us - we could hear their L.G's firing,- Had the Manchesters from Carpeza Copse x simply retired and with the Battalion formed a defensive flank, which was in touch with 24th Division? or had the 50th Division, which we believed had been in reserve behind us and Cavalry been brought up and was there only a dent in the line the south of us?, Might we not expect a counter attack?, if one was made to straighten the line to the south, we should be invaluable for it to rest its flank on, and if no counter attack was ready for an attack which was known to be coming, why had our position been changed from a continuous line to an isolated position where the whole Boche army could have gone round us?. And if we were not known to be there and considered sufficiently useful to be worth protecting why did our own field artillery shell us in an obvious attempt to put a protective barrage in front of us?. During 24hours we had'nt seen the boche gain one yard where we had been resisted - if we were put in a strong point, it was to be presumed that we were expected to defend ourselves from the rear and not leave when the enemy got behind us.

We could have gone up to that time with a loss of perhaps 50% but all immediately to the north must have gone also and the 16th Div. flank would have been open.

This effusion was more or less my answer to Collier's remark, that ready as he was to stay, and he had remained when his own battalion hadv left him without warning, we were damned fools to stay. We shall never know whether, on the facts as we saw them, we were right or wrong, there can never be an enquiry, those who put themselves in the wrong by being taken know far too much - and the true story of the time will never be told.

Shortly after the last attack I had a message from Collier that his men were troubled by the idea that the enemy were in some partly dug trenches to the rear and were digging - I thought this impossible as we had a post which covered them - so I took two men to look and found nothing - I then worked to the right and saw Collier, I mention this because whilst we were talking I looked at my watch to see how long the S.A.A. had to last until dark, and the time was 1.40. I left him with renewed mutual assurances that we would stick it to the last. I found the men in great spirits - some are suggesting that they could hear the boche guns far in the rear (an Officer afterwards told us that at this time their field guns were in the Roisez - Montigny road) and suggested that we were far enough behind their lines to capture a General and Staff! I had covered about a quarter of the Redoubt when a message reached me that the men of the 66th Div. on our left were surrendering. Without believing it I hurried as much as the bullets which were passing over would allow. Up to that time these men can hardly have seen the Boche.

When I got to the left I found what seemed about 50 men lined up across our left flank about 130 yards distant, there was one Boche M.G. in the midst of them and one in a dip in the ground just in front pointed at us - we could just see the top of the Boche helmets - this flank had seemed comparatively easy to defend there was a long field of fire over open ground - if these swine had not been there we should have been quite right on that flank, they must have watched the enemy approach and held their fire. We refused a summons to surrender brought by an N.C.O., but it was useless. The Boche came on strongly on their right and rear and with the greater part of the men held to the trench by these protected guns, no weight of fire could meet them. The men on the right met them on the parapet amongst them Capt. Collier and his men. From what I have learnt from information collected by his father, Collier and many of his men were shot in the back by these M.G's on the left. Capt. Collier had been sent up to join us from Capeza Copse by his C.O., he might very well have left us when the remainder of his Battalion retired from the Copse, but he elected to stay, the part he held had been included in most of the attacks and he and his men had fought splendidly, ever cheery and with a complete grasp of the situation, the help he gave was invaluable.

The men on the right were simply overwhelmed and it seemed as if none would get out - the ground in the centre of the Redoubt was higher and there the Boche met their own covering fire from the left, they halted and stopped the fire by waving flags.

This was the end of C. Coy's. effort. I have only mentioned the chief incidents it would take too long to write of the little efforts of the various posts to prevent parties of Boche from establishing themselves too close, and the constant exchange of rifle and M.G. fire.

Even to me who knew them well and expected much of them, the spirit which the men showed to the end was something of a revelation. For 24 hours they had seen the enemy advancing until they were lost to view in the rear, and no unit except our own seemed to offer any resistance or even to stay - they were surrounded and gave up expectation of any relief - the mist gave a feeling of blind helplessness - they were shelled by their own artillery and even for the wounded for some 6 hours there was no way out, and yet they never for a moment considered that there was any other job for them but to stay and fight until the ever increasing numbers round them should find the courage to overwhelm them, to the end they held themselves better men than the enemy and to the end they jeered and dared him to come on.

The fact that their efforts ended so badly was no fault of theirs - it was entirely due to the failure of the Officer in charge of them. There was plenty of evidence from which he might have foreseen that it was probable that the men on the left would surrender if threatened, and if he had allowed himself to be less oppressed by the absence of the usual and well proved Platoon Commanders and not tried to do their work, he might have foreseen and guarded against it.

If only the whole battalion could have been in line with its flanks secured, what a fight there would have been.

- - - - - - - - - - - - - - - - -

73rd Inf.Bde.
24th Div.

WAR DIARY

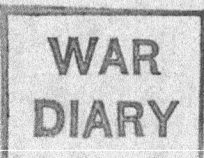

9th BATTN. THE ROYAL SUSSEX REGIMENT.

A P R I L

1 9 1 8

Attached:

Casualty Lists.

Army Form C. 2118.

WAR DIARY
or
~~INTELLIGENCE SUMMARY.~~
(Erase heading not required.)

Vol 32

Instructions regarding War Diaries and Intelligence Summaries are contained in F. S. Regs., Part II. and the Staff Manual respectively. Title pages will be prepared in manuscript.

Place	Date	Hour	Summary of Events and Information	Remarks and references to Appendices
Confidential				
			9th Bn Royal Sussex Regt	
			for the month of	
			April 1918	
				33.I 3 sheet

A6945 Wt. W11422/M1160 350,000 12/16 D. D. & L. Forms/C./2118/14.

April 1918.

9th Royal Sussex Regiment

WAR DIARY
or
INTELLIGENCE SUMMARY.
(Erase heading not required.)

Army Form C. 2118.

RS/G/47.

Instructions regarding War Diaries and Intelligence Summaries are contained in F. S. Regs., Part II. and the Staff Manual respectively. Title pages will be prepared in manuscript.

Place	Date	Hour	Summary of Events and Information	Remarks and references to Appendices
Field	April 1		Battalion was relieved from positions held at Bridgeheads at BERTEAUCOURT and THENNES, by 7th NORTHAMPTONS, and returned to billets in THEZY GLIMONT.	H.C.C.
	2		"B" Coy relieved 1 Coy of 7th Northamptons in original position. "B" Coy relieved forward Coy. (3rd)	H.C.C.
	4		Battalion less "B" Coy marched off to BOIS de GENTILLES at 5 am. where it bivouacked until 2 pm. "B" Coy rejoined at 1.30 pm. At 2 pm Battalion went forward and took up support positions in depth to 24th Divisional Depot Battalion in front of BOIS de GENTILLES on S.W. side of AMIENS-ROYE road	H.C.C.
	5.		Battalion withdrew at 11 pm. and marched to billets in LONGEAU	H.C.C.
	6.		Battalion met 'busses at 5 am. and was conveyed to SALEUX where it entrained at 7 pm.	H.C.C.
	7.		At 3 am train arrived at ST. VALERY, where Battalion had tea at CHURCH ARMY Hut, and went into billets until 2 pm. when it proceeded by march route to FRIVILLE (SOMME)	H.C.C.
	8		Draft of 1 Off. + 365 ORs joined Battalion.	H.C.C.
	9.		Day spent in reorganization, inspections &c.	H.C.C.
	10.		Lieut Col. W. R. CORRALL, M.C. assumed command of Battalion	H.C.C.
	11 to 15		Intensive training particular stress being laid on the training of platoon + section commanders 'Rouse' Parade 6.45 am - 7.15 am Battalion Parade 9.0 am. after which platoon training till 12.30 pm. Organised games, 2.0 - 3.30 pm. All platoon commanders to keep a diary of training. Conference of all officers and N.C.Os platoon commanders, daily.	H.C.C.
	16		Battalion paraded at 11.10 pm and marched to WOINCOURT	H.C.C.
	17		Battalion entrained at WOINCOURT about 3 am. and proceeded to PERNES, arriving about 11 am. and detrained. Breakfasts were served in a field outside PERNES after which Battalion marched to LA COMTE arriving about 4.30 pm.	H.C.C.

A5834 Wt. W4973/M687 750,000 8/16 D. D. & L. Ltd. Forms/C.2118/13.

II

Army Form C. 2118.

Instructions regarding War Diaries and Intelligence Summaries are contained in F. S. Regs., Part II. and the Staff Manual respectively. Title pages will be prepared in manuscript.

WAR DIARY
or
INTELLIGENCE SUMMARY.
(*Erase heading not required.*)

Place	Date	Hour	Summary of Events and Information	Remarks and references to Appendices
Field	April 18		Parades under Company arrangements for kit inspections etc.	H.C.C
	19 to 28		Training at LA COMTE. Voluntary Church parade only on Sundays.	H.C.C
	21		1 Platoon formed guard of honour to M. CLEMENCEAU visiting the area.	H.C.C
	27		Ceremonial parade at 9.0 am. Divisional Band attended.	H.C.C.
	29		Battalion paraded at 9 am to move to LES BREBIS area. Busses arrived about 11 am and Battalion embussed. Cyclist orderly arrived with orders cancelling move. Battalion debussed and returned to billets.	H.C.C
	30		Battalion under orders to move. Paraded at 3.0 pm and moved by lorries to LES BREBIS where orders were received for 3 Coys. of Battalion to go on in the lorries to MAROC where they were billeted. 1 Coy remained and occupied billets at LES BREBIS.	H.C.C

A5834 Wt. W4973/M687 750,000 8/16 D. D. & L. Ltd. Forms/C.2118/13.

C A S U A L T Y   L I S T S .

[illegible]alion Orders By
Captain C.V. NEWTON. M.C.
Commanding 9th Royal Sussex Regiment.

No. 87.

[illegible].4.18.

STRENGTH DECREASE.

9th BN. ROYAL SUSSEX REGT.
No.....................
Date...................

CASUALTIES.

OFFICERS.

KILLED IN ACTION.

MAJOR. J.J. BANHAM. 27.3.18.
2/LIEUT. E.C. REGAN. [illegible] ✓
2/Lieut. A.E. GOLDER. [illegible]
2/LIEUT. A.W. BISHOP. [illegible]
E.L. HALL 27.3.18

WOUNDED IN ACTION.

LIEUT.COL. M.V.B. HILL. D.S.O. M.C. [illegible]
CAPTAIN. A.V. NEWELL. [illegible]
CAPTAIN A.W. COLLINGBOURNE. [illegible]
CAPTAIN. A.F. WEST. [illegible]
LIEUT. F.J. SURRIDGE. [illegible]
LIEUT. W.R. JOHNSTONE-WILSON. [illegible]
~~2/LIEUT. E.L. HALL. [illegible]~~
2/LIEUT. S.L. CHAPMAN. [illegible]
2/LIEUT. H.C. LISSIMAN. [illegible]
2/LIEUT. J. MANN. [illegible]
2/LIEUT. R.G. CHICHESTER. [illegible]
2/LIEUT. J.C. HALLEY. [illegible]
2/LIEUT. R.P. WILLETT. [illegible]
2/LIEUT. F.V. PELLINGER. [illegible]

WOUNDED AND MISSING

2/LIEUT. C.F.P. CLERIHEW. [illegible]
2/LIEUT. W.E. PALING. [illegible]

MISSING BELIEVED PRISONER OF WAR.

CAPTAIN. H. SAXON. M.C.

MISSING. Believed KILLED.

CAPTAIN. R.E. YOUNG. [illegible]

H. C. Coleman

Captain & Adjutant.
for O.C. 9th Royal Sussex Regiment.

Battalion Orders By
Captain C.V. NEWTON. M.C.
Commanding 9th Royal Sussex Regiment.

No. 66.

10.4.18.

STRENGTH DECREASE.

C A S U A L T I E S.

"A" COMPANY.

KILLED IN ACTION.

15169.	Pte.	H. Barber.	26.3.18.
17581.	Pte.	F. Cole.	22.3.18.
10572.	Pte.	G.V. Hope.	21.3.18.
10405.	Pte.	T. Hinch.	21.3.18.
10212.	Pte.	J. Smith.	25.3.18.
3646.	L/C.	A. Joseph.	27.3.18.

WOUNDED IN ACTION.

1497.	Cpl.	R. Ashford.	28.3.18.
10542.	L/C.	D.J. Baker.	27.3.18.
2186.	Pte.	H. Bagge.	27.3.18.
8535.	L/C.	J. Beasey.	23.3.18.
2832.	Pte.	T. Burchell.	22.3.18.
12614.	Pte.	E. Brown.	27.3.18.
5875.	Cpl.	E. Carter.	21.3.18.
11542.	Sgt.	S. Darling.	20.3.18.
12026.	Cpl.	H. Danyer.	25.3.18.
17175.	Pte.	E. Fewer.	22.3.18.
14948.	Sgt.	H. Felgate.	26.3.18.
7758.	Pte.	F.C. Graimes.	22.3.18.
17129.	Pte.	A. Guntrip.	22.3.18.
17556.	Pte.	F.B. Hardiman.	26.3.18.
3665.	Sgt.	V.G. Haskell.	25.3.18.
1413.	Pte.	H. Hewell.	22.3.18.
10026.	Pte.	W. Pearson.	27.3.18.
1586.	Pte.	C. Pocock.	25.3.18.
16642.	Pte.	A. Parsons.	28.3.18.
12544.	Pte.	H. Pearson.	26.3.18.
10527.	Pte.	G. Roberts.	22.3.18.
3708.	Cpl.	F.P. Selly.	22.3.18.
10976.	Pte.	J. Summers.	27.3.18.
2811.	Pte.	G. Sillence.	23.3.18.
3652.	Pte.	G.D. Sullivan.	24.3.18.
1282.	Pte.	E.G. Smith.	25.3.18.
6201.	Pte.	V.G. Wood.	27.3.18.

WOUNDED AND MISSING.

3846.	Pte.	A. Coppard.	22.3.18.
11525.	Pte.	G. Dunkley.	22.3.18.
10142.	L/C.	W.T. Wall.	22.3.18.

MISSING during period 21.3.18 - 3.4.18.

12162.	Pte.	W. Attfield.
16183.	Sgt.	L. Abel.
21520.	Pte.	E. Ashby.
12178.	Pte.	W. Adsett.
7510.	Sgt.	R. Bungard.
12874.	Pte.	H. Beegrman
4138.	Pte.	H. Baldwin.
5631.	L/C.	H. Baker.
759.	Pte.	C. Baldwin.
202522.	Pte.	J. Bennett.
17738.	Pte.	E. Balday.
3610.	Sgt.	E. Beard.

11670 Pte R. G. Hall

Continued.

MISSING during period 21.3.18 - 6.4.18.

3516. Pte. F. Coombs.
12946. Pte. E. Cheeseman.
3474. U/L/Cpl. A.D. Collier.
[illegible]. Pte. F. Coote.
1235. Cpl. L. Dancer.
15006. Cpl. E. Ellis.
12175. Cpl. H.G. Filmer.
2806. Pte. W. Fretwell.
12116. Pte. P. Fears.
1083. Pte. H. Finch.
14518. Pte. R. Fiddler.
15411. Pte. R.H. Freeman.
17822. Pte. H. Fensicka.
5556. Cpl. P. Gardner.
11602. Pte. W. Green.
201911. Pte. J. Gardiner.
14527. Pte. H. Goodman.
14802. Pte. C. Harben.
14307. Pte. F. Hood.
15230. Pte. H.G. Halliday.
15487. Pte. H.G. Hall.
14412. Pte. T.J. Hill.
[illegible]. Pte. W. Howlett.
[illegible]. Pte. W. Judge.
20715. Pte. T.J. Jewell.
8282. Pte. H. Martin.
[illegible]. Pte. E. Magann.
8934. Pte. W. Perry.
156 4. Pte. C.G. Parker.
12216. Pte. A. Prasnell.
14204. Pte. J.F. Playford.
18642. Pte. S. Pattinson.
18641. Pte. G. Piggott.
8342. L/C. A. Rose.
18052. Pte. G. Rogers.
5511. Pte. A. Rooker.
6287. Pte. A. Stevenson.
5007. Pte. A. Swan.
207038. Pte. J.C. Saltmarsh.
6882. Pte. A. Stace.
[illegible]. Pte. A. Stevenson.
13880. Pte. J. Tomlinson.
15404. Pte. S. Vennell.
10882. Pte. F. Wright.

H. C. Coleman

Captain & Adjutant.
for O.C. th Royal Sussex Regiment.

10th April. 1918.

Battalion Orders By
Captain C.V. [illegible]. M.C.
Commanding [illegible]th Royal Sussex Regiment.

No. 60.

[illegible].4.18.

STRENGTH DECREASE.

C A S U A L T I E S.

"B" COMPANY.

KILLED IN ACTION.

[illegible]. Pte. W.H. Cozens. 21.3.18.
[illegible]. Pte. A. David. 26.3.18.
[illegible]. Pte. C.H. Page. [illegible].3.18.

WOUNDED IN ACTION.

[illegible]. Sgt. A. Abrahams. 27.3.18.
[illegible]. Sgt. R.D. Billings. MM. [illegible].
[illegible]. Pte. [illegible]. Buckman. [illegible].3.18.
11024. Pte. F. Burden. 22.3.18.
[illegible]. Pte. J.S. Bourne. [illegible].3.18.
[illegible]. Pte. F. Barden. 22.3.18.
[illegible]. Pte. E. Boxall. 21.3.18.
[illegible]. L/C. H. Burroughs. [illegible].3.18.
[illegible]. Pte. H. Botting. 21.3.18.
[illegible]. Pte. L. Bailey. [illegible].3.18.
[illegible]. Sgt. E.W. Cutting. [illegible].3.18.
[illegible]. L/C. F. Cooper. [illegible].3.18.
[illegible]. Pte. E. Cannon. 25.3.18.
[illegible]. Pte. G.S. Collins. [illegible].3.18.
[illegible]. C.L. F. Cooper. MM. 21.3.18.
[illegible]. Pte. A. Dorman. 21.3.18.
[illegible]. L/C. F.G. Edwards. [illegible].3.18.
~~[illegible]. Pte. [illegible]. Ellis. [illegible]~~
[illegible]. Pte. J.H. Fast. 22.3.18.
[illegible]. Pte. E. Evershed. [illegible].3.18.
[illegible]. Pte. F. French. 24.3.18.
[illegible]. L/C. A.W. Freeman. [illegible].3.18.
[illegible]. Pte. F. Griffin. [illegible].3.18.
[illegible]. Pte. F. Garton. 21.3.18.
[illegible]. Pte. R. Goldfinch. [illegible].3.18.
[illegible]. C.L. J.A. Games. [illegible].3.18.
[illegible]. Pte. F. Holewell. 22.3.18.
[illegible]. Pte. D. Hatcher. [illegible].3.18.
[illegible]. L/C. G.W. Heaton. [illegible].3.18.
[illegible]. Pte. W. Izzard. [illegible].3.18.
[illegible]. Pte. A. Jones. [illegible].3.18.
[illegible]. Pte. A. James. [illegible].3.18.
[illegible]. Pte. W. Killick. [illegible].3.18.
[illegible]. Pte. H. Knight. [illegible].3.18.
[illegible]. Pte. A. Lindsay. [illegible].3.18.
[illegible]. Pte. E. Mitchell. [illegible].3.18.
[illegible]. C.L. F.C. Pestell. [illegible].3.18.
[illegible]. Pte. W.J. Poole. [illegible].3.18.
[illegible]. Pte. H.F. Peskett. [illegible].3.18.
[illegible]. Pte. J. Richardson. [illegible].3.18.
[illegible]. Pte. F. Richardson. [illegible].3.18.
[illegible]. Pte. J. Russell. [illegible].3.18.
[illegible]. Pte. W.J. Sorense. 21.3.18.
[illegible]. Pte. A. Standen. [illegible].3.18.
[illegible]. Pte. G. Slaughter. [illegible].3.18.
[illegible]. Pte. L. Standing. [illegible].3.18.
[illegible]. Pte. W. Stanbridge. 21.3.18.
[illegible]. Sgt. J. Tedman. MM. [illegible].3.18.
[illegible]. Pte. H. Tutt. [illegible].3.18.
[illegible]. Pte. A. Tillstone. [illegible].3.18.

Continued.

WOUNDED IN ACTION.

10874. Pte. H. Taylor. 22.3.18.
10341. L/C. F. Voice. 27.3.18.
4186. Pte. R. Watts. 22.3.18.
4803. Pte. S. Watt. 22.3.18.
7764. Pte. W. Ward. 31.3.18.
10267. Pte. H. Wright. 22.3.18.
5407. Pte. A. Wickens. 25.3.18.

WOUNDED AND MISSING.

4808. Pte. W. Pearcey. 22.3.18.
5024. Pte. H. Tomlinson. 22.3.18.

MISSING during period 21.3.18 - 3.4.18.

10466. Pte. W. Farnell.
10664. Pte. A.L. Crouch.
202128. Pte. M. Cattell.
77[illegible]. Pte. H. Dowling.
6483. Pte. D. Ellis.
6446. Pte. W. Henson.
10540. Pte. W. Hollis.
200417. Pte. A.G. Marsh.
10340. Pte. J. Weddings.
10683. Pte. H. Randall.
10678. Pte. H. Vickers.

DIED OF WOUNDS.

265182. Cpl. R.H. Clybous. 28.3.18.
4186. Pte. W.J. Strong. 24.3.18.

H. C. Coleman

Captain & Adjutant.
for O.C. 9th Royal Sussex Regiment.

10th April. 1918.

Battalion Orders By
Captain C.V. NEWTON. M.C.
Commanding 9th Royal Sussex Regiment.

No. [illegible].

[illegible].4.18.

STRENGTH DECREASE.

C A S U A L T I E S.

"C" COMPANY.

KILLED IN ACTION.

[illegible]. Pte. R.S. Batchup. [illegible].3.18.
11952. Pte. F. Dye. 22.3.18.
8134. Pte. F.F. Nicholls. [illegible].3.18.

WOUNDED IN ACTION.

8140. Pte. F. Andrews. 25.3.18.
14825. Pte. S. Buchan. 25.3.18.
18273. Pte. A.W. Cooper. 22.3.18.
8523. Pte. G. Dunn. 22.3.18.
18881. Pte. A.S. Dickens. 21.3.18.
[illegible]1. Pte. F. Elliott. 25.3.18.
11136. Pte. W.A. Goodman. 22.3.18.
18288. Pte. C. Goundry. 21.3.18.
4843. Pte. F. Godsmark. 22.3.18.
8134. Cpl. S.A. Humphress. 21.3.18.
[illegible]66. Pte. H. Hyman. 22.3.18.
8233. L/C. J. Hudson. 22.3.18.
18532. Pte. S. Hales. 22.3.18.
2462. Pte. W.H. Johnson. 22.3.18.
8841. Pte. R. King. 22.3.18.
182. Pte. J. Millham. 25.3.18.
11524. Pte. G.L. Munn. 22.3.18.
18844. Pte. H.S. Mills. 25.3.18.
8188. Pte. R.A. Munday. 22.3.18.
18348. L/Cpl. F.H. Norris. 22.3.18.
8391. Pte. C. Parbery. 22.3.18.
7270. Pte. G. Palmer. 21.3.18.
7655. Pte. H. Peddlesden. 22.3.18.
17871. Pte. A. Rogers. 22.3.18.
18858. Pte. S. Ruler. 21.3.18.
8148. L/C. E. Sheppard. 21.3.18.
18532. Pte. E.A. Stares. 21.3.18.
7898. L/C. R. Stuart. 25.3.18.
8855. Sgt.Drmr. E. Trussler. DCM. [illegible].
18638. Pte. A.E. Vickery. 21.3.18.
18558. Pte. H.S. Ward. 25.3.18.

MISSING believed PRISONER OF WAR.

2814. Cpl. R. Anderson. 22.3.18.
18948. Pte. A. Beer. 22.3.18.
12850. Pte. W. Brown. 25.3.18.
14168. Pte. C. Boorman. 25.3.18.
[illegible]976. Pte. F. Baker. 27.3.18.
[illegible]120. Pte. E. Parker. 22.3.18.
14858. Pte. L. Block. 22.3.18.
12468. Pte. G. Boothroyd. 22.3.18.
8323. Pte. F.H. Booth 22.3.18.
14836. Pte. F. Brown. 22.3.18.
5618. Sgt. H. Campbell. 22.3.18.
1725. Pte. W. Coussens. 22.3.18.
576[illegible]. Pte. G.W. Collins. 22.3.18.
21751. Pte. T. Coney. 22.3.18.
1[illegible]467. Pte. W.J. Cissell. 22.3.18.
18452. Pte. C. Collins. 22.3.18.
[illegible]. Pte. R. Cooper. 22.3.18.
[illegible]. Pte. C. Chidwick. 22.3.18.

Continued.

MISSING believed PRISONER OF WAR.

14371. Pte. G. Cowdrey. 22.3.18.
14226. Pte. F.L. Chapman. 22.3.18.
[illegible]07. Pte. E. Deakin. 22.3.18.
265288. Cpl. E.C. Donovan. 22.3.18.
14243. Pte. T.W. Dickerson. 22.3.18.
2175. Pte. F. Davey. 22.3.18.
13252. Pte. H.J. Daxter. 22.3.18.
14243. Pte. A. Duffield. 22.3.18.
10811. Pte. S.A. Eve. 22.3.18.
9768. Sgt. C. Fuller. 22.3.18.
15423. Pte. R. Faulkner. 22.3.18.
265279. Pte. S. Fenwicke. 22.3.18.
16576. Pte. A.W. Gibling. 22.3.18.
4833. Sgt. F. Greenfield. 22.3.18.
[illegible]. Pte. L.J. Garbutt. 22.3.18.
15274. Pte. W. Guston. 22.3.18.
16331. Pte. C.F. Gurney. 22.3.18.
2136. Pte. H. Hatherall. 22.3.18.
1258. Pte. G. Haselden. 22.3.18.
15922. Pte. J. Hutson. 22.3.18.
9558. Cpl. G.H. Hills. 22.3.18.
8235. Sgt. C.V. Holter. 22.3.18.
4032. Pte. J. Hibbard. 22.3.18.
1271. Pte. F.W. Homewood. 22.3.18.
20287. Sgt. J. Harris. 22.3.18.
1490. Pte. C. Hammond. 22.3.18.
13822. Pte. G. Jarman. 22.3.18.
14273. Pte. V. Knights. 22.3.18.
3224. Pte. H. Lelliott. 22.3.18.
8625. Pte. L. Lmoan. 22.3.18.
15227. Pte. J. Lee. 22.3.18.
[illegible]. Pte. J.W. L e. 22.3.18.
[illegible]. Pte. J. Leaves. 22.3.18.
714. Pte. H. McNally. 22.3.18.
7518. Cpl. W.H. Martin. 22.3.18.
2458. Cpl. J. Macey. 22.3.18.
16625. Pte. A.G. Miles. 22.3.18.
889. Pte. R.F. Pullinger. 22.3.18.
[illegible]. Pte. G.W. Pentecost. 22.3.18.
4248. Pte. T.R. Pain. 22.3.18.
15824. Pte. A. Pullen. 22.3.18.
13282. Pte. J. Raynor. 22.3.18.
3368. Pte. A. Rowlands. 22.3.18.
16818. Cpl. J. Robinson. 22.3.18.
13849. Pte. A. Rossiter. 22.3.18.
16654. Pte. F. Ridgley. 22.3.18.
2176. L/C. R. Steele. 22.3.18.
[illegible]. Pte. J. Stenning. 22.3.18.
170 " J Driscoll 22.3.18

MISSING believed KILLED.

[illegible]1. L/C. R. Coslick. 22.3.18.

MISSING during period 21.3.18 - 5.4.18.

[illegible]. L/C. R.H. Clarke. 22.3.18.
[illegible]74. Pte. R. Smith. 22.3.18.
[illegible]. Pte. G.S. Sendall. 22.3.18.
[illegible]. Cpl. J. Sutton. 22.3.18.
[illegible]. Pte. J. Spicknell. 22.3.18.
[illegible]. Pte. J. Sillett. 22.3.18.
[illegible]. Pte. A. Turner. 22.3.18.
[illegible]. Pte. S. Tasker. 22.3.18.
[illegible]. Pte. G. Virtue. 22.3.18.
[illegible]. Pte. J. Whitman. [illegible]
[illegible]. Pte. [illegible].E. Waller. 22.3.18.
[illegible]5. Pte. C. Webb.

9th BN. ROYAL SUSSEX REG
No. ......
Date ......

Continued.

MISSING during period 21.3.18 - 3.4.18.

[illegible]5. Pte. F. Ward. 22.3.18.
[illegible]. Pte. A. Watkins. 22.3.18.

DIED OF WOUNDS.

[illegible]. L/C. A.J. Dell. DCM. 24.3.18.
17547. Cpl. J. Ryder. 24.3.18.

WOUNDED AND MISSING.

[illegible]. Pte. A. Trussler. 22.3.18.
18874. Pte. R. Watson. 22.3.18.

N. C. Coleman

Captain & Adjutant.
for O.C. 9th Royal Sussex Regiment.

[illegible]th April. 1918.

Battalion Orders By
Captain C.V. NEWTON. M.C.
Commanding 9th Royal Sussex Regiment.

No. 7[illegible].

[illegible].4.18.

STRENGTH DECREASE.

C A S U A L T I E S.

"D" COMPANY.

KILLED IN ACTION.

192.	Pte.	A.E. Balchin.	22.3.18.
24535.	Pte.	G. Pinckney.	21.3.18.
6887.	L/C.	E. Hurrell.	22.3.18.
3452.	Pte.	E.L. Martin.	21.3.18.
5482.	Pte.	C. Radford.	21.3.18.
3212.	Cpl.	S. Stevens.	22.3.18.
7832.	Pte.	C. Towler.	22.3.18.
202688.	Sgt.	F. Whitmer.	21.3.18.

WOUNDED IN ACTION.

3441.	Pte.	F. Abbott.	25.3.18.
5121.	Pte.	S. Anelli.	22.3.18.
8933.	Pte.	H. Burfield.	21.3.18.
5571.	Pte.	W. Burley.	26.3.18.
13465.	Pte.	F. Burden.	22.3.18.
6686.	Pte.	A. Baker.	22.3.18.
24328.	Pte.	S. Blakey.	21.3.18.
10157.	Pte.	G. Clark.	22.3.18.
5802.	Pte.	J. Crockett.	26.3.18.
7236.	L/C.	V. Carter.	22.3.18.
16827.	UL/C.	W. Dunkerley.	22.3.18.
3147.	Pte.	H.J. Dawdney.	26.3.18.
22877.	Pte.	F. Darnell.	28.3.18.
7713.	Pte.	W. Ford.	22.3.18.
6571.	Pte.	H. Gower.	22.3.18.
202852.	Pte.	J. Gowen.	23.3.18.
8821.	Pte.	F. Gardner.	22.3.18.
15134.	Pte.	W. Holden.	22.3.18.
16533.	U/L/Cpl.	W.W. Hill.	26.3.18.
16926.	Pte.	E.P. Juffs.	22.3.18.
10318.	Pte.	J. Keys.	22.3.18.
448.	Pte.	H. Kennard.	21.3.18.
24438.	Pte.	G. Knight.	21.3.18.
10344.	Pte.	C. Ling.	21.3.18.
5824.	Pte.	T. Lloyd.	21.3.18.
1[illegible].	Pte.	T.H. Mitten.	21.3.18.
3424.	Pte.	A.W. Mundy.	22.3.18.
6987.	Pte.	E. Mitchell.	22.3.18.
889.	C.l.	W. Polling.	22.3.18.
15783.	L/C.	H. Pomley.	27.3.18.
10338.	Pte.	H. Pauiger.	21.3.18.
24428.	Pte.	A.W. Perry.	21.3.18.
16339.	Pte.	J.G. Robinson.	27.3.18.
4750.	U/L/Cpl.	J. Ridley.	25.3.18.
224 6.	Pte.	E. Raynor.	21.3.18.
10622.	Pte.	G. Raines.	22.3.18.
16582.	Pte.	F. Smith.	21.3.18.
14380.	Pte.	J. Soutter.	21.3.18.
5036.	Sgt.	W. Skinner.	22.3.18.
10141.	Pte.	W. Santer.	21.3.18.
3215.	Pte.	A.H. Streeter.	21.3.18.
16662.	L/C.	C. Shepheard.	21.3.18.
12657.	Pte.	E.G. Skinner.	22.3.18.
7568.	Pte.	T. Trevett.	4.4.18.

Continued.

WOUNDED IN ACTION.

	6032.	Pte. H. Vowles.	21.[illegible].18.
	3490.	L/C. G. White.	21.3.18.
	[illegible].	Pte. J.P. Weston.	22.3.18.
	16[illegible].	L/C. S. Wilkinson.	26.3.18.
	3576.	Sgt. E.A. Williams.	27.3.18.
(Sgt)	3370.	Sgt. F.C. Weaver.	26.3.18.
	13501.	Pte. H. Weeks.	21.3.18.
	18064.	Pte. W. Woodhouse.	21.3.18.
	1[illegible]16.	Pte. G. Wren.	21.3.18.

WOUNDED AND MISSING.

12819.	Sgt. R. Golds.	28.3.18.
24375.	Pte. J. Hales.	22.3.18.
8133.	Pte. H. Holcombe.	[illegible].3.18.
5742.	Sgt. P. Larking.	[illegible].3.18.
12405.	Pte. F. Lovegrove.	27.3.18.
18402.	Cpl. R.D.J. Seal.	25.3.18.

MISSING during period 21.3.18 - 3.4.18.

6838.	Sgt. W. Bailey. MM.	22.3.18.
24457.	Pte. E. Burtenshaw.	22.3.18.
13006.	Pte. W.F. Cooke.	21.3.18.
2[illegible]61.	Pte. A. Chambers.	25.3.18.
5750.	Pte. A.J. Canning.	25.3.18.
3[illegible]4.	L/C. H.O. Dean.	25.3.[illegible].
8[illegible].	U/L/Cpl. F. Ellis.	27.3.18.
18122.	Pte. [illegible] Gravett.	26.3.18.
14086.	L/C. F. Harvey.	25.3.18.
2631.	Pte. F. Middleton.	25.3.18
11477.	Cpl. A. Nash.	25.3.18.
18842.	Pte. H. Purser.	24.3.18.
7534.	Pte. [illegible] Salgeman.	23.3.18.
8532.	Pte. W. Stoner.	21.3.18.
10211.	Pte. J. Smith.	21.3.18.
18372.	Pte. F.A. Smith.	21.3.18.
18664.	Pte. S. Sealey.	21.3.18.
18642.	Pte. G. Sharp.	21.3.18.
18580.	Pte. G. Smith.	21.3.18.
18814.	Pte. A.R. West.	25.3.18.
18221.	Pte. H. Wright.	21.3.18.
[illegible].	Pte. E. Ward.	22.3.18.
[illegible].	Pte. R. Young.	22.3.18.

H.C. Coleman

Captain & Adjutant
for O.C. 9th Royal Sussex Regiment.

[illegible] April 1918.

Army Form C. 2118.

Instructions regarding War Diaries and Intelligence Summaries are contained in F. S. Regs., Part II. and the Staff Manual respectively. Title pages will be prepared in manuscript.

WAR DIARY
or
~~INTELLIGENCE SUMMARY.~~
(*Erase heading not required.*)

Vol 33

Place	Date	Hour	Summary of Events and Information	Remarks and references to Appendices
Confidential			9th Bn The Royal Sussex Regiment	
			for the month of	
			May 1918	

34-I
5 sheet

MAY 1918

9th BN. ROYAL SUSSEX REGT.
No. RS/A15/15
Date 3/6/18

9th Royal Sussex Regiment

Army Form C. 2118.

WAR DIARY
or
INTELLIGENCE SUMMARY.
(Erase heading not required.)

Instructions regarding War Diaries and Intelligence Summaries are contained in F. S. Regs., Part II. and the Staff Manual respectively. Title pages will be prepared in manuscript.

Place	Date	Hour	Summary of Events and Information	Remarks and references to Appendices
Field	1st May	-	Battalion situated in Cellars at S. MAROC. Battalion moved up at 8.30pm to relieve 3rd CANADIAN MOUNTED RIFLES in support to HILL 70 sector. "B" Coy HARRISONS CRATER – "C" Coy HARTS CRATER – "D" Coy CHALK PIT ALLEY – "A" Coy and Bn HQ VILLAGE LINE. Capt. B. WHITEMAN MC cross-posted to 12th SHERWOOD FORESTERS	H.C.C.
	2nd		Relief complete 5.30am	H.C.C.
	2nd to 5th		Quiet tour. Battalion engaged on Working parties – improving fire positions and LG positions. Casualties 2 ORs accidentally wounded	H.C.C.
	6th		Battalion relieved 7th NORTHANTS in left sub-sector from HEAVEN TRENCH to O.B.1. "A" Coy Right Front – "C" Coy Centre – "D" Coy Left Front – "B" Coy Support in TOSH ALLEY. Bn HQ LOOS TRENCH. Relief complete 11.5pm	H.C.C.
	9th		Inter-Coy Reliefs. Bn HQ took over "B" Coys quarters in TOSH ALLEY. "B" Coy moved to LOOS TRENCH. Casualties 2 ORs wounded	H.C.C.
	10th 12th		Casualties Wounded OR 2 and OR 1 self inflicted	H.C.C.
	13th		"A" Coy relieved by Company of 13th MIDDLESEX Regt and moved to VILLAGE LINE relieving a Coy of 7th NORTHANTS. This shortened the Battalion front to HUMBUG ALLEY to O.B.1. "B" Coy relieved "D" Coy.	H.C.C.
	14th		Casualties Wounded OR 7 and OR 1 accidentally injured	H.C.C.
	15th		"C" Coy relieved by "A" Coy	H.C.C.
	17th		Casualties Wounded OR 2 and OR 1 accidentally injured	H.C.C.
	16th to 18th		A quiet tour in the line. Very little shelling except lightning bombardments of dumps and selected trench targets by 7.7cm Batteries.	H.C.C.
			Work. Battalion concentrated on wiring and improving fire positions	

I

A5834 Wt. W4973/M687 750,000 8/16 D. D. & L. Ltd. Forms/C.2118/13.

May 1918

Sheet II

WAR DIARY
or
INTELLIGENCE SUMMARY.
(Erase heading not required.)

1st Royal Sussex Regt

Army Form C. 2118.

Instructions regarding War Diaries and Intelligence Summaries are contained in F. S. Regs., Part II. and the Staff Manual respectively. Title pages will be prepared in manuscript.

Place	Date	Hour	Summary of Events and Information	Remarks and references to Appendices
Loos	6–18		especially wiring in the Front line trench which was held by day by snipers and Observers at Posts at heads of C.Ts and at night by Posts dug in behind the Parados. Active patrolling was kept up.	H.C.C.
	19 to 24		Battalion in Rest Billets at LES BREBIS. Training carried out under Company arrangements though this was seriously interfered with by Working parties having to be found. Baths were allotted on the 19th. Ammunition, Kit and other inspections were carried out.	H.C.C.
	20		Battalion had a practice Stand to moving off at dusk to assembly trenches. This was done fairly satisfactorily.	H.C.C.
	24		Battalion relieved 7th NORTHANTS in Right Sub-sector. "C" Coy Right Front "D" Coy left Front – "B" Coy Support in Loos 'L' "A" Coy Reserve in VILLAGE LINE. Battalion HQ at HATCHETTS Loos subsequently moving to ST PATRICKS on 28th.	H.C.C.
	25		Casualties Wounded OR 1.	H.C.C.
	27		Lieut H.V. ALDER proceeded to England for transfer to R.A.F.	H.C.C.
			Lieut C.W. HAMMOND proceeded to England for transfer to R.A.F. on 19th.	H.C.C.
	28		Vickers Guns were withdrawn from HYTHE TUNNEL and L.G's substituted.	H.C.C.
			Casualties OR 1 wounded and OR 1 accidentally injured.	H.C.C.
	29		Casualties Lieut F.H. BRAY accidentally killed whilst patrolling and Missing believed Killed OR 1. Wounded OR 1.	H.C.C.
	30		"B" Coy relieved "D" Coy – "A" Coy relieved "C" Coy.	H.C.C.
			Casualties. Lieut D.C. WESTALL Wounded and OR 1 Killed.	H.C.C.
	31		About 400 Gas projectors fired on to Battalion Sector at about 11.45pm and about 20 at 12.35am (1/6/18) These were of large size and produced a great concentration of gas. Casualties were rather heavy 21 OR in Killed and wounded.	H.C.C.

A5834 Wt. W4973/M687 750,000 8/16 D. D. & L. Ltd. Forms/C.2118/13.

May 1918.

Sheet 111

WAR DIARY
or
INTELLIGENCE SUMMARY.
(Erase heading not required.)

9th Royal Sussex Regiment

Army Form C. 2118.

Instructions regarding War Diaries and Intelligence Summaries are contained in F. S. Regs., Part II. and the Staff Manual respectively. Title pages will be prepared in manuscript.

Place	Date	Hour	Summary of Events and Information	Remarks and references to Appendices
Field	24th to 31st		Active patrolling was kept up. Lighting bombardments with T. Mor. Batteries kept up especially on HYTHE ALLEY and O.G.1. Work:- Wiring, improving fire positions and digging in HUXLEY TRENCH. also consolidating Defences of HYTHE TUNNEL.	H.C.C.
			The following Officers joined Battalion during the month. Lieut. P.A. HILL on 17.5.18 and Lieut. G.A. WALFORD on 13.5.18.	
			HONOURS and AWARDS	
			The undermentioned have been awarded decorations for gallantry and devotion to duty during the German Offensive on the SOMME.	
			Bar to DSO	
			T/Lieut. Col. M.V.B. HILL. DSO. MC.	
			Bar to M.C.	
			a/Captain D.W.G. MAY MC.	
			Military Cross	
			Capt. A.V. REWELL Lieut. I. FRASER.	
			Lieut. J. MANN Lieut. H.H. L'ESTRANGE attached 73rd T.M.By.	
			Do P.V. PULLINGER Lieut. S. HORSCROFT — 24th D.T.M.B.	
			Distinguished Conduct Medal	
			No 3359 Cpl. G.F. HEAD.	H.C.C.

111

A5834 Wt. W4973/M687 750,000 8/16 D. D. & L. Ltd. Forms/C.2118/13.

May 19

Instructions regarding War Diaries and Intelligence Summaries are contained in F. S. Regs., Part II. and the Staff Manual respectively. Title pages will be prepared in manuscript.

Sheet IV

WAR DIARY
or
INTELLIGENCE SUMMARY.
(Erase heading not required.)

1st Royal Sussex Regt

Army Form C. 2118.

Place	Date	Hour	Summary of Events and Information	Remarks and references to Appendices
			Honours and Awards (Continued).	
			Military Medals.	
			1671. Pte. S. Stokes. — 14365. Pte. W. Issard. — 5427. Corpl. C. J. Bliss.	
			5985. L/Cpl. A. Parkes. — 5212. " J. Bourne — 27245. " W. H. Hadley	
			8148. Pte. H. Bagge. — 16755. " J. Dunk. — 8065. Sergt. V. C. Haskell.	
			12725. L/Cpl. C. Taplin. — 16762. L/Cpl. S. Wilkinson. — 13582. Pte. R. H. Weeks.	
			4197. Corpl. R. Ashford — 17612. Corpl. F. Pestell — 10924. " E. Paley.	H.C.
			6019. Pte. O. Leighton.	

A5834 Wt. W4973/M687 750,000 8/16 D. D. & L. Ltd. Forms/C.2118/13.

Army Form C. 2118.

Instructions regarding War Diaries and Intelligence Summaries are contained in F. S. Regs., Part II, and the Staff Manual respectively. Title pages will be prepared in manuscript.

WAR DIARY
or
INTELLIGENCE SUMMARY.
(Erase heading not required.)

Vol 34

Place	Date	Hour	Summary of Events and Information	Remarks and references to Appendices
Confidential			War Diary for month of June.	35 I 12 sheet
			9th Battalion Royal Sussex Regt.	

A6945 Wt. W11422/M1160 350,000 12/16 D. D. & L. Forms/C./2118/14.

JUNE 1918

9th Battn ROYAL SUSSEX Regiment

WAR DIARY
or
INTELLIGENCE SUMMARY.
(Erase heading not required.)

Instructions regarding War Diaries and Intelligence Summaries are contained in F. S. Regs., Part II. and the Staff Manual respectively. Title pages will be prepared in manuscript.

9th BN. ROYAL SUSSEX REGT. No. RS/A.2/52 Date ......

Army Form C. 2118.

Place	Date	Hour	Summary of Events and Information	Remarks and references to Appendices
Field.	1st to 5th June	-	Battalion in the line N. of LOOS. A fairly quiet tour especially towards the end. Work was chiefly directed to filling front line Trench with wire and digging saps forward of line of Resistance to provide fire positions	H.C.C.
	3rd	-	A party of 30 O.R. under Lieut. R. HUDSON and Lieut. C.W. MANFIELD raided the enemy trenches at HUMBUG ALLEY - E. of PUITS 14 BIS. Artillery, Trench Mortars and Machine Guns co-operated in the raid which resulted in the capture of 2 Privates of the 1st BAVARIAN Reserve Division. Our casualties were 4 O.R. wounded and 2 O.R. Missing. Operation Orders for the Raid are attached.	H.C.C.
	5th	-	Battalion relieved by 13th MIDDLESEX Regiment and moved to Billets at LES BREBIS.	H.C.C.
	5th to 11th	-	Battalion in Reserve. Training was carried out, especially Lewis Gun Classes. Working parties took about two Companies daily	H.C.C.
	8th	-	Raiding party went to Canadian Concert Party at CHATEAU de la HAIE.	H.C.C.
	9th		Lieut. S. HORSCROFT M.C. transferred to R.A.F. and proceeded to England	
	11th		Battalion relieved 7th NORTHAMPTONSHIRE Regiment in the line.	
	11th to 23rd		An uneventful tour, except for an outbreak of influenza owing to which 5 Officers and about 250 men were sent to Hospital. Work was hindered by sickness but considerable progress was made	

A5834 Wt. W4973/M687 750,000 8/16 D. D. & L. Ltd. Forms/C.2118/13.

I

June 1918 — 9th Royal Sussex Regiment — Sheet II

Instructions regarding War Diaries and Intelligence Summaries are contained in F. S. Regs., Part II. and the Staff Manual respectively. Title pages will be prepared in manuscript.

WAR DIARY
or
INTELLIGENCE SUMMARY.
(*Erase heading not required.*)

Army Form C. 2118.

Place	Date	Hour	Summary of Events and Information	Remarks and references to Appendices
Field	11th to 23rd Continued		in wiring in unoccupied part of front line and also in digging saps to provide fire positions in line of resistance.	H.C.C.
	23rd		Battalion was relieved by 13th MIDDLESEX Regiment and moved to Reserve Billets at ES BREBIS.	H.C.C.
	25th		Lieut. Col. W. R. CORFIELD MC. proceeded on leave to England. Major T. FOSTER assumed command of the Battalion.	H.C.C.
	28th		Lieut. C. W. MANFIELD transferred to R.A.F.	H.C.C.
			About 12 Officers and all signallers attended a practice in signalling to aeroplane by the Popham Panel. Practice was very successful.	H.C.C.
	29th		Battalion relieved 7th NORTHAMPTONSHIRE Regiment in the line.	H.C.C.
			HONOURS.	
			MILITARY CROSS: Capt. A. F. BEST. Capt. C. HARRIS. RAMC (attached). Lieut. R. HUDSON. (awarded for Raid on 3rd June).	
			Mentioned in Dispatches. Capt. C. V. NEWTON MC. Capt. N. E. YOUNG. Lieut. H. C. LISSIMAN. No. 16509. Pte. T. J. HIGHAM. 5985. L/Cpl. A. PARKES.	

A5834 Wt. W4973/M687 750,000 8/16 D. D. & L. Ltd. Forms/C.2118/13.

June 1918 — 9th Royal Sussex Regiment — Sheet III

Army Form C. 2118.

WAR DIARY
or
INTELLIGENCE SUMMARY.
(Erase heading not required.)

Instructions regarding War Diaries and Intelligence Summaries are contained in F. S. Regs., Part II. and the Staff Manual respectively. Title pages will be prepared in manuscript.

Place	Date	Hour	Summary of Events and Information	Remarks and references to Appendices
	HONOURS (continued)		DISTINGUISHED CONDUCT MEDAL 9010. T/RS.M. H.A. COLES. MILITARY MEDAL (awarded for Raid on 3rd June) No 14848. Sergt. W. C. NORMAN. " 7896. Lce. Cpl. R. E. STUART. " 80. Pte. A. S. LIGHTFOOT.	W.C.

H.C. Coleman
Captain & Adjt.
Comdg. 9th Royal Sussex Regiment.

A5834 Wt. W4973/M687 750,000 8/16 D. D. & L. Ltd. Forms/C.2118/13.

S E C R E T.

BATTALION ORDER NO 5
by
Lieut. Colonel N.I. Whitty, D.S.O.
Commanding 24th Bn, Machine Gun Corps.

I.6.18.

I. The guns detailed below will fire a barrage in co-operation with a raid by the 9th R. Sussex Regt on the enemy post about the Junction of **HUMBUG ALLEY** and NASH SWITCH on the night of 3rd/4th June, at a time to be notified later (approximately II p.m.)

2. Officers Commanding A and C Companies will reconnoitre and prepare gun positions at the positions shown on attached table.

3. At Zero minus 30 seconds one battery of I8 pdrs will open intense fire on enemy trench and lift at Zero, when the machine guns detailed will open fire, with the remaining artillery detailed, at the rate of one belt per two minutes.

4. The raid will last approximately IO minutes and the signal for all barrages to cease will be three red lights fired from Infantry Coy Hd Qrs in HUMBUG ALLEY at H.3I.b.56.65.

5. The signal for withdrawal of the raiding party will be one green light fired horizontally by each of the three Infantry group commanders. This will be repeated by the firing of a rocket from the junction of HUMBUG ALLEY with HUGO TRENCH followed by three Very lights in quick succession.

6. Group No I consisting of batteries A B and D will be under the control of Capt Tibbett.
Group No 2, consisting of batteries C and E will be under the control of Major Anderson, M.C.

7. Watches will be synchronised by arrangement between O.C. Companies and O.C. 9th R. Sussex Regt.

8. ACKNOWLEDGE.

H.A. Robinson

Captain and Adjutant,
for O.C. 24th Bn, M.G.C.

<u>DISTRIBUTION</u>:-

I. 24th Division 'G'
2. I7th Infantry Bde.
3. 73rd Infantry Bde.
4. A. Co, 24th Bn, M.G.C.
5. C. Co, 24th Bn, M.G.C.
6. D. Co, 24th Bn, M.G.C.
7. 24th Divnl Artillery.
8. IIth Bn, M.G.C.
9. 9th Bn, R.Sussex Regt.
IO. File.

APPENDIX TO BATTALION ORDER NO 5.

Battery	No of M G	M.G to be used	Gun Position.	Target	Range	Q E	Grid bearing.	Traverse
A	2	CRAP I & II	English Alley G.36.a.80.30	H.26.d.I5.70 to H.26.b.22.I5	2350	6° 35′	68° 30′	I° R & L.
B	2	PREVITE CASTLE	GUN TRENCH SWITCH G.30.a.90.50.	HULLUCH TRENCH H.26.b.22.I5 to H.26.b.99.05.	2175 to 2550	6° 20′ and 7° I5′	95°	Fixed Lay Separate Elev'n for each gun. Zones will overlap.
C	2	BANKER I & II	G.36.b.95.45	BOIS deQUATORZE H.27.d.05.70 to H.27.a.00.90.	2I50	5° 25′	72°	30′ R & L.
D	2	STUD II & CY-CLONE I	G.30.a.75.30	H.26.d.20.70 to H.26.d.65.70.	2225 to 2450	6° I5′ & 7°.	97°	Fixed Lay. Separate elev'n for each gun Zones will overlap.
E	4	POKER WHIST CRATER I CRATER 2	N.I.a.40.30	H.32.b.90.60 to H.27.c.25.I5.	2I00 to 2400	4° 30′ 5° I0′ 5° 45′ 6° 20′	56° 55° 20′ 54° 40′ 54°	Fixed Lay.

At least I0 belts will be at each gun position on commencement.

TABLE "A".

UNIT	No. of Guns	PHASE 1 Zero –30 secs. to Zero.	PHASE 2 Zero to Zero +15 mins
. Advd.	2	H.26.d.28.04 – H.32.b.42.91.	H.26.d.15.72 – H.26.d.90.40 following line of trench. (both rows)
.	4	* H.26.d.35.25 – H.26.d.45.00	
B.	6	H.32.b.42.91 – H.26.d.45.04.	H.26.d.14.34 – H.26.d.15.72.
C. Advd.	2	H.26.d.45.04 – H.26.d.50.17. (both rows)	H.26.d.70.20 – H.26.d.85.30
.	4		H.32.b.47.69. – H.32.b.72.80
. Advd.	2	H.26.d.28.04 – H.26.d.15.25.	H.26.d.85.30 – H.27.c.02.42.
D. 4	2	1 – H.26.d.35.25 – H.26.d.50.17 1 – H.26.d.38.14 – H.26.d.50.17	H.32.b.72.80 along HUT TR to H.32.b.90.60.
	2	H.26.d.45.04 – H.26.d.50.17.	
/106	6	NIL	H.32.b.90.60 – H.27.c.22.16.
/48th	1	H.27.c.02.42.	As for Phase 1.
	2	H.26.d.90.40.	
	3	H.26.d.15.72.	
	4	H.27.c.22.16.	
	5	H.32.b.90.60.	
	6	H.32.b.55.40.	

*

M.P.I. + 75 yds. from F.L.T.

RATES of FIRE.	18 pdrs. 1st PHASE.	18 pdrs. 2nd PHASE.	4.5" HOWS.
	C + B. Gun Fire	1st 2 mins = Normal	Normal.
	A + D. Intense.	8 " = Rapid	
		5 " = Normal.	

W. T. Jones 2/Lieut.
Staff Officer
Left Group.

1st June 1918.

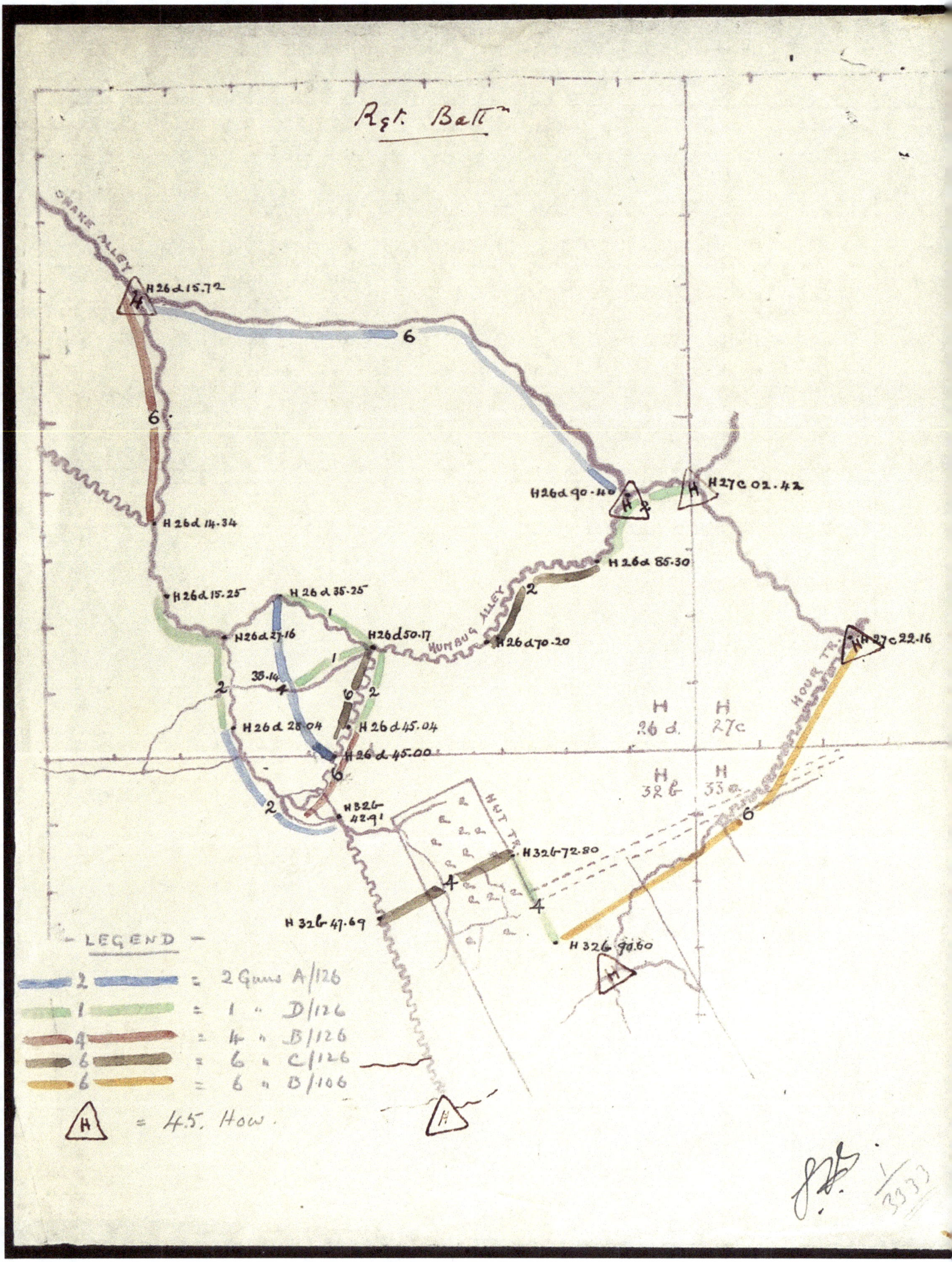

Rgt. Batt.
SNAKE ALLEY
H26d15.72
6
6
H26d14.34
H26d15.25
H26d35.25
H26d27.16
H26d50.17
HUMBUG ALLEY
H26d70-20
H26d85.30
H26d90-40
H27c02.42
H27c22.16
HOUR TR.
35.14
H26d28.04
H26d45.04
H26d45.00
H32b 42.91
H32b-72.80
H32b 47.69
H32b 90.60
NUT TR.
H 26 d.
H 27c
H 32b
H 33a
LEGEND
2 = 2 Guns A/126
1 = 1 " D/126
4 = 4 " B/126
6 = 6 " C/126
6 = 6 " B/106
H = 4.5. How.

SECRET.

COPY NO:- 9

Ref. sheet 36 C, N.W.3. 1/10,000.

73rd. INFANTRY BRIGADE ORDER NO.194.

H.Q. 73 I.B., June 1st.1918.

1. A raid will be carried out by the 9th. Bn.Royal Sussex Regiment on night 3/4th. June 1918 on the enemy trenches at about H.26.d.30.00.

2. Detailed arrangements have been drawn up by the Officer Commanding, 9th. Bn.Royal Sussex Regiment. A copy of those orders is attached (to units marked * on Distribution List only).

3. ZERO HOUR will be notified later. Probable hour 11 p.m.

4. The Left Group of the 24th. Divisional Artillery will co-operate in the raid. Detailed arrangements have been drawn up by Lt.Col. STALLARD, C.M.G., D.S.O., R.F.A.

At ZERO minus 30 seconds the Artillery will fire at intense rates on the area to be raided.

At ZERO hour a box barrage will be formed round the raiding party.

5. Medium T.M's, Stokes and Machine Guns will open fire at ZERO hour on selected targets.

6. The signal for all barrages to cease will be three RED Very Lights fired from Company Headquarters in HUMBUG ALLEY at H.31.b.56.65.

This will be confirmed by a PRIORITY wire to Brigade Headquarters, Code word - NOW.

7. Signal for withdrawal of raiding party.

A GREEN Very Light fired horizontally by each of the three Group Commanders. An Officer will be at the junction of HUMBUG ALLEY and HUGO TRENCH, and, on seeing the GREEN very lights will at once send up a Golden Rain Rocket followed by three WHITE Very Lights in quick succession.

8. In the event of all the raiders not returning within a reasonable period three WHITE Very Lights will be fired in quick succession every ten minutes from the junction of HUMBUG ALLEY and HUGO TRENCH.

9. Synchronisation of Watches.

The Brigade Signalling Officer will arrange for watches to be synchronised at Right Battalion Headquarters and Left Group Headquarters at 6 p.m. and 9.30 p.m. on the 3rd. June 1918.

Representatives from the Medium T.M.Battery, 73rd. Light T.M.Battery and "A" Coy., 24th. M.G.Battn. should be at Right Battalion Headquarters at the above hours.

10. The following Code Words will be used between Battalion and Brigade Headquarters:-

Raiding party in position	HUDSON.
Raiding party all back	MANFIELD.
No identifications secured	NOTHING DOING.
Number of prisoners captured...	COLEMAN ....
Our casualties ,.........	PAUL ....

11. On night 3/4th. June rations etc. will not arrive at PRATT DUMP before 12 midnight.

12. No working parties will be out in the Brigade area between 11 p.m. and 12 midnight on night 3/4th. June 1918. This does not

apply to ....

apply to parties working at HYTHE TUNNEL and : . on FOSSE 7 Defences.

P. T. Chenevix

ISSUED AT 7 p.m.

Captain,
Brigade Major, 73rd. Infantry Brigade.

Copy No.1. File.
2. War Diary.
3. " "
o 4. "G" 24 Div.
5. 24th. Divl.Artillery.
* 6. 17th. Inf. Bde.
* 7. Left Flank Bde.
8. 3rd. Aust.T.Coy.R.E.
9. 9th. Royal Sussex.
o 10. 7th. Northamptons.
o 11. 13th. Middlesex.
o 12. 73rd. Light T.M.Battery.
13. 129th. Fd. Coy R.E.
14. 73rd. Fd. Ambulance.
15. D.T.M.O., 24th. Div.
16. B.T.O., 73rd. I.B. (for action as regards para 11.).
* 17. Left Group, 24th. Divl. Art'y.
* 18. "A" Coy., 24th.Bn.M.G.Corps.

o Copies of detailed scheme already sent to these units.

Right Battn

SECRET.

O.O. No. 13.
Copy No. 1....

OPERATION ORDERS by Lieut. Colonel S.F. Stallard, C.M.G., D.S.O.
Commanding Left Group Artillery,

....

1. OBJECT. A raid will be carried out on the 3rd June by the Right Battalion for purpose of capturing the Machine Gun Post at H.26.d.25.20 and two other posts about the junction of HUMBUG ALLEY and HOOK TRENCH, and in conjunction with the Artillery, to inflict losses on the enemy.

2. ZERO HOUR. This will be notified later (approx. 11.0 p.m.)

3. ARTILLERY. The Batteries of the 48th, 126th, and 106th Brigades R.F.A. will act in accordance with TABLE "A" and diagram attached.

4. SIGNALS. The signal for withdrawal of Infantry will be single green lights fired by Commanders of Infantry Groups.
The signal for all barrages to ceasewill be three red lights fired from Company Headquarters in HUMBUG ALLEY. This will be confirmed by wire from this Office.

5. WATCHES. Watches will be synchronized at 7 p.m. and 10 p.m. on the 3rd June at these H.Qrs.

W Webley Jones 2/Lieut.
Staff Officer,
LEFT GROUP.

2nd June, 1918.

SECRET.   O.O. No.30.

Copy No. 15

OPERATION ORDERS by Lieut.Col W.R.CORRALL, M.C. for a Raid on enemy trenches on night 3rd/4th June 1918.

1. OBJECT OF RAID. To obtain identification by capturing Machine Gun post known to be at H.26.d.25.20, also two other posts about junction of HUMBUG ALLEY and HOOK TRENCH, and in conjunction with the Artillery, to inflict losses on the enemy.

2. STRENGTH OF RAIDING PARTY. 2 Officers and 30 O.R. divided into three groups of 10, called "Right", "Centre" and "Left" groups respectively. The right group will be commanded by 2/Lieut. R. HUDSON; the centre group by a selected N.C.O. and the left group by 2/Lieut. C.W. MANFIELD. 2/Lieut. HUDSON will be O.C. Raiding Party. In addition, two Lewis guns, each with a team of four men, 2 sections of infantry will be held in readiness in dugouts in HUGO TRENCH to assist the raiding party should they get into difficulties.. (This latter para. is subject to alteration).

3. ZERO HOUR. This will be notified later. (Approx 11.0. p.m.).

4. ARTILLERY CO-OPERATION. Arrangements have been made for five batteries (30 guns) 18-pdrs. to form a box barrage at ZERO hour round the section to be raided, as follows : On HAKE ALLEY from junction with enemy front line, to a point H.26.d.20.70 - on trench in H.26.d. central from HAKE ALLEY to HUMBUG ALLEY - on HUMBUG ALLEY from junction at HARD TRENCH to trench junctions at H.26.d.50.12.
In addition a barrage will be placed on HOUR TRENCH from junction with HARD TRENCH to junction with HOG TRENCH, thence along HUT TRENCH to a point H.32.b.70.84, and from that point to front line at H.32.b.48.78, a battery of 4.5" hows. will also engage the following points (Trench junctions) H.27.c.08.42; H.27.c.21.17; H.32.b.53.46 and H.32.b.93.65.
At ZERO minus 30 seconds, two batteries (12 guns) 18-pdr. will open with intense fire along trench running south-west, from H.26.d.51.20 to H.32.b.44.91. One battery (6 guns) 18 pdr. will sweep with intense fire enemy trench from H.26.d.15.25. to H.32.b.40.95. One gun (18-pdr) on trench running back from enemy front line at H.33.d.38.19 to H.2y.d.50.20., and one gun 18-pdr. on trench from H.26.d.23.13. to H.26.d.50.20
At ZERO these guns (20 guns) cease, and join box barrage.

5. MEDIUM TRENCH MORTARS. The 6" T.M. (3 guns) will at ZERO hour engage enemy machine guns at H.26.c.60.64. and H.26.c.80.65.

6. STOKES GUNS. The Stokes guns at ZERO hour will put a barrage on enemy trenchs from H.26.d.08.44. to H.26.c.30.60.

7. MACHINE GUNS. Arrangements have been made with O.C. "A" Coy, 24th Divl. Machine Gun Battn. to fire on the following targets :

4 guns searching HOUR TRENCH from junction at enemy front line to junction with HARD TRENCH.

4 guns searching on trench in H.26.d.central, from HAKE ALLEY to HUMBUG ALLEY.

2 guns searching HORSE ALLEY from H.26.d.00.80. to H.26.b.20.10

2 guns traversing western end of BOIS de QUATORZE.

2 guns searching HULLUCH TRENCH from junction with HORSE ALLEY to BOIS de QUATORZE.

Th signal for all barages to cease will be three red lights fired from Coy. H.Q. in HUMBUG ALLEY at H.31.b.56.65. A message will also be/

be sent by wire to Brigade H.Q. for communication to batteries. It is estimated the raid will be over at ZERO plus 10 minutes.

8. ASSEMBLY. Raiding party will assemble in HUMBUG ALLEY, 10 minutes before ZERO hour in the following order :- Right group, - centre group - left group. Head of party to be 10 yards short of trench junction at H.32.b.14.98

9. DETAIL. The three groups will rush in at ZERO hour, blocking parties each of three men will be formed as follows :- For the right group at the trench junction H.32.b.40.95; Centre group at H.26.d.30.12 Left group at H.26.d.15.25. On reaching the trench, the right and left group will work left and right respectively, the centre group outwards. The right group will push down the trench running from H.32.b.44.81, to H.26.d.51.20, and clear up any dugouts before working towards the centre group. The signal for withdrawal will be one green light fired horizontally by each group commander. Each man will then find his own way back to our lines, via HUMBUG ALLEY. The signal for withdrawal will be repeated by firing a rocket from the junction of HUMBUG ALLEY with HUGO TRENCH, followed by three Very lights in quick succession, to enable men to pick up their direction.
The two Lewis guns mentioned in para.3. will take up a position in HUMBUG ALLEY at about H.32.a.90.95. These guns will only open fire in the event of the enemy attempting to outflank the raiding party. They will not withdraw until the last of the raiding party has returned. The order for withdrawal will be given to them by an officer. An Officer will be posted at junction of HUGO TRENCH and HUMBUG ALLEY, to count the raiders as they come in, and direct them to dugouts in HUGO TRENCH where the roll will be called. Prisoners will be taken to Coy. H.Q. in HUMBUG ALLEY.

10. DRESS. Soft caps, rifles, belts, bayonets and 20 rounds S.A.A. (10 rounds in magazine and 10 rounds in trouser pocket) Each man will carry 4 bombs, 2 in each bottom jacket pocket. Armbands of white tracing tape will be worn on the right arm above the elbow.

11. SYNCHRONIZATION of WATCHES. Watches will be synchronised at 8.0.p.m. and 9.30 p.m. on ZERO day, from Brigade H.Q.

This cancels Operation Order No. 36 dated 30/5/18.

H.C. Coleman Capt. & Adj.
for Lieut.Col.
Commanding 9th Royal Sussex Regiment.

31/5/18

DISTRIBUTION.

Copy No. 1. To H.Q.73rd.Inf.Bde.
2. O.C. "A" Coy.
3. O.C. "B" Coy.
4. O.C. "C" Coy.
5. O.C. "D" Coy.
6. 2/Lieut. R. HUDSON.
7. 2/Lieut. MANFIELD.
8. O.C.7th NORTHANTS.
9. O.C. 1st R.FUSILIERS.
10. (Bde) Heavy Liaison Officer.
11. 126 Bde. R.F.A. Liaison Officer.
12. O.C. 24th M.G.Battn.
13. 73rd. L.T.M.Batty.
14. O.C. 73rd. Medium T.M.Bty.
15. Commanding Officer.
16. War Diary.
17. File.

ACKNOWLEDGE.

Instructions regarding War Diaries and Intelligence Summaries are contained in F. S. Regs., Part II. and the Staff Manual respectively. Title pages will be prepared in manuscript.

WAR DIARY
or
~~INTELLIGENCE~~ SUMMARY.
(*Erase heading not required.*)

Army Form C. 2118.

Vol 35

Place	Date	Hour	Summary of Events and Information	Remarks and references to Appendices
Confidential				
			9th Bn Royal Sussex Regiment	
			for the month of	
			July 1918	
				36.I [illegible]

A6945 Wt. W11422/M1160 350,000 12/16 D. D. & L. Forms/C./2118/14.

Instructions regarding War Diaries and Intelligence Summaries are contained in F. S. Regs., Part II. and the Staff Manual respectively. Title pages will be prepared in manuscript.

9TH BATTALION Royal Sussex Regt

WAR DIARY

or

INTELLIGENCE SUMMARY.

(Erase heading not required.)

JULY. 1918.

Army Form C. 2118.

Place	Date	Hour	Summary of Events and Information	Remarks and references to Appendices
Field.	JULY 1		Battalion in Right sub-section, Left Sector, HILL 70. Battalion H.Q. St. Patricks. Major T. Foster commanded Battalion in absence of Lt. Col. W.R. Corrall on leave.	H.C.C
	2.		Draft of 20. O.R from BASE. These were badly needed owing to the large number of men in Hospital with P.U.O. epidemic.	H.C.C
	4.		Short hurricane bombardments on front line and LOOS CRASSIER. Little damage.	H.C.C
	5		Inter Company reliefs were carried out.	H.C.C
	8		1 Officer and 5. O.R. sent to Army Rest Camp at AUDRESSELLES. Draft of 50. O.R. from Base. CSM. Butcher MC. DCM rejoined Battalion from 2nd Batt.	H.C.C
	9		About 200 5.9"s in vicinity of LOOS chiefly on Battery Positions	H.C.C
	10		Tour of Inspection by CORPS COMMANDER. He visited HYTHE TUNNEL and the forward positions held by the Battalion.	
	11		Battalion relieved by 13TH Middlesex Regt. and moved to Reserve billets in LES BREBIS.	H.C.C
	12.		Lieut Col. W.R. CORRALL. M.C. rejoined Battalion from leave.	H.C.C
	13.		Visit by CORPS COMMANDER. He inspected Platoon training, billets and cookers and was very pleased with the Battalion and the method in which the training was being carried out.	H.C.C
	12th to 19th		During the tour in reserve, Platoon training under the direct supervision of the Platoon Commander was carried out. Firing on LES BREBIS range, Inspections, Classes etc. were also detailed each day. A good allotment of Baths was received enabling every man in the Battalion to have a Bath and clean change of clothing.	H.C.C
	16th.		A Smoking Concert was given by the Sergeants in their Mess to which all Officers were invited. A very successful and enjoyable evening was spent.	H.C.C

A5834 Wt. W4973/M687 750,000 8/16 D. D. & L. Ltd. Forms/C.2118/13.

Instructions regarding War Diaries and Intelligence Summaries are contained in F. S. Regs., Part II. and the Staff Manual respectively. Title pages will be prepared in manuscript.

9TH BATTALION Royal Sussex Regt.

Army Form C. 2118.

WAR DIARY
or
INTELLIGENCE SUMMARY.

(Erase heading not required.)

JULY. 1918.

Place	Date	Hour	Summary of Events and Information	Remarks and references to Appendices
FIELD	JULY. 17.		Battalion relieved 7th Northamptonshire Regt. in Left. Sub. Section. Battalion H.Q at PREVITE CASTLE	H.C.C
	17th to 29th		A quiet tour during which a considerable amount of work was done. Co operation with the Left Battalion was placed on a good footing. During the tour ruses were adopted by the Battalion to deceive the enemy and put the "wind-up" him. Active patrolling was carried out. Our heavy artillery was very active on enemy back areas.	H.C.C
	26.		Lieut. Col. M.V.B. HILL. D.S.O. M.C. rejoined from England and assumed command of the Battalion.	H.C.C
	27.		Capt. G.M. SHACKEL. M.C. rejoined Battalion and was posted to command A Company	
	29.		Battalion relieved by 19th Middlesex Regt. and moved to billets in LES BREBIS and became Brigade Reserve.	H.C.C

A5834 Wt. W4973/M687 750,000 8/16 D. D. & L. Ltd. Forms/C.2118/13.

9th Battalion Royal Sussex Regiment

Army Form C. 2118.

Instructions regarding War Diaries and Intelligence Summaries are contained in F. S. Regs., Part II. and the Staff Manual respectively. Title pages will be prepared in manuscript.

WAR DIARY
or
INTELLIGENCE SUMMARY.
(Erase heading not required.)

JULY 1918.

Place	Date	Hour	Summary of Events and Information	Remarks and references to Appendices
FIELD	JULY. 30.		The day was devoted to BATHS, cleaning up and inspections. Party of 40. O.R and a few officers visited 2ND Battalion Sports at NOEUX-LES-MINES and the C.O and 6 other officers dined with 2ND Battalion in the evening.	H.C.C
	31.		Training was carried out under Platoon Commanders. Classes were started for Lewis Gunners, Observers and young N.C.O's. Lieut J.E. PAUL rejoined from sick leave.	H.C.C

H.C. Colman
Captain & Adjutant
for O.C. 9th Royal Sussex Regt.

A5834 Wt. W4973/M687 750,000 8/16 D. D. & L. Ltd. Forms/C.2118/13.

Instructions regarding War Diaries and Intelligence Summaries are contained in F. S. Regs., Part II. and the Staff Manual respectively. Title pages will be prepared in manuscript.

WAR DIARY

~~or~~

~~INTELLIGENCE SUMMARY.~~

(*Erase heading not required.*)

Army Form C. 2118.

Vol 36

Place	Date	Hour	Summary of Events and Information	Remarks and references to Appendices
Confidential				
			9th Bn Royal Sussex Regiment	
			for the month of	
			August 1918	
				87. I

A6945 Wt. W11422/M1160 350,000 12/16 D. D. & L. Forms/C./2118/14.

9th Battalion Royal Sussex Regiment

WAR DIARY
or
INTELLIGENCE SUMMARY.
(*Erase heading not required.*)

Instructions regarding War Diaries and Intelligence Summaries are contained in F. S. Regs., Part II. and the Staff Manual respectively. Title pages will be prepared in manuscript.

AUGUST. 1918.

G14/64 Army Form C. 2118.

Place	Date	Hour	Summary of Events and Information	Remarks and references to Appendices
Field.	1.8.18.		Battalion in Brigade Reserve at LES BREBIS. 1 Company engaged on working parties, remainder on training. A Company marched to MARQUEFFLES Range for Firing Practice. Captain G. R. Duffield was wounded by a blow-back from a defective rifle and evacuated to C.C.S.	H.C.
	3.8.18.		Day spent in platoon training. At 8.45 p.m. "TEST PREPARE FOR ACTION" received. The message "Test MAN BATTLE POSITIONS" was delayed and not received till 10.4 pm. The Battalion turned out in fighting kit and moved to assembly positions clear of LES BREBIS in vicinity of GRENAY-NOYELLES Line. From here 1 officer per Company and 2 O.R per platoon were sent forward to Battle Company H.Q. and from there reported to Battle Battalion H.Q. LENS Road REDOUBT. The practice was carried out very successfully	H.C.C.
	4.8.18.		Battalion relieved 7th NORTHAMPTONSHIRE Regiment in Right Sub Sector.	H.C.C.
	4.8.18 to 17.8.18.		A very quiet tour except for harassing fire on LOOS and shelling at night of HYTHE Tunnel. The chief work undertaken was the siting of Battle Positions for all L.G. and rifle sections. Blocks and "straight shoots" were made in trenches leading to posts and progress was made in wiring defensive positions. On the 8th the Brigade on our left raided the enemy lines and captured 2 wounded prisoners and a M.G. Several casualties were inflicted on the enemy who removed his wounded across the open under cover of a Red Cross flag. On the 10th a dummy raid was carried out in the same area.	H.C.C.

A5834 Wt. W4973/M687 750,000 8/16 D. D. & L. Ltd. Forms/C.2118/13.

9th Battalion Royal Sussex Regiment

C14/64

Army Form C. 2118.

WAR DIARY
or
INTELLIGENCE SUMMARY.

(*Erase heading not required.*)

AUGUST. 1918.

Instructions regarding War Diaries and Intelligence Summaries are contained in F. S. Regs., Part II. and the Staff Manual respectively. Title pages will be prepared in manuscript.

Place	Date	Hour	Summary of Events and Information	Remarks and references to Appendices
Field	10.8.18.		Hon Lieut & Quartermaster T. MARTIN proceeded to England. He had served with the Battalion since it was first formed in September 1914. first as C.Q.M.S. of "D" Company. then as R.Q.M.S and finally as Quartermaster	H.C.C.
	17.8.18.		Battalion relieved by 13th MIDDLESEX Regiment and moved to billets at LES BREBIS.	H.C.C.
	18.8.18.		Lieut. J.C.WIGGS rejoined the Battalion and appointed Assistant Adjutant. Lieut. J.E. GALE also rejoined and posted to "C" Company.	H.C.C.
	18.8.18 to 23.8.18.		Three Companies were available each day for training, the other Company being detailed for working parties. Training at LES BREBIS was confined to Platoon training but on two days the Range at MARQUEFFLES was allotted to the Battalion, musketry practice being carried out and Company Schemes practised. On the 22nd. the G.O.C. 24th Division inspected the Battalion paying special attention to the organisation. On this day the Mine Buildings at LES BREBIS were heavily shelled.	H.C.C.
	24.8.18.		Major. J.C.D. BIRTWHISTLE was attached to the Battalion. Major. T. FOSTER assumed command of Divisional Reception Camp at MAISNIL BOUCHE. Battalion relieved 7th NORTHAMPTONSHIRE Regiment in Left Sub Sector LOOS.	H.C.C.

G14/64.

Army Form C. 2118.

Instructions regarding War Diaries and Intelligence Summaries are contained in F. S. Regs., Part II. and the Staff Manual respectively. Title pages will be prepared in manuscript.

9th Battalion Royal Sussex Regiment

WAR DIARY

or

INTELLIGENCE SUMMARY.

(Erase heading not required.)

AUGUST 1918.

Place	Date	Hour	Summary of Events and Information	Remarks and references to Appendices
Field.	27.8.18.		Battalion relieved by 1/9th ROYAL SCOTS, 15th Division and moved to billets at BULLY GRENAY, D Company being billeted at CITÉ CALONNE.	H.C.C.
	28.8.18.		Battalion relieved 8TH ROYAL WEST KENT Regiment in the line in front of LENS with Battalion H.Q in the Chateau de RIAUMONT. LIEVIN. The 8th ROYAL WEST KENTS had taken over the line the night before from the 20th Division. This re-adjustment was rendered necessary by the move forward in front of ARRAS and consequent extension of the front at that point. These two reliefs were carried out very easily and without casualties. Transport Lines and Q.M. Stores remained at BULLY GRENAY. which was very inconvenient.	H.C.C.
	29.8.18.		Enemy artillery active at intervals during early morning, otherwise a quiet day.	H.C.C.
	30.8.18.		A quiet day except for hostile shelling during early morning. 2/Lieut CHILDS led a patrol of "D" Coy toward the enemy posts at night. He located a post from which lights were sent up in response to which enemy artillery opened fire.	H.C.C.
	31.8.18.		Raid carried out by Battalion on our left was not successful. After dark 2/Lieut CHILDS took out 2 sections and established posts on the LENS - LA BASSEE Road. in N.14.c. An enemy patrol was seen but not engaged. The 7th NORTHAMPTONSHIRE Regiment on our right attempted to occupy GREEN CRASSIER but failed owing to extreme darkness and the obstacles in position	H.C.C.

H.C. Coleman

Captain & Adjutant

for. O.C. 9th Royal Sussex Regiment.

4.9.1918.

A5834 Wt. W4973/M687 750,000 8/16 D. D. & L. Ltd. Forms/C.2118/13.

21

Confidential

Vol 37

9th Royal Sussex Regt

WAR DIARY.

38.I
6 months

9th BN. ROYAL SUSSEX REGT.
No. G14/47
Army Form C. 2118.
Date.

Instructions regarding War Diaries and Intelligence Summaries are contained in F. S. Regs., Part II. and the Staff Manual respectively. Title pages will be prepared in manuscript.

9th Battalion Royal Sussex Regiment. **WAR DIARY** or ~~INTELLIGENCE SUMMARY.~~ (*Erase heading not required.*) September. 1918

Place 1918	Date	Hour	Summary of Events and Information	Remarks and references to Appendices
September. Field.	1		Battalion in the line on western outskirts of LENS. Information was given by prisoner captured by 7th Northamptonshire Regt. that the 36th GERMAN Reserve Division had evacuated LENS the previous night leaving pioneers to blow up dug-outs. The line to be held was said to be the OPPY - MERICOURT - VENDIN line. Patrols were pushed forward in conjunction with 72nd Infantry Brigade on left and a line of posts was established on the LA BASSEE Road. A readjustment of Brigade dispositions was carried out at dusk and the Battalion held the line as follows: Front Coy. 'B' Left Support Coy. 'D'. Right Support Coy. 'C' Reserve Coy. 'A'	A.O.C.
	2.		A slight increase in enemy activity was noticed. Patrols found that the enemy withdrew his forward posts by day, but that they were in position at night. 'B' Coy took over positions on the GREEN CRASSIER from 7th Northamptonshire Regiment. Lieut C.E. Edlington rejoined Battalion and was posted to 'A' Coy	A.O.C.
	3.		An uneventful day on our front. 72nd Brigade on left had several encounters with the enemy.	A.O.C.
	4.		Very active patrolling was carried out by three parties under 2/Lieut F. CHEW, Lieut J. E. GALE and 2/Lieut. A.G. WALFORD. The following points were reached - SALAD TR (N 27.c. central) FOSSE 5. and LENS STATION. None of the enemy were encountered but a post was located in vicinity of N. 21.a. 1.7. The patrol to SALAD TRENCH found a section of the SCOTTISH RIFLES who had been missing for two days. An artillery shoot was carried out on front of Brigade on left, followed by a gas operation. Enemy shelled Green CRASSIER and posts on LA BASSEE Road during morning. Mr. HARRY LANDER visited Battalion H.Q. (Chateau de RIALIMONT) in order to obtain a view of LENS.	A.O.C.
	5.		During the night 4th/5th. CITE des GARENNES and vicinity was heavily shelled with Mustard Gas and Green X shells. The Battalion had no casualties but 7th Bn. Northamptonshire Regt suffered about 70 casualties. A patrol (under	

A5834 Wt. W4973/M687 750,000 8/16 D. D. & L. Ltd. Forms/C.2118/13.

Instructions regarding War Diaries and Intelligence Summaries are contained in F. S. Regs., Part II. and the Staff Manual respectively. Title pages will be prepared in manuscript.

9th Battalion ROYAL **WAR DIARY** SUSSEX Regiment
or
INTELLIGENCE SUMMARY.
(Erase heading not required.)

Army Form C. 2118.

SEPTEMBER 1918.

Place	Date	Hour	Summary of Events and Information	Remarks and references to Appendices
Field	September 5		under 2/Lieut. S.E. Gibbs met an enemy patrol. Rifle shots and Bombs were exchanged. Two of our party were slightly wounded. They were taken back to our line and the patrol then returned to the scene of the fight in the hope of meeting the enemy again. They waited for about 2 hours without any result.	H.C.C.
	6		The Battalion was relieved by 13th MIDDLESEX Regt and moved to Support. 'A' Coy - BOIS de RIAUMONT 'B' and 'C' Coys - CITE DE CALMONT 'D' - Vicinity of CRAZY POST. Battn. H.Q. - QUARRY S.W. of BOIS de RIAUMONT CITE des CARENNES was not occupied owing to gas shelling on 5th. This locality was shelled at intervals for several days following the gas bombardment. The 'TIMES' Correspondent visited Battn. H.Q.	H.C.C.
	7-13.		Battalion carried out Company Training. Companies at CITE de CALMONT got through some very useful work. The other 2 Coys. were restricted to Lewis Gun Classes, Musketry and Bombing as they were in close support to Front Battalion.	H.C.C.
	11		Battalion H.Q and 'D' Coy moved to CITE de ROLLENCOURT. The vicinity of new billets was shelled during the move and 2 O.R. were wounded. The shelling continued steadily through the night but no further casualties were caused. Major T. Foster rejoined Bn from Divisional Reception Camp.	H.C.C.
	13.		Officers reconnoitred Battle Positions of Battalion in Divisional Reserve and routes forward from assembly positions. Major T.C.L. Burtchaell left Bn. to join 13th North Staffordshire Regt. as 2ND in command.	H.C.C.
	14.		Battalion relieved by 13th MIDDLESEX Regt and became Battalion in Divisional Reserve at MARQUEFFLES FARM.	H.C.C.
	15.		The day was spent in cleaning up and Baths. The range was used in the morning and several Officers attended a demonstration given by 14th Infantry Brigade of co-operation between Infantry and Tanks.	H.C.C.
	16.		Company Training. Special attention was given to learning formations for advancing in open fighting and to teaching the principles of fire and movement.	H.C.C.

9th Battalion ROYAL **WAR DIARY** SUSSEX Regiment

or

~~**INTELLIGENCE SUMMARY.**~~

(Erase heading not required.)

Army Form C. 2118.

Instructions regarding War Diaries and Intelligence Summaries are contained in F. S. Regs., Part II. and the Staff Manual respectively. Title pages will be prepared in manuscript.

Place	Date	Hour	Summary of Events and Information	Remarks and references to Appendices
Field.	17th		Coy Training. In the afternoon a Tactical Scheme without troops was carried out under the direction of the B.G.C. and was attended by C.O. Adjutant, Coy Commanders and Signalling Officer. The Bn. played the Divisional Train at football in the afternoon and won by 4 goals to nil. The Divl. Concert Party gave a Concert in the evening.	
	18th		Battalion paraded for Ceremonial Drill. A lecture was given by O C TANKS to all Officers and N.C.Os on the Co-operation between Infantry and Tanks. The BAND played at 8th Corps. H.Q. 2/Lieut. D FRASER MC proceeded to England for transfer to the R.A.F. A telegram was received from 1st ARMY H.Q. saying German prisoners stated German withdrawal from LENS.	H.C.C.
	19th		Training was carried out under Company arrangement. A tactical scheme with Tanks was carried out in afternoon to demonstrate duties of infantry assisted by Tanks. New Brigade Scheme issued in case of enemy withdrawal. The Bn. Played D.A.C. at football in the afternoon and lost 1-2.	H.C.C.
	20th		Battalion Route March in the morning. The Divl. Education Officer gave a lecture in the afternoon to all Officers and 50 men per Coy. Judging of Transport in the Corps Competition held. This was attended by the C.O.	H.C.C.
	21st		All Coys. on Range during the day. The CO and Adjutant reconnoitred the line during the day. Battalion played A.S.C at football and won. 3-1. Lieut. A.G.A. VIDLER MC joined Battalion and was posted to 'C' Coy.	H.C.C.
	22		The Battalion went into line relieving the 4th NORTHAMPTONSHIRE REGT in the LENS SECTOR Right Brigade. A larger frontage was taken over making a 2 Coy. front disposed as follows:- B. Coy. RIGHT FRONT — 'C' Coy LEFT FRONT D. SUPPORT — 'A' SUPPORT BATTN. H.Q. Constitution Hill.	H.C.C.
	23.		Situation very quiet. Little aerial activity on both sides, weather wet. During the past week the Battalion purchased 213? War Savings Certificates at 15/6d. each.	H.C.C.
	24.		Our Artillery very active during the morning. Considerable aerial activity during day.	H.C.C.

3.

A5834 Wt. W4973/M687 750,000 8/16 D. D. & L. Ltd. Forms/C.2118/13.

Instructions regarding War Diaries and Intelligence Summaries are contained in F. S. Regs., Part II. and the Staff Manual respectively. Title pages will be prepared in manuscript.

9th Battalion ROYAL **WAR DIARY** SUSSEX Regiment
or
~~**INTELLIGENCE SUMMARY.**~~
(Erase heading not required.)

Army Form C. 2118.

SEPTEMBER. 1918

Place	Date 1918.	Hour	Summary of Events and Information	Remarks and references to Appendices
Field	September 25		Extremely quiet day although there was unusual aerial activity. Orders received for feint attack on 73 I.B. front. This was cancelled later. Night 25/26 was observed as a silent night by the Artillery.	H.C.C.
	26.		73 I.B. order No 202 received for feint attack on 24th Divisional front to be carried out during the night 26/27. The Artillery did a good deal of wire cutting during the day and the 72nd I.B. raided enemy post at N.8.d.5.4. at 3.0pm. Raid successful. 1 German officer killed, a dug out which sheltered several Germans was blown up and M.G. captured. Enemy machine flew very low over our lines and was engaged by A.A and M.G. fire which succeeded in driving it off. Inter Coy relief as follows took place at dusk. Dispositions after relief. 'D' Coy Right Front. A Coy Left Front. B Coy Right Support. C Coy Left Support.	H.C.C.
	27.		Feint attack carried out. ZERO being 5.5. AM. Heavy Artillery & 6" Newtons bombarded selected points on whole Div. Front from ZERO to ZERO plus 30 minutes. At ZERO plus 30 minutes coloured lights were fired and from ZERO plus 30 to plus 40 a creeping barrage of 18 pounders on selected areas. After ZERO + 55 normal Artillery activity was resumed. The enemy did not retaliate very much. The usual Artillery and Aerial activity during the day.	H.C.C.
	28.		At about 4.10. A.M. enemy raided one of 'D' Coy. post capturing 1 man and wounding 2 others and also taking the Lewis Gun. This post gave a good account of themselves but the enemy were too strong and bombed very freely getting direct hits on the post.	H.C.C.
			Casualties 2 O.R. Wounded and 1. Missing. Artillery active at night. The 12th K.R.R.C. carried out a raid on our right. Orders received for move of Battalion and relief by 9th LONDON Regt. on night of 30/31st.	H.C.C.
	29.		Enemy planes active over our line during the morning. Patrols out during night but nothing was seen or heard of the enemy. Relief Orders and entraining orders for Oct. 1. 1918 were issued.	H.C.C.

H.

A5834 Wt. W4973/M687 750,000 8/16 D. D. & L. Ltd. Forms/C.2118/13.

Instructions regarding War Diaries and Intelligence Summaries are contained in F. S. Regs., Part II. and the Staff Manual respectively. Title pages will be prepared in manuscript.

9th Battalion ROYAL **WAR DIARY** SUSSEX Regiment
or
INTELLIGENCE SUMMARY.
(Erase heading not required.)

SEPTEMBER 1918

Army Form C. 2118.

Place	Date 1918.	Hour	Summary of Events and Information	Remarks and references to Appendices
Field	September 30.		Battalion relieved by 9th LONDON Regt and proceeded to SOUCHEZ from whence the Battalion was conveyed to COUPIGNY huts by Motor busses. Good relief - no casualties. This relief was preliminary to the transfer of the 24th Division to the 3RD ARMY - DOULLENS Area	H.C.C.
			AWARD. No 17146 Pte. W. CAMPLIN 'A' Coy. awarded the M.M. for good patrol work doing particularly well, although wounded.	H.C.C.
			H.C. Coleman Captain & Adjutant for O.C. 9th Royal Sussex Regt. October 4. 1918.	

A5834 Wt. W4973/M687 750,000 8/16 D. D. & L. Ltd. Forms/C.2118/13.

Instructions regarding War Diaries and Intelligence Summaries are contained in F. S. Regs., Par. II. and the Staff Manual respectively. Title pages will be prepared in manuscript.

WAR DIARY

or

~~INTELLIGENCE SUMMARY.~~

(Erase heading not required.)

Army Form C. 2118.

Vol 38

73/24

Place	Date	Hour	Summary of Events and Information	Remarks and references to Appendices
			Confidential	
			9th Bn Royal Sussex Regiment	
			for the month of	
			October 1918	
			—	
				39.T 9 sheets

A6945 Wt. W11422/M1160 350,000 12/16 D. D. & L. Forms/C. 2118/14.

9th BN. ROYAL SUSSEX REGT.
No. G14/35
Date

Instructions regarding War Diaries and Intelligence Summaries are contained in F. S. Regs., Part II. and the Staff Manual respectively. Title pages will be prepared in manuscript.

— 9th Battalion ROYAL SUSSEX Regiment —

WAR DIARY
or
~~INTELLIGENCE SUMMARY.~~
(*Erase heading not required.*)

October. 1918.

Army Form C. 2118.

Place	Date	Hour	Summary of Events and Information	Remarks and references to Appendices
Field	October 1		Battalion under orders to proceed to MONDICOURT and stationed at COUPIGNY HUTS near HERSIN. COUPIGNY HUTS were left about 1 p.m and the Battalion entrained at HERSIN leaving about 2.40 p.m. MONDICOURT was reached just after 9.30 p.m. Billets for the Battalion were located close to the detraining station. The 24th Division was located in this area being transferred to the 3rd Army.	H.C.C.
	2-4.		Battalion at MONDICOURT. These three days were spent in cleaning up, Baths, Kit inspections etc. Training was carried out and included a Battalion Scheme which took place on the 4th and involved the general principles of successful attack etc. Orders were received on the 4th for the transfer of the 73rd Infantry Brigade Group to the FREMICOURT - HERMIES Area on the 6th inst and advance parties under Lieut. P.W. CHAPMAN proceeded to the new area accordingly.	H.C.C.
	5		The Transport of the 73rd Brigade Group moved by march route to MOEUVRES, halting night 5/6 October at BOISLEUX-AU-MONT. A Company Commanders' conference was held by the C.O in the evening at H.Q Mess. followed by a meeting of all Officers.	H.C.C.
	6.		Battalion under orders to proceed to XVII Corps AREA and left MONDICOURT about 2 p.m. and detrained at HERMIES. The Battalion then proceeded by March route to camp of bivouacs just E. of MOEUVRES arriving at about 9 p.m. Night 6/7th was spent here. The 24th Division, in operations commencing 8th inst, was to be in support of the 63rd Division and to be ready to pass through if needed.	H.C.C.
	7.		Battalion moved at 3 p.m to camp in L.1. just S.W. of CANTAING. Here bivouacs were erected and the 190th Infantry Brigade (63rd Division) relieved. Brigade move completed by 8 p.m. The B.G.C., Battalion and Coy. Commanders reconnoitred area through which Brigade would probably pass. The night 7/8th was spent at this camp.	H.C.C.
	8.		The 63rd Division captured NIERGNIES by 8 A.M. At 2 pm. 73rd Inf. Brigade moved forward and concentrated E. of CANAL de ST. QUENTIN in G.7 and G.8. Batt. H.Q were established in a dugout E. of NOYELLES. Four casualties from shell fire, all wounded, were suffered here. Otherwise the move was completed without incident.	H.C.C.
	9.		The 72nd Inf. Brigade attacked at 5.20. am and pushed forward to their final objectives supported by a heavy artillery barrage. AWOINGT and Railway to the E. were captured. The Battalion in conjunction with the rest of the Bde. moved forward at 6 am. in close support of the 72. I. Bde. The Battalion was leading with the 7th Northamptons in support and the 13th Middlesex in reserve. Two Stokes Guns moved forward with the Battalion which was also accompanied by the 'Fighting' portion of the 1st line Transport. Two sections 'A' Coy. 24th M.G.C. also moved forward in close support of the Battalion.	

A5834 Wt. W4973/M687 750,000 8/16 D. D. & L. Ltd. Forms/C.2118/13.

Instructions regarding War Diaries and Intelligence Summaries are contained in F. S. Regs., Part II. and the Staff Manual respectively. Title pages will be prepared in manuscript.

— 9th Battalion ROYAL SUSSEX Regiment. —

WAR DIARY
or
INTELLIGENCE SUMMARY.
(Erase heading not required.)

October 1918.

Army Form C. 2118.

Place	Date	Hour	Summary of Events and Information	Remarks and references to Appendices
Field	October 9.		The Battalion moved forward by way of RUMILLY due N.E through NIERGNIES to AWOINGT where the leading Battalion held the line of the Railway relieving the 73rd I. Bde. The Battalion was then ordered to move forward and occupy CAUROIR which had been reported clear of the enemy by cavalry. The Brigade were to occupy the general line CAUROIR-CAGNONCLES. Leading troops of the Battalion crossed CAMBRAI-CAUDRY Road at 11 am. and met slight M.G. opposition from outskirts of CAUROIR. Batt. H.Q established in cellar near junction of CAMBRAI-LE CATEAU and AWOINGT-CAUROIR Road. H.Q came under fire here and suffered casualties. 1 runner being killed. Orders were issued by B.G.C for attack on CAGNONCLES, the Battalion having to move through CAUROIR and attack enemy positions to the E. of the village. By 6pm advanced troops of the Battalion had reached Cemetery E. of CAUROIR. Casualties very slight. Orders were received for advance to be continued at 5 A.M on the 10th. - Captain C.E. Goad. M.C. rejoined Battn. (at Divnl. Reception Camp) from 6 months tour of duty in England	M.R.C.
	October 10.		At dawn the artillery barrage opened and at 5 a.m. the advance was resumed with the Battalion on the right, 7th Northamptons on the left, 13th Middlesex in Support. No opposition was encountered in the early stages of the advance. Cavalry reported RIEUX clear of the enemy but high ground North of AVESNES-les-AUBERT strongly held by the enemy. At 9.35 a.m the 13th Middlesex passed through the two leading Battalions and was directed on AVESNES and RIEUX. By 1 pm. infantry patrols were east of these two villages. In pushing forward in support Batt. H.Q and Coys. came under shell fire and had casualties. Lieut. T.E. PAUL being wounded, 1 H.Q runner killed and several wounded. Cover was obtained in sunken road between AVESNES-les AUBERT and BIEFVILLERS. Soon after Bn. H.Q were established in cellars close by. Meanwhile at 4.45 pm. 13th Middlesex moved forward to attack high ground N. of AVESNES-les-AUBERT and 1 Coy. of the Battalion were placed at the disposal of the O.C. 13th Middlesex to support his left flank. By 9 pm advanced troops of Battalion had reached western outskirts of St AUBERT. Orders were issued for 13th Middlesex to hold high ground during the night and that the 17th I. Bde. would pass through the 73rd I. Bde at dawn and resume the advance. The Battalion remained in its positions during the night	M.R.C.
	October 11		Early in the morning orders were received that all Units would remain in their present positions until the 17th I. Bde had reached the line VILLERS-en-CAUCHIES - ST. AUBERT when they would be ordered to withdraw to billets in RIEUX and AVESNES-les-AUBERT. Instructions were received for the Brigade to be withdrawn to Reserve. Accordingly all forward troops were withdrawn and the Battalion billeted in AVESNES-les-AUBERT. Battn. H.Q. moved forward from its previous position to AVESNES-les-AUBERT. The advance of the 17th I. Bde. was held up by strong enemy opposition and during the night the enemy effected his withdrawal to the line of the SELLE River closely followed by the 17th I.B.	

A5834 Wt. W4973/M687 750,000 8/16 D. D. & L. Ltd. Forms/C.2118/13.

2.

Instructions regarding War Diaries and Intelligence Summaries are contained in F. S. Regs., Part II. and the Staff Manual respectively. Title pages will be prepared in manuscript.

9th Battalion ROYAL SUSSEX Regiment.

WAR DIARY
or
INTELLIGENCE SUMMARY.
(Erase heading not required.)

Army Form C. 2118.

October. 1918

Place	Date	Hour	Summary of Events and Information	Remarks and references to Appendices
Field	October 12.		Battalion at AVESNES-les-ALBERT. Rear H.Q. and Q.M. Stores rejoined Battalion and billets were occupied by the whole Battalion in AVESNES. The day was spent in sleep, cleaning up etc. and a conference of Commanding Officers was held at Bde H.Q. at 5 p.m. Orders were received from Division that the 17th Bde. would attack to capture high ground E. of SELLE River at 9.0 am on the 13th. and that 73rd I.B. coming into support were to maintain close touch.	H.C.C.
	13.		Battalion at AVESNES-les-ALBERT. It was understood that the Bde. would be required to pass through and capture high ground E. of HAUSSY. 2/Lieut. R.A. DICKER and 2/Lieut. H.C. SARGENT joined Battalion to day	H.C.C.
	14.		The whole Brigade was concentrated in the AVESNES-les-ALBERT area as Bde. in Support. The B.G.C. held conference of Commanding Officers with regard to intended attack. Orders were now received that the 24th Division would be relieved by the 19th Division	H.C.C.
			Total casualties to date were determined as follows:- Officers. Lieut. J.E. PAUL (Signalling Officer). Wounded. 10.10.18. 2/Lieut. G.A. WALFORD. Wounded (Gas) O.R. Killed. 6. Died of Wounds 4. Wounded in Action 53. Wounded in Action (GAS) 28	H.C.C.
	15-16.		During these two days general training was carried out including the practice of the intended attack on MAISON BLANCHE. Orders were received for the relief of the 24th Division and the move of the 73rd I.B. to CAUROIR on the 17th. Billeting party under Lieut. G. KINNEIR proceeded to CAUROIR.	H.C.C.
	17.		At 2.0 pm. the Battalion moved by march route to CAUROIR arriving at 3.30 pm. Bde. H.Q. were also located at CAUROIR	H.C.C.
	17-24.		Battalion at CAUROIR. The period was spent in training and recreation. Lewis Gun and N.C.O's classes were held and recreational training took place in the afternoons. Several concerts were given in the evenings by different concert parties. A Brigade Church service was held on Sunday 20th. and attended by 200 men per Battalion. Lieut. H.G. WELHAM. MC. rejoined Battalion from six months tour of duty and was posted to 'C' Coy. On the 23rd. a 'NAIL HUNT' was carried out in the vicinity of billets and resulted in the collection of over 80 lbs. of nails. Football matches against Brigade and other Battalions were played during this period.	H.C.C.
	25.		A Battalion Scheme was carried out this morning by 'A', 'B' and 'D' Coys. Stokes Mortars co-operated with 'B' Coy. The general idea was to illustrate the enveloping of a strong point which is holding up an advance. Notification was received that the 24th. Division would be required to relieve the Support Division at an early date. Arrangements were made for the dumping of surplus kits etc.	H.C.C.
	26.		Advance parties left for HAUSSY-MONTRECOURT Area at 5 A.M. this morning. The 73. I. Bde. Group moved to HAUSSY. Reveille 5. A.M. Breakfast 6 A.M. Battalion paraded at 7.40 a.m and proceeded by march route via AVESNES-les-ALBERT and ST. AUBERT to HAUSSY.	

A5834 Wt. W4973/M687 750,000 8/16 D. D. & L. Ltd. Forms/C.2118/13.

3.

9th Battalion ROYAL SUSSEX Regiment.

Army Form C. 2118.

WAR DIARY
or
INTELLIGENCE SUMMARY.
(Erase heading not required.)

Instructions regarding War Diaries and Intelligence Summaries are contained in F. S. Regs., Part II. and the Staff Manual respectively. Title pages will be prepared in manuscript.

October. 1918.

Place	Date	Hour	Summary of Events and Information	Remarks and references to Appendices
Field	October 26.		HAUSSY arriving at 12.15 p.m. Battalion rested during the afternoon. Lieut C.H. DUDENEY rejoined Battalion from six months tour of duty in England.	H.C.
	27th-31		Battalion at HAUSSY. During this period training was carried out including Battalion and Company Schemes. On Sunday 27th a Brigade Church Service was held and attended by Battalions. After the service a March past took place the B/G.C. taking the salute. On Tuesday 29th the Brigade Sports were held in the afternoon and attended by most Officers of the Battalion, which had a good number of entries in the various events. On the 31st a Brigade Scheme was carried out in the morning. 'B' Coy. represented the enemy. The 73. I. Bde were attacking high ground E. of HAUSSY. The attack was made as realistic as possible, imitation tanks being used. The 7th Northamptonshire Regt. and 13th Middlesex Regt. opened the attack, the Battalion (A, C and D Coys) passing through and securing the final objectives.	H.C.
	31		It was understood that the 73rd Inf. Bde would shortly be leaving HAUSSY for the forward area.	
			No. 19148. Pte. W.A. HYDE, 'A' Company, a H.Q. runner, was awarded the MILITARY MEDAL for devotion to duty and gallantry during the operations of 8th-14th inst.	
			73rd Infantry Brigade Summary of Operations October 5th-17th is attached (to original copy of War Diary only).	

6.11.18.

H.C. Coleman
Captain & Adjutant
for O.C. 9th Royal Sussex Regiment.

A5834 Wt. W4973/M687 750,000 8/16 D. D. & L. Ltd. Forms/C.2118/13.

G6

Headquarters 73rd. Inf. Bde.
Nos. B.M. 97.
27. 10. 18.

SUMMARY OF OPERATIONS.

Ref. Maps. OCTOBER 5th to OCTOBER 17th 1918.

57.C., 57.B.
51.A. 1/40,000

OCTOBER 5th. 1. The Transport of the 73rd Infantry Brigade Group, which included 129th Field Company R.E., 73rd Field Ambulance, 197th Company A.S.C., and "A" Company, 24th Battalion M.G. Corps, moved by march route to MOEUVRES, halting night 5th/6th October at BOISLEUX AU MONT.

OCTOBER 6th. 2. Personnel of 73rd Infantry Brigade Group proceeded by train to XVII Corps Area detraining at HERMIES and FREMICOURT. Units accommodated in bivouacs night 6th/7th October in Staging Area "D" (just East of MOEUVRES).

Divisional Commander held conference and outlined role of 24th Division in operations commencing on 8th instant.

24th Division was to be in support to 63rd Division and be ready to pass through and follow up the enemy if he withdrew.

OCTOBER 7th. 3. Moved into bivouacs in Staging Area "C" (just S.W. of CANTAING) relieving 190th Infantry Brigade (63rd Division). Move completed by 8 p.m.

B.G.C., Battalion and Company Commanders reconnoitred area through which the brigade would probably be ordered to pass.

OCTOBER 8th. 4. 63rd Division attacked and captured NIERGNIES and by 8 a.m. 72nd Infantry Brigade was concentrated just N.W. of RUMILLY.

Later in day 72nd Infantry Brigade ordered to relieve 63rd Division.

At 2 p.m. 73rd Infantry Brigade and "A" Company 24th Bn. M.G. Corps moved forward and concentrated East of CANAL DE ST QUENTIN in G.7. and G.8. Concentration completed by 8 p.m. without incident.

5. Orders received from Division that 72nd Infantry Brigade was to attack at 05.20 hours 9th instant and capture AWOINGT and line of railway just East of it, forming a defensive flank facing CAMBRAI. 73rd Infantry Brigade to keep in close touch with 72nd Infantry Bde. and be prepared to go through 72nd Inf. Bde. and capture CAUROIR. Latter operation not to take place until ordered by 24th Division. 72nd and 73rd Infantry Brigade Headquarters both established in QUARRY at MT. SUR L'OEUVRE.

OCTOBER 9th. 6. At 0520 hours 72nd Infantry Brigade attacked supported by a heavy artillery barrage, and meeting with no opposition pushed forward to their final objectives on the Railway East of AWOINGT.

73rd Infantry Brigade started moving forward at 06.00 hours in close support to 72nd Inf. Brigade with 9th Bn. Royal Sussex Regiment leading, 7th Bn. Northamptonshire Regiment in support and 13th Bn. Middlesex Regiment in reserve.

Two Stokes Guns....

Two Stokes Guns moved forward with 9th BnlRoyal Sussex Regiment and two with 7th Bn. Northamptonshire Regiment, Battery H.Q. remaining with Brigade H.Q. 'Fighting' portions of 1st Line 'Transport accompanied their own units.

Two Sections "A" Company 24th Bn. M.G.Corps moved forward in rear of 9th Bn. Royal Sussex Regiment ready to assist 9th Bn. Royal Sussex Regiment and 7th Bn. Northamptonshire Regiment when required. Remainder of Company moved with Brigade Headquarters.

Two companies XVII Corps Cyclists under command of B.G.C. 73rd Infantry Brigade at RUMILLY were placed at 15 minutes notice from ZERO hour onwards.

Brigade Headquarters moved at 6.45 a.m. to about 1 mile S.W. of NIERGNIES.

On finding 72nd Infantry Brigade were meeting with no opposition, B.G.C. rode forward to ascertain plans of B.G.C. 72nd Inf. Bde. On learning that B.G.C. 72nd Inf. Bde. did not consider it advisable to push on himself owing to the extent of front his Battalions were on and disorganisation owing to the attack, B.G.C. decided to push through without awaiting orders. Division notified to this affect at 0930 hours. Verbal instructions were issued to battalion commanders as follows -

Leading Battalion to line of Railway.
Support Battalion to just N.W. of AWOINGT.
Reserve Battalion to follow Support Battn.
The Cyclist Battn.was directed on CAUROIR.

Brigade H.Q. moved to SHRINE just S.E. of NIERGNIES, and after short halt,to Railway Bridge just N.E. of AWOINGT.

7. At 12.00 hours orders received from Division that 73rd Infantry Brigade with Corps Cyclist Bn., 1 troop of 6th Dragoon Guards, 2 companies Machine Guns, 2 Sections 104th Field Coy.R.E. and 56th and 181st Bdes. R.F.A. under Brigadier General COLLINS to form advance guard and push forward at once to the general line CAUROIR - CAGNONCLES. 6th Dragoon Guards, less 1 troop, to act as Corps Cavalry on instructions issued direct.

8. On receipt of these orders 9th Bn.Royal Sussex Regiment, who were in position just East of NIERGNIES at 09.45 hours, ordered to move forward and occupy CAUROIR which at 10.30 hours was reported by Cavalry as being free of enemy.

7th Bn. Northamptonshire Regiment ordered to follow at distance of 1500 yards and 13th Bn.Middlesex Regiment 2000 yards behind them. Leading troops 9th Bn. Royal Sussex Regiment crossed CAMBRAI - CAUDRY Road at 11.00 hours and at 12.10 hours patrols approaching S.W. outskirts of CAUROIR met with slight M.G. opposition from the Sunken Road just South of CAUROIR. In touch with Guards Division on right but not with Canadians on left, who at 12.15 hours were reported to have established a line of posts along the Eastern outskirts of CAMBRAI.

At 13.00 hours 7th Bn. Northamptonshire Regt. were concentrated at B.19.d. just N.W. of AWOINGT, and 13th Bn.Middlesex Regiment about 500 yards due West of AWOINGT.

9. At 13.45 hours.

9. At 13.45 hours orders were issued by B.G.C. 73rd Infantry Brigade for following attack to be carried out at 16.15 hours.

In conjunction with Guards Division who were attacking CARNIERES, 9th Royal Sussex Regiment to pivot on their Southern flank, move through CAUROIR and attack enemy positions on the spur in 17.a. (500 yards East of the village).

7th Bn. Northamptonshire Regiment to attack CAGNONCLES from the South West, at the same time moving along the spur in B.9., 1 troop 6th Dragoon Guards being ordered to protect their left flank.

XVII Corps Cyclists were to take up positions on the high ground East of CAMBRAI Station to protect rear and Northern flank of the 7th Bn.Northamptonshire Regiment, watching the East exits of CAMBRAI which had not been reported clear of enemy. On gaining touch with Canadians East of CAMBRAI they were to move along the NAVES Road and cover the left flank of the Brigade.

Attack was postponed until 16.30 hours to enable 7th Bn. Northamptonshire Regiment to get into their assembly positions.

10. At 18.00 hours after overcoming considerable M.G. opposition which was met with from the N.E., 7th Bn. Northamptonshire Regiment has captured the high ground west of CAGNONCLES overlooking the village, but patrols which had pushed, after dusk, down into the village were forced to withdraw owing to strong opposition.

9th Bn.Royal Sussex Regiment had reached the Cemetery East of CAUROIR and were in touch with Guards Division on their right. Enemy Artillery retaliated heavily on CAUROIR and Western outskirts of CAGNONCLES. 7th Bn. Northamptonshire Regt., casualties during this operation amounted to 3 Officers and about 80 Other Ranks.

9th Royal Sussex Regiment casualties were very slight.

Owing to shelling Brigade Headquarters moved at 16.30 hours to North edge of AWOINGT, remaining there for the night.

Orders received at 23.50 hours from Division that advance was to be resumed by 73rd Infantry Brigade at 05.00 hours 10th October, 6th Dragoon Guards to act independently.

Arrangements made with O.C. 6th Dragoon Guards for Cavalry to move along high ground on right of the Corps front. O.C. Cyclist Battalion ordered to move on RIEUX and ascertain if held or not and to keep touch with Canadians on CAMBRAI - SAULZOIR Road.

<u>OCTOBER 10th.</u> 11. At 05.00 hours advance was resumed with 9th Bn. Royal Sussex Regiment on right, 7th Bn.Northamptonshire Regiment on left, 13th Bn.Middlesex Regiment in reserve.

At 06.40 hours reports were received from leading Battalions that no opposition was being met with and troops of 7th Bn.Northamptonshire Regiment were 200 yards East of CAGNONCLES.

At 09.00 hours.

At 09.00 hours Cavalry and Cyclist patrols entered RIEUX and AVESNES LEZ AUBERT. RIEUX was found evacuated but some M.G. opposition met with in Western outskirts of AVESNES LEZ AUBERT. 09.30 hours Cavalry patrols reported high ground North of AVESNES LES AUBERT in U.15. and 16. strongly held by enemy.

Brigade H.Q. moved at short intervals by bounds along the CAUROIR - ST VAAST Road reaching Tr.de RIEUX about 1030 hours.

12. At 09.35 hours 13th Bn. Middlesex Regiment were ordered to pass through the two leading battalions which were now 2000 yards East of CAGNONCLES, and march on AVESNES LEZ AUBERT and RIEUX.

At 11.15 hours 13th Bn. Middlesex Regiment had reached line of Railway South of RIEUX and high ground 1000 yards S.W. of AVESNES LEZ AUBERT.

At 13.50 hours infantry patrols were East of RIEUX and AVESNES LEZ AUBERT and in touch with Canadians on North. Our infantry came under heavy artillery fire on southern outskirts of RIEUX and Western outskirts of AVESNES LEZ AUBERT, in addition to considerable M.G. fire from the high ground to the N.E. and N.

13. On receipt of verbal instructions from G.O.C. Division that the advance was to be pressed on, B.G.C. went forward to see O.C.13th Bn.Middlesex Regt.

At 16.45 hours, in accordance with verbal orders issued to O.C., 13th Bn. Middlesex Regiment moved forward to attack the high ground in U.15 and 16. 1 Company 9th Bn.Royal Sussex Regiment, at request of O.C. 13th Bn.Middlesex Regiment, being placed at his disposal, moved up to support the left flank of the attack.

In conjunction with this attack 1 Company 9th Bn.Royal Sussex Regiment was pushed forward to occupy AVESNES LEZ AUBERT Station and maintain touch with Guards Division on the Southern flank.

14. This attack met with very heavy machine gun fire and considerable shell fire on left flank, and gas shelling of the valley between RIEUX and AVESNES LEZ AUBERT.

At 18.00 hours our troops had reached the high ground in U.15 and 16, but had not gained touch with the Canadians.

By 20.15 hours troops of 9th Bn.Royal Sussex Regiment were reported to have reached the Western outskirts of ST AUBERT, and Cyclist patrols were in touch with Guards Division West of ST HILAIRE.

Orders were issued to 13th Bn.Middlesex Regt. to hold on to high ground during the night and that 17th Infantry Brigade would pass through them at dawn, and resume the advance.

OCTOBER 11th. 15. At 03.00 hours orders were issued from H.Q. 73rd I.B. that all Units would remain in their

present.....

present positions until 17th Infantry Brigade had reached the line VILLERS EN CAUCHIES - ST AUBERT, when they would be ordered to withdraw to billets in RIEUX and AVESNES LEZ AUBERT.

During the early morning news was received that Lt.Col. A.N. HINGLEY, M.C. Commanding 13th Bn. Middlesex Regiment, was severely wounded by a M.G. bullet. Major R.S.DOVE, M.C. was ordered forward to assume command.

The attack of the 17th Infantry Brigade carried out at 05.45 hours met with heavy resistance from enemy M.Gs. from high ground in U.16.a., U.22.a. and b. and no further advance was made.

The enemy artillery barrage on the slopes and villages of RIEUX and AVESNES LEZ AUBERT was heavy.

16. Instructions were received for the Brigade to be withdrawn to Brigade in Reserve; accordingly during the afternoon verbal orders were issued to 13th Bn.Middlesex Regiment and 9th Bn.Royal Sussex Regiment to withdraw all forward troops by driblets and to concentrate entire battalions in RIEUX and AVESNES LEZ AUBERT respectively.

7th Bn.Northamptonshire Regiment and 73rd Lt. T.M.Battery were also ordered to move to billets in RIEUX. Brigade H.Q. moved to RIEUX at 15.00 hours.

The total casualties of units up to 20.00 hours 11th instant were as follows :-

9th Royal Sussex Regt.	- 2 Offrs.	38	O.Rs
7th Northamptonshire Regt.	- 6 "	85	"
13th Middlesex Regiment.	- 6 "	141	"
73rd Light T.M.Battery.	- - -	1	"

OCTOBER 12th. 17. During the course of the night 11th/12th the enemy effected his withdrawal to the line of the SELLE RIVER closely followed by 17th Infantry Bde. who succeeded in securing and constructing crossings over the SELLE RIVER.

The day was spent in sleep, re-organisation and cleaning up, and at 17.00 hours a conference of all Commanding Officers was held by B.G.C. at Brigade Headquarters.

Instructions received from 24th Division that advance to capture high ground East of RIVER SELLE was to be continued by 72nd Inf. Brigade at 02.00 hours on the 13th instant, and that the 73rd Infantry Brigade coming into support were to maintain close touch.

OCTOBER 13th. 18. Instructions received from 24th Division that after 72nd Infantry Brigade had secured bridgeheads on SELLE RIVER that 73rd Inf. Brigade would probably be ordered to pass through and capture the high ground on the general line MAISON BLANCHE - P.35.central - P.29.

B.G.C. requested to submit a plan of attack, and carried out a personal reconnaissance of the

area accordingly.

area accordingly.

13th Bn.Middlesex Regiment ordered to move to AVESNES LEZ AUBERT.

OCTOBER 14th. 19. 7th Bn.Northamptonshire Regiment, 73rd Light T.M.Battery and H.Qrs. 73rd Inf. Brigade moved to AVESNES LEZ AUBERT, the entire Brigade now being concentrated in this area as Brigade in Support.

B.G.C. held conference of Commanding Officers and as many Officers as possible ordered to reconnoitre forward area with reference to their respective roles for the attack as indicated by the B.G.C.

Orders received from 24th Division that tactical situation permitting, the 19th Division would relieve the 24th Division, the 73rd Infantry Bde. moving to CAUROIR on the 17th instant.

OCTOBER 15th. 20. B.G.C. inspected Battalions at training - practice attacks over ground attacked on the 11th instant being carried out.

OCTOBER 16th. 21. 72nd Infantry Brigade attacked high ground East of LA SELLE RIVER with the object of establishing bridgeheads for future operations. All objectives were gained and 400 prisoners captured.

At 09.00 hours 7th Bn.Northamptonshire Regt. were moved up into close support and placed under orders of B.G.C. 72nd Infantry Brigade, being disposed as follows :-

"H.Qrs. and 2 Companies. - ST AUBERT.
"2 Companies. - High ground West of LA SELLE RIVER.

22. At 13.00 hours Right Battalion, 72nd Infantry Brigade were heavily counter attacked and forced back to West bank of the River at HAUSSY, the line of the left ~~division~~ battalion being withdrawn slightly with posts East of the River and crossings intact.

At 16.00 hours 7th Bn.Northamptonshire Regt. were ordered to relieve remaining elements of 9th Bn.East Surrey Regiment and 8th Bn.R.W.Kent Regt. with 2 companies. This was successfully carried out.

At 01.00 hours (17th inst) information received that two forward companies of 7th Bn.Northamptonshire Regiment were forced to withdraw to West bank of RIVER SELLE, the enemy having penetrated the right flank under cover of darkness and threatened the remaining river crossings.

OCTOBER 17th. 23. 73rd Infantry Brigade (less 7th Northamptonshire Regiment) moved to CAUROIR.

7th Bn.Northamptonshire Regiment were relieved by a Battalion of the 56th Infantry Brigade and accommodated in AVESNES LEZ AUBERT for the night 17th/18th, coming under orders of 73rd Inf.Bde.

OCTOBER 18th.

__OCTOBER 18th.__ 24. 7th B .Northamptonshire Regiment moved to CAUROIR, the entire Brigade being concentrated in this area.
B.G.C. inspected 13th Bn.Middlesex Regiment at training.

T.T. Chevallier Captain
for Brigadier General,
Commanding 73rd Infantry Brigade.

Instructions regarding War Diaries and Intelligence Summaries are contained in F. S. Regs., Part II. and the Staff Manual respectively. Title pages will be prepared in manuscript.

WAR DIARY

~~or~~

~~**INTELLIGENCE SUMMARY.**~~

(Erase heading not required.)

Army Form C. 2118.

VR 39

Place	Date	Hour	Summary of Events and Information	Remarks and references to Appendices
Confidential				
			9th Bn The Royal Sussex Regiment	
			for the month of	
			November 1918.	E.W.
				40-I 6 sheets

A6945 Wt. W11422/M1160 350,000 12/16 D. D. & L. Forms/C./2118/14.

9th Battalion ROYAL SUSSEX. Regiment. G14/57

— WAR DIARY —

NOVEMBER 1918.

FIELD Nov. 1. 1918. Orders received for the 73rd Infantry Brigade to relieve the 184th Infantry Brigade (61st. Div) The Battalion was to move off from HAUSSY at 14.00 hours to BERMERAIN. A Conference was held at Battalion H.Q. Open Warfare training carried out during the morning. M.

Nov. 2. The Battalion left HAUSSY at 14.00 hours for BERMERAIN via MAISON BLANCHE, MAISON BLEUE, St. MARTIN arriving about 16.30 hours. The Transport followed in rear of the Battalion. Battle Surplus personnel proceeded from HAUSSY at 09.45 hours under 2/Lieut. L.R. BAXTER to Divnl. Reception Camp. Lieut. C.H. DUDENEY proceeded at 10.00 hours to vicinity of SEPMERIES to select a site S. of the Railway for Trench shelters. The 13th MIDDLESEX Regt. relieved front line troops of the 184th. Inf. Bde. M.

Nov. 3. The Battalion left BERMERAIN at 05.00 hours and marched by Companies to SEPMERIES, becoming Support Battalion. Information was received that there were indications of an enemy withdrawal in the early morning and the leading Battalion had pushed forward patrols. The Battalion remained at SEPMERIES until 16.00 hours when orders were received for the Battalion to move forward. 'C' & 'D' Coys. to MARESCHES and 'A' & 'B' Coys. to Sunken road about 400 yds. E. of MARESCHES. The Battalion was to be prepared to continue the advance going through the following morning. M.

Nov. 4. Orders issued to Companies for attack through the 13th MIDDLESEX Regt. to take High Ground N. of WARGNIES le PETIT and WARGNIES le GRAND and to make good, if possible, the crossings over the RHONELLE River. ZERO Hour 05.30 hours. The advance was to be made through a creeping Barrage. The Battalion was disposed as follows :-

'C' Coy. on left. 'A' Coy. in centre. 'B' Coy. on ~~left.~~ right.

'D' Coy. in Support.

The march to the Assembly Positions was made through a good deal of enemy shelling particularly in the vicinity of VILLERS POL. Enemy Machine guns were very active whilst Companies were actually getting into their positions. A number of casualties were sustained before ZERO by these M.Gs. During the advance enemy artillery was not directed very much against front troops but M.Gs. were very numerous and caused a number of casualties particularly on High ground N.W. of Brick-field. The advance was successful but 'A' & 'B' Coys. were held up on the right by M.Gs. on both sides of the River until 11.00 hours when the enemy was forced to retire and these Coys. consolidated on the High ground W. of WARGNIES le PETIT. The 13th MIDDLESEX pushed forward on the left through WARGNIES le GRAND and the 5th NORTHAMPTONSHIRE Regt. advanced to the East edge of Wargnies le PETIT outskirting the Village on the M.

Northern

FIELD Nov. 4 (contd). Northern side during the afternoon. 'D' Company pushed forward patrols under Lieut. F. M. HILL and 2/Lieut. W. ALDRIDGE through WARGNIES le PETIT at 16.00 hours and finding no opposition established touch with the 7th. Northamptonshire Regt. E. of the Village at 17.30 hours. The Casualties sustained during these operations were estimated at

Lieut. H. G. WELHAM 'C' Killed in Action & 35 Killed, 95 Wounded, 6 Missing } O.R's

Nov. 5. The 17th. Inf. Bde. passed through the 73rd. Inf. Bde. at 07.30 hours and continued the advance on the Divisional Front. The 73rd. Inf. Bde became support Brigade and was billeted in WARGNIES le PETIT. 'C' Echelon Transport arrived from Maresches about 14.00 hours and joined the Battalion at WARGNIES le PETIT. The enemy shelled WARGNIES le PETIT at intervals during the day. M.

Nov. 6. The 73rd. Inf. Bde. became Brigade in reserve and Battalion remained at WARGNIES le PETIT. Day was spent in cleaning up etc. The enemy continued shelling of the Village and caused casualties to 'D' Coy. (1 Killed 3 Wounded) M.

Nov. 7. The 72nd. Inf. Bde. reported to have reached Eastern outskirts of BAVAI and the 73rd Inf. Bde were ordered to move to the St. VAAST Area. The Battalion moved off at 14.45 hours and owing to the continued advance of the 72nd. Bde. was ordered to continue its march to BAVAI where it arrived about 19.00 hours and was billeted for the night. Some shelling was experienced during the march but no casualties were sustained. Owing to several bridges having been blown up the transport could not proceed further than ST. VAAST where it remained until 03.00 hours (8th) when it was able to proceed to BAVAI by cross country route. The news was received that German Parliamentaires bearing the Flag of Truce might be expected to pass through the British lines. This was afterwards amended to read French lines. M.

Nov. 8. The 73rd. Inf. Bde. was now in support and the Battalion at BAVAI. Orders received that owing to the rapid advance of the Franco-American troops on the SEDAN-MEZIERES Railway the 3rd. Army was to continue the advance with the utmost vigour in order to cut the last remaining line of the enemy. Bde. H.Q. and the 7th Northamptonshire Regt. moved to LONGUEVILLE. Orders were received that the 73rd. Infantry Bde. would pass through the 72nd Inf. Bde and continue the advance on the morning of the 9th. This order was afterwards cancelled. M.

Nov. 9. The 24th Division took over the whole of the Corps front the 73rd Infantry Brigade being in the front line. The Battalion moved from BAVAI at 06.00 hours and passed through the 72nd. Brigade and the 19th Division at 09.00 hours. The Brigade then advanced as follows:- 7th Battalion NORTHAMPTONSHIRE Regt. on the right, 13th MIDDLESEX Regiment in the centre and the Battalion M.

FIELD. Nov. 9. (contd) the Battalion on the left. The Battalion objective was the MONS-MAUBEUGE Road and this was reached without opposition at 12.00 hours and patrols were then sent into BETTIGNIES.
Definite orders were given by Brigade that the Battalion was not to advance East ~~than~~ of the MONS-MAUBEUGE Road. Later instructions were issued that a Company was to occupy BERSILLIES
This was done and the Battalion was disposed as follows:-

'B' Company in BERSILLIES } Front Line
'D' Company in BETTIGNIES }
'A' Company at MONBERSON'S FARM }
'C' Company and Battalion H.Q. at St. PIERRE FONTAINE FARM } Support.

'B' Coy were shelled rather heavily in BERSILLIES, 1 O.R. being killed.

Nov. 10. The 73rd. Infantry Brigade was relieved by the 60th Infantry Brigade, the relief being complete by 13.30 hours. and Battalion marched by Companies to LES VENTS where the Battn. was billeted for the night. Casualties from midnight 2 November to date were determined as follows :-

Officers Lieut. H.G. WELHAM MC. Killed in Action 4.11.18.

Other Ranks Killed in Action 47. Wounded in Action 95. Missing 8.

Orders were received for an early morning move to LOUVIGNIES-BAVAI.

Nov. 11. Battalion left LES VENTS at 06.00 hours and marched to LOUVIGNIES-BAVAI arriving there at 09.30 hours. Orders were received at 10.00 hours that hostilities would cease at 11.00 hours owing to the acceptance by GERMANY of the terms of the armistice.

Nov. 12.-16th. Battalion at LOUVIGNIES-BAVAI. Day spent in cleaning up and re-organisation.
During this period general training was carried out by the Battalion. On the 13th. the Battalion found a Guard for Brigade H.Q. The Commanding Officer inspected Companies. 'A' & 'D' Companies on the 14th. and 'B' & 'C' Companies on the 15th. N.COs classes under the Regimental Sergeant Major were held on the 15th and 16th. On the 16th. The Brigadier General Commanding inspected the Battalion at 09.30 hours. and general training was carried out during the day. It was indicated that the Battalion would shortly move to the DENAIN Area. A Billeting Party under Lieut. P.W. CHAPMAN was sent to WARGNIES le GRAND on the afternoon of the 16th.

Nov. 17. The Battalion marched to WARGNIES le GRAND leaving LOUVIGNIES at 09.30 hours and arrived about 13.00 hours. This move was preliminary to the transfer of the 24th Division to the First Army. Orders were issued for the Battalion to continue the march to DENAIN Area on the morning of the 18th.

The Battalion

9th Battalion ROYAL SUSSEX Regiment.

FIELD Nov. 18. The Battalion left WARGNIES le GRAND at 08.30 hours and proceeded via VILLERS POLMARESCHES ARTRES, MAING, and THIANT to PROUVY where the Battalion was billeted for the night. Orders were issued for the march to be continued on the morning of the 19th. M.

Nov. 19. The Battalion left PROUVY about 11.30 hours and proceeded via DENAIN & ABSCON to AUBERCHICOURT. Captain A.V. RENNELL MC. rejoined Battalion from England and was appointed Battalion Sports Officer. M.

Nov. 20-24. During this period the Battalion remained at AUBERCHICOURT and general training was carried out as far as possible. Conferences were held at Headquarters to discuss training, education and recreation. On the 21st. a Thanksgiving Service was held in the Theatre, AUBERCHICOURT and attended by 300 men per Battalion. Several concerts were given during the stay of the Battalion in this area notably by the Brigade and Divisional Concert Parties. On the morning of the 23rd. orders were received that the 73rd. Infantry Brigade would move to RUMEGIES on the 25th. and from thence to MOUCHIN on the 26th. On the 24th Lieut. Col. M.V.B. HILL DSO.MC. took command of the Brigade during the absence of the B.G.C. on leave, Major T. FOSTER assuming command of the Battalion. Orders issued for the move to RUMEGIES on the morning of the 25th. M.

Nov. 25. The Battalion left AUBERCHICOURT at 08.10 hours and proceeded to RUMEGIES via SOMAIN-MARCHIENNES-BRILLON-ROSULT. A halt was made at 12.30 hours for dinners and the march resumed at 14.00 hours. The Battalion arrived at RUMEGIES about 15.30 hours. No men fell out during the march. Orders issued for the march to be continued to MOUCHIN Area on the 26th. M.

Nov. 26. Battalion left RUMEGIES at 10.30 hours and arrived at MOUCHIN at 12.30 hours. A conference was held at H.Q. Mess to discuss Training, Education and Recreation. The Battalion was billeted at BERCU. M.

Nov. 26-30. The remainder of the month was spent in the usual training and recreational hours were allotted in the afternoons. Several conferences were held to consider the important questions of education and the Rev. T.F. BAKER C.F. was appointed Battalion Education Officer and steps taken to start classes in the various subjects as soon as possible. Recreational training also claimed a considerable amount of attention. M.

H. Hopp Lt. for
Captain & Adjutant
December 4th 1918. for O.C. 9th Royal Sussex Regiment.

9th Royal Sussex Regiment

APPENDIX to WAR DIARY NOVEMBER 1918-

the following awards were made to N.C.Os and men of this Battalion for gallantry during the operations commencing November 4th. 1918.

MILITARY MEDAL

886. Sgt. M. Luff	'C' Coy.
5943. Sgt. A. Whitlock	'D' Coy.
1432. Cpl. R.H. Peirce	'A' Coy.
19276. Cpl. G.F. Davis	'C' Coy
475. Cpl. C.F. Bridger	'C' Coy.
19273. L/C. W. Durling	'B' Coy.
11824. L/C. G.L. Mann	'C' Coy.
3523. Sig. AA. Collier	'A' Coy.
19188. Pte. R. Martin	'A' Coy.
16427. Pte. A.F. Greene	'A' Coy.
19341. Pte. H. Throckston	'B' Coy.
4153. Sig. B. Hearn	'D' Coy.
290480. Pte. F.A. Joyce	'B' Coy.

Instructions regarding War Diaries and Intelligence Summaries are contained in F. S. Regs., Part II, and the Staff Manual respectively. Title pages will be prepared in manuscript.

9th Battalion

WAR DIARY
or
INTELLIGENCE SUMMARY.
(Erase heading not required.)

ROYAL SUSSEX Regiment.

Army Form C. 2118.

968 40

Place	Date	Hour	Summary of Events and Information	Remarks and references to Appendices
Field.	Dec. 1st.		Battaliom at MOUCHIN in Billets awaiting orders tomove to final area . A Voluntary Church Service was held at H.Q. at 11.00 hours. 2/Lieut. F.N. WALKER joined Battalion and was posted to 'C' Company.	H.C.C.
	2nd – 17th		During this period 2 hours training under Company Commanders was carried out in the morning and recreational training and football League matches held in the afternoon. On the 2nd. the terms of re-engagement in the new Regular Army were explained to men by their Company Commanders. A Battalion Parade was ordered for the morning of the 3rd. but was cancelled owing to the inclement weather. Lectures and organisation of Educational Classes being proceeded with instead. 2/Lieut. H. B. DRURY was struck off the strength on Medical Board being ordered by the War Office. A Draft of 45.O.Rs. joined the Battalion from ENGLAND on the 3rd. Most of them had not been out to FRANCE before. On the 4th. a Lecture was given by the Divisional Educational Officer to all Officers at 73rd. L.T.M. Battery H.Q. at 14.15. hours. The subject of the Lecture was the Educational Scheme being introducedinto Battalions and hints were given on the Method of Teaching. A Football Match on the 5th. between 'D' Coy. & the 73rd. L.T.M. Battery resulted in a draw 2 goals each. League matches on the 6th. by 'B' and 'A' Companies were both lost to 'B' Coy 7th. Northamptonshire Regt. and 73rd. Field Ambulance respectively, the scores being 6 - 3 and 3 - 0 in the respective matches. On the 7th. the Commanding Officer , Adjutant, 8 other Officers and 18 N.C.Os. and men per Company journeyed by lorry to line the road near TOURNAI on the occasion of the King's visit. It was arranged for the King to stop, but owing to a misunderstanding he did not do so His Majesty was heartily cheered and the men were able to see him and the Princes very well. A league match on the 7th. resulted in 'C' Company losing 5 - 0 against 'A' Coy. 13th. Middlesex Regiment. On Sunday Dec. 8th the usual Church Services were held and a Conference regarding Education took place in the H.Q. Mess in the evening. All Companies reported that they were ready to start classes in spite of the lack of Books and Stationery. On Monday the 9th. Education Classes started in earnest being held on most mornings from 10.30.- 12.15. hours. Voting Ballot papers commenced to arrive on this day. Lectures had been given on the arrangements for voting. Each man received a Ballot paper and also a Declaration of Identity These were completed and sent by post to the Returning Officer of the respective constituencies. The arrangements on the whole were good. It was unavoidable that men should know less than they wished of the Candidates in their constituencies, but Election Adresses reached most men and lists of Candidates were posted up by each Company. A League Match was won by 'D' Company against 'A' Coy 13th. Middlesex Regt. by 6goals to 1 goal. 2/Lieut. A.F. CHILDS was struck off the strength on the 11th. Medical Board being ordered by the War office. On this.	41. I 3 sheet

Instructions regarding War Diaries and Intelligence Summaries are contained in F. S. Regs., Part II. and the Staff Manual respectively. Title pages will be prepared in manuscript.

9th Battalion **WAR DIARY** *or* **INTELLIGENCE SUMMARY.** *(Erase heading not required.)* ROYAL SUSSEX Regiment. DECEMBER 1918. Army Form C. 2118.

Place	Date	Hour	Summary of Events and Information	Remarks and references to Appendices
Field	2nd-17th		this day a Race meeting took place at MOUCHIN under the auspices of the I CORPS but the weather was extremely unfavourable. Only a certain proportion of the Battalion took an interest in the races. There were 3 entries from the Battalion but they met with no success. The first man from the Battalion to be demobilised was sent to England on the 11th. to report to Dispersal Centre (SHORNCLIFFE). He was No.18843.Pte.H.G.Carswell and was sent home as a Coal Miner. On the 12th. about 20 N.C.Os and men of the Battalion visited LILLE and spent an interesting day. On the 13th. 3 Coalminers proceeded to report to Dispersal Centre (OSWESTRY) for demobilisation. Lieut.Colonel.M.V.B.HILL DSO. MC. rejoined fom Commanding 73rd. Infantry Brigade and assumed Command of the Battalion. Lieut. S .J.CHESTER joined Battalion and was posted to 'B' Company. The 73rd. Infantry Brigade defeated 'B' Company by 2 goals to NIL after a strenuous game. On the 14th. 'D' Company salvaged a large number of bricks from an old German Aerodrome. These were carried to TAINTEGNIES to be used in making ovens in our new Billets. On Sunday 15th. a Voluntary Service was held at H.Q. at 11.00 hours. Platoon football matches took place in the afternoon good games being played. I Coalminer proceeded to Dispersal Centre (SHORNCLIFFE) for demobilisation. A very exciting football match took place on the 16th. between 73rd. Inf. Bde and 'D' Company, resulting in a draw 1 goal all. On the 17th. another Coalminer proceeded to England for demobilisation.	H.C.C.
	18th		On this day the Battalion moved to the final rest Area at TAINTEGNIES, parading at 11.00. hours and proceeding by March Route arriving about 1.30.pm. Billets were very much better than those at MOUCHIN and with a certain amount of work it was hoped to make them very comfortable. 3.O.Rs. proceeded to report to Dispersal Centre (RIPON) for demobilisation as Coal Miners.	H.C.C.
	19th-31st.		This period was marked by a great increase in Educational Classes and Lectures were given on several days. On the 19th. Companies generally cleaned up Billets and arranged Recreation Rooms . 37 O.Rs. joined Battalion from the Base; they were mostly young soldiers detained at the Base on acount of their age. 'D' Company 7th. Northamptonshire Regt were beaten by 'B' Company, the score being 3 goals to 2 goals. On the 20th. 'C' Company defeated 'A' Coy. by 3 goals to NIL. On the 24th. Sgnr. Wickens 'A' Company. proceeded to Dispersal Centre (OSWESTRY) for demobilisation on account of Long Service with the B.E.F. ON the 25th. Christmas Day, Church Services were held in the morning. Company Dinners were held Battn. H.Q. dining with their respective Companies. The Commanding Officer visited Companies whilst dining. Every dinner was a great success. The chief items in the MENU were pork and Christmas Pudding. Concerts were held in the afternoon and in the evening Sergeant's Messes held	

(A9175) Wt W2358/P360 600,000 12/17 D. D. & L. Sch. 52a. Forms/C2118/15.

Instructions regarding War Diaries and Intelligence Summaries are contained in F. S. Regs., Part II, and the Staff Manual respectively. Title pages will be prepared in manuscript.

9th Battalion **WAR DIARY** *or* **INTELLIGENCE SUMMARY.** ROYAL SUSSEX Regiment. DECEMBER 1918.

(Erase heading not required.)

Army Form C. 2118.

Place	Date	Hour	Summary of Events and Information	Remarks and references to Appendices
Field.	1918 31st.		held their dinners. All Officers of the Battalion attended a dinner which was held at Brigade H.Q. on the evening of Christmas Day. The Brigade Orchestra played very well throughout the evening. A few speeches were made after dinner, which was followed by a Dance Lieut.Colonel M.V.B.Hill DSO.MC. proceeded on leave to U.K. 26th In the evening of the 26th. dinners were arranged for the Cooks and Officer's Servants who had not been able to join in the Xmas.Day dinners. On the 28th.2.O.R.proceeded to report to Dispersal Centre (SHORNCLIFFE) for demobilisation on account of Long Service with the B.E.F. The Commanding Officer's servant L/C.J.Keys had served continuously for 51 months with the B.E.F. and had been the C.Os.servant for that period.On the 29th 1.O.R.proceeded to Transfer Centre WATFORD to assist in the work of demobilisation . A Lecture was given by Major DELANY , the subject being Boxing. This lecture,which took place on the 31st. was very well attended and was very enthusiastically received. Arrangements were made at once for nightly instruction in Boxing.	H.C.C.
			HONOURS	
			Mentioned in Sir.Douglas Haig's Despatch of November 8th.1918.	
			Lieut.Colonel.M.V.B.HILL, DSO.MC. No.5730.Pte.A.BRAY 'A' Coy.	
			H.C. Coleman Captain & Adjutant for O.C.9th Royal Sussex Regiment.	

(A9175) Wt W2358/P360 600,000 12/17 D. D. & L. Sch. 52a. Forms/C2118/15.

Instructions regarding War Diaries and Intelligence Summaries are contained in F. S. Regs., Part II. and the Staff Manual respectively. Title pages will be prepared in manuscript.

11/3

24

WAR DIARY

~~or~~

~~INTELLIGENCE SUMMARY.~~

(*Erase heading not required.*)

RgP

Army Form C. 2118.

VS41

Place	Date	Hour	Summary of Events and Information	Remarks and references to Appendices
Confidential				
			9th Bn Royal Sussex Regiment	
			for the month of	
			January 1919	
				42.I 4 sheets

A6945 Wt. W11422/M1160 350,000 12/16 D. D. & L. Forms/C./2118/14.

Instructions regarding War Diaries and Intelligence Summaries are contained in F. S. Regs., Part II, and the Staff Manual respectively. Title pages will be prepared in manuscript.

9th Battalion

WAR DIARY
or
INTELLIGENCE SUMMARY.
(Erase heading not required.)

ROYAL SUSSEX Regiment.

Army Form C. 2118.

JANUARY, 1919.

Place	Date	Hour	Summary of Events and Information	Remarks and references to Appendices
Field	Jan 1/31st		The Battalion spent the whole of the month at TAINTEGNIES, Belgium, during which period no outstanding events occurred.	
			Training and Educational Classes were carried out on most mornings, the afternoons being devoted to Football and other Recreation. Several concerts were given during the month by the Brigade Concert Party, one at RUMES on the 4th. being attended by 12 Officers and 150 Other Ranks. The Brigade Party also gave 4 performances of 'ALADDIN' at TAINTIGNIES and these were particularly/well attended by the Battalion and other troops in the neighbourhood.	
			Within the Battalion many pleasant evenings were arranged generally taking the form of card tournaments in whist, bezique, cribbage and other games. A dance ~~xxxxx~~ usually terminated the proceedings.	
			Demobiliation, which was proceeding rather slowly at the commencement of the month, speeded up considerably towards the finish attaining an average rate of 10 to 12 per diem.	
			A table is attached shewing the number demobilised during the month, giving dispersal stations and reasons for the release of the men.	
			On Wednesday January 8th an Agriculteral Discussion on 'Small Holdings' was held in the Schoolroom. Major T.FOSTER and Captain PASSMORE.MC made the opening speeches after which discussion was invited from those present.	
			ON January 9th.Captain G.M.SHACKEL.MC.proceeded to U.K.to attend Course at S.O.School ALDERSHOT. and was struck off the strength.	
			On the 24th.Major BRISCOE R.A.M.C. gave a lecture to 'A' and 'C' Coys on medical subjects.	
			The following awards were notified during the month. :-	
			<u>MENTIONED in Sir Douglas Haig's despatch of November 8th.1918.</u>	
			Lieut.Col.M.V.B.HILL D.S.O. M.C. 5730.Pte.A.Bray.	
			<u>New Year's HONOURS</u>	
			Lieut.A.W.COLLINGBOURNE awarded the MILITARY CROSS 3590.Sergeant.A.J.Newnham awarded the DISTINGUISHED CONDUCT MEDAL.	

(A9175) Wt W2358/P363 600,000 12/17 D. D. & L. Sch. 52a. Forms/C2118/15.

Instructions regarding War Diaries and Intelligence Summaries are contained in F. S. Regs., Part II. and the Staff Manual respectively. Title pages will be prepared in manuscript.

9th Battalion ROYAL SUSSEX Regiment. Army Form C. 2118.

WAR DIARY or INTELLIGENCE SUMMARY.

JANUARY 1919.

(Erase heading not required.)

Place	Date	Hour	Summary of Events and Information	Remarks and references to Appendices
Field	Jan 1/31st.		Awarded the MILITARY CROSS — Awarded the D.C.M.	
			Captain F.J.BURROWS. 'C' Coy. — 899.Sgt.W.Pelling "B" Coy.	
			Lieut.H.R.BATE 'A'Coy.	
			~~2/Lieut.S.J.A.BRIDGER 'C' Coy.~~	
			Awarded the MERITORIOUS SERVICE MEDAL.	
			3289.Sgt.A.C.R.Hayes. Battalion H.Q.	
			The following Officers were demobilsed during the month.	
			Lieut.H.R.BATE M.C. Group 43.	
			Lieut.G.KINNEIR Group 43.	
			2/Lieut.F.DAVISON. Group 1.	
			4.2.19.	
			[illegible] Lieut. & A/Adjutant for O.C.9th Royal Sussex Regiment.	

Ripon	Shorncliffe	Prees Heath	Harrowby	Thetford	Purfleet	Fovant	George-town	Clipstone	Chiseldon	Wimbledon	TOTAL	
	15	1	1			4		2		2	25	Long Service
2	1	8		1	1	2					15	Releasable Groups
	19		1	2	3	1	1	1	1		29	Group 1
		1									1	Group 3
	6	1	1		5					2	15	Pivotal
										2	2	Serving Soldiers
	13				1						14	Re-enlisted Soldiers
									1		1	Over 41
		3						1			4	Guarantee Letters
2	54	14	3	3	10	7	1	4	2	6	106.	

Instructions regarding War Diaries and Intelligence Summaries are contained in F. S. Regs., Part II. and the Staff Manual respectively. Title pages will be prepared in manuscript.

WAR DIARY
or
INTELLIGENCE SUMMARY.
(Erase heading not required.)

Army Form C. 2118.

Vol 42

Place	Date	Hour	Summary of Events and Information	Remarks and references to Appendices
			War Diary	
			9th Bn Royal Sussex Regt	

43. I

A6945 Wt. W11422/M1160 350,000 12/16 D. D. & L. Forms/C/2118/14.

9th Battalion ROYAL SUSSEX REGIMENT.

WAR DIARY
or
INTELLIGENCE SUMMARY.
(Erase heading not required.)

Instructions regarding War Diaries and Intelligence Summaries are contained in F. S. Regs., Part II. and the Staff Manual respectively. Title pages will be prepared in manuscript.

Place	Date	Hour	Summary of Events and Information
TAINTEGNIES.	1st/28th Feb. 1919.		The Battalion has been in billets at TAINTEGNIES (BELGIUM) during the whole of the month. A certain amount of Training and Education has been carried out but work has been considerably impeded by demobilization and preparing drafts for the Army of Occupation. On the 6th. we were ordered to prepare a draft of 10 Officers and 200 Other Ranks for the Rhine, Volunteers to be taken first and the remainder to be made up with men retainable under Army Order XIV. The following Officers volunteered, together with 151. Other Ranks. Capt. A.V. Rewell.MC. Lieut.R.T.Bryan. Lt.S.J.Chester. Lt.R.Hudson.MC. 2/Lt.W.G.Booker. 2/Lt.M.Taylor. Lieut.R.S.Hoath. 2/Lt.S.F.Gibbs. 2/Lieut.W.Aldridge. 2/Lieut.F.N.Walker. CSM.J.McClymont and CQMS.W.Collier were amongst the Volunteers. On the 21st. the draft was reduced to 2 Officers and 150 Other Ranks. No further orders have been received and the draft is still standing by. During the month 3 Officers and 217 Other Ranks have been demobilized. The three Officers are 2/Lieut.R.Lister. 4th. 2/Lieut.R.Aldington. 9th. A/Capt. C.H. Knight. 17th inst. ~~On the~~ On the 14th. orders were received that the King's Colours would be consecrated on the 19th and afterwards presented to all the Battalions in the Brigade by the Army Commander, General Sir H.S. Horne, KCB. KCMG. On the 15th and 17th. a Battalion Practice was carried out. On the 18th. the Brigade Practice was carried out on the Champs des Manoeuvres. On the 19th. the ceremony took place on the same ground as the Brigade Practice the previous day. The parade was in every way quite satisfactory and all ranks were congratulated on the general turn out of the Brigade. The address by General Sir. H.S. Horne. KCB.KCMG. and Brigadier General R.J. Collins. CMG. D.S.O. reply are given below. **<u>Address by General Sir. Henry H.S.Horne. KCB. KCMG.</u>** It is my proud duty today to present the King's Colour to each of the three Battalions in the 73rd Infantry Brigade. I present the Colour in the name of His Majesty the King and I charge you to guard it and honour it in accordance with the traditions of your Regiment and of the British Army. When the Battalions now standin on parade were formed they became part of a very distinguished Regiments and they inherited the great traditions of those Regiments. The ROYAL SUSSEX (35th and 107th Foot) The NORTHAMPTONSHIRE (48th and 58th Foot) The MIDDLESEX (57thDiehards and 77th Foot). Battalions that have served in all parts of the world, that have established splendid records and made their names famous in every corner of the globe, GIBRALTAR, CANADA;

(1)

9th Battalion ROYAL SUSSEX REGIMENT.

WAR DIARY
or
INTELLIGENCE SUMMARY.
(Erase heading not required.)

Instructions regarding War Diaries and Intelligence Summaries are contained in F. S. Regs., Part II, and the Staff Manual respectively. Title pages will be prepared in manuscript.

Place	Date	Hour	Summary of Events and Information
TAINTEGNIES.	1/28th. Feb. 1919.		EAST INDIES, INDIA, PENINSULA, CRIMEA, NEW ZEALAND, EGYPT, and SOUTH AFRICA. The past history of your Regiments have been written for you but it has been your duty since your formation 4½ years ago to write your own history. This you have done and have done it well. Formed in September. 1914, and came out to this country a year later in time to take part in the Battle of LOOS, and the heavy fighting at FOSSE 8. In 1916 you were in the Battle of the SOMME and fought well at GUILLEMONT and DELVILLE WOOD. In the British Offensive in the Spring of 1917, you played a most important part on the North of the VIMY RIDGE at ANGRES and LEIVIN. In June you fought at MESSINES and in the Autumn took part in the Third Battle of YPRES. In the Great Offensive launched by the Germans in the Spring of 1918 you played an important part in holding up the enemy and then in the Autumn in the final phase of the war followed him up beyond MAUBEUGE. A fine record and I know you are proud of it, and your esprit is high. The Colour presented to you today is the embodiment of the spirit of your Battalion - the emblem of your Loyalty and the symbol of your tradition. Men come and men go, faces change in the ranks but the colour remains. It is the spirit of a Battalion. That is what the Colour means. That is why men in days gone by rallied round the Colour. Conditions have changed and though now in war we are unable to carry the Colour still the sentiment remains unchanged and men fight to the last for the honour of the Battalion. I have no doubt that you will guard and fight for these Colours in war and that is the spirit you should carry into Peace. We have gained a great Victory over the Germans but Peace is not yet assured. Great difficulties lie before us. There is great unrest throughout Europe and that unrest has spread in a minor degree to England. Remember that the Army represents the pick of the nation. Remember that the Army will have great power at home and with that power we have our responsibility. Having fought and beaten the Germans in war we must stand solid and ensure the bringing about of a successful peace, such a peace as will enable us to improve the conditions both moral and social of life in our own country. To those of you who are going home, therefore I have this to say :- You will have much power and with that power remember there comes responsibility. The German has been beaten war but he still hopes to gain a victory in peace. Agents are at work at home striving to upset the conditions of life. Some of them are doing it unintentionally, others are in German pay. It is those we want to beat. If we approach our task in the spirit which we have shown out here we shall put things right in a very short time. Do your duty at home in peace as you have done it in war. Demobilization is going ahead fast. It is a sad

(A9175) Wt W2358/P360 600,000 12/17 D. D. & L. (Sch. 52a. Forms/C2118/15.

9th Battalion ROYAL SUSSEX REGIMENT.

WAR DIARY
or
INTELLIGENCE SUMMARY.

(Erase heading not required.)

Instructions regarding War Diaries and Intelligence Summaries are contained in F. S. Regs., Part II. and the Staff Manual respectively. Title pages will be prepared in manuscript.

Place	Date	Hour	Summary of Events and Information
TAINTEGNIES.	1st/28th Feb. 1919.		time when comrades have to part and I know well that that sentiment inspires a great many of you, but although this Brigade and these Battalions will be broken up I feel sure that the sentiment of comradeship will still remain. In bidding farewell to the 73rd Infantry Brigade I thank you from the bottom of my heart for the splendid work you have done throughout the war and especially during the period when you have served in the First Army. I thank you and I bid you all collectively and individually Godspeed.

<u>Address by Brigadier General R.J. Collins. CMG. D.S.O.</u>

I would like to thank you Sir, on behalf of the Brigade and on my own behalf for the honour you have done us in coming today to present these Colours. This will probably be the last parade on which the Brigade will appear as a whole, but I can assure you Sir, that all ranks will carry with them wherever they go the spirit of discipline and good comradeship which has been the keynote of the Brigade throughout its service in France, and if at any time the Brigade is again called into existence I am equally sure that it will under these Colours do its very best to maintain its present high position and that it will fight as gallantly in the future as it has in the past.

A good deal of inter-Company football has been played during the month. On the 26th. 'D' Coy. defeated 'A' Coy. by 5 goals to 1. and on the 27th. 'B' Coy. by 4 goals to 2. On the 28th. 'D' Coy. played 'The Rest' of the Battn. and after a very exciting game the 'Rest' proved Victors by 3 goals to 2.

The 'Stickits' (73rd Brigade Concert Party) gave several performances which were always well attended and thoroughly appreciated.

On the evening of the 28th. at the Officers Club. TOURNAI. a farewell dinner was given by Officers of the Brigade to Captain. P.T. Chevalier. D.S.O. M.C. Brigade Major. 73rd Infantry Brigade. Lieut.Col. M.V.B. HILL. D.S.O. M.C. Major. C.F. Goad. M.C. and Captain. H.C. Coleman. M.C. represented the Battalion.

-=-=-=-=-=-=-=-=-=-

Instructions regarding War Diaries and Intelligence Summaries are contained in F. S. Regs., Part II. and the Staff Manual respectively. Title pages will be prepared in manuscript.

9th. Battalion. **WAR DIARY** *or* **INTELLIGENCE SUMMARY.** *(Erase heading not required.)* ROYAL SUSSEX Regiment. MARCH 1919.

ORDERLY ROOM. 9th Bn. ROYAL SUSSEX REGT. No. C14/26. Date

Army Form C. 2118.

NL 43

Place	Date	Hour	Summary of Events and Information	Remarks and references to Appendices
TAINTIGNIES. Belgium.	1/31. March		The Battalion remained at TAINTIGNIES for the whole month. The gradual process of reduction to Cadre strength was carried on and the strength of the Battalion was reduced from 31 Officers 419 Other Ranks at the beginning of the month to 14 Officers 189 Other Ranks at the end. The Cadre was completed at the beginning of the month. The chief causes of decrease in strength were :- 1. Draft to the 4th. Battalion ROYAL SUSSEX Regiment of 2 Officers and 150 Other Ranks 2. Demobilisation during the month of 5 Officers and 74 Other Ranks. (This included 50 Other Ranks for Re-enlistment in the New Regular Army). On the 24th. 45 men were demobilised, this being the record number demobilised in one day. The reduction in strength of the Battalion was not confined to personnel. At the beginning of the month there were 46 animals with the Battalion transport. All these were sent away during the month, some to ENGLAND for sale, some for further service in the Army, and some for sale in TOURNAI to civilians. The Battalion Stores were checked in accordance with the Demobilisation Store Table and indents made out for all deficiencies. All vehicles that could be spared were loaded up and sent ot the Divisional Vehicle Park at BAISIEUX which is to be the Cadre Railhead. After this rations and supplies were delivered by lorry. The reduction in the strength of the Battalion made it no longer necessary for the Companies to be scattered through the long length of the village. Accordingly billets were closed up round Battalion H.Q. and 'A' & 'D' Coys. were amalgamated in one area and 'B' & 'C' Coys. in another. The organisation of the higher command was completely changed during this month and the Battalion came into a Brigade Group of Cadres under the command of Brig.Gen. R.W.Morgan DSO. Corps H.Q. was replaced by H.Q. DOUAI Cadres under the command of Brig.Gen.F.G.Maunsell. CB.CMG. RA. On the 12th a draft of 150 O.Rs. under Captain.A.V.Rewell.M.C. and Lieut.R.S.Hoath left to join.	

(1).

D. D. & L., London, E.C. (10340) Wt W5300/P713 750,000 3/18 E 2688 Forms/C2118/16.

App. I 4 sheets

Instructions regarding War Diaries and Intelligence Summaries are contained in F. S. Regs., Part II. and the Staff Manual respectively. Title pages will be prepared in manuscript.

9th Battalion **WAR DIARY** *or* **INTELLIGENCE SUMMARY.** ROYAL SUSSEX Regiment. MARCH 1919.

(*Erase heading not required.*)

Army Form C. 2118.

Place	Date	Hour	Summary of Events and Information	Remarks and references to Appendices
TAINTIGNIES Belgium.	March. 1/31		join the 4th. Battalion ROYAL SUSSEX Regiment on the RHINE. A Roll of the Draft is attached (to Records only). This draft had been standing by for some time and was originally intended to be 200 strong. In consequence of this reduction 'C' Company only contributed 6 men to make up the full number and the Other Companies sent all available men. The draft paraded at 10.am. and were inspected by the Commanding Officer who afterwards addressed them and recounted the outstanding performances to the credit of the Battalion which it behoved them to remember and of which they had every reason to be proud.	

After this official farewell they marched through the main street of the village and their many friends turned out to give them a good send off. At the top of the street they marched past and saluted the King's Colours. They left about 11.am. in lorries for RAISMES where they entrained. News came later that they had a good journey and were settling down happily with their new Battalion.

The following table shews the number of men of the Battalion who re-enlisted in the Post-Bellum Army :-

Company.	Four years	Three years.	Two years.	Total.
'A' Coy.	5.	8.	1.	14.
'B' Coy.	7.	5.	11.	23.
'C' Coy.	-	18.	-	18.
'D' Coy.	2.	17.	-	19.
TOTAL.	14.	48.	12.	74.

The following is a list of Officers who left the Battalion during the month :-

D. D. & L., London, E.C.
(10340) Wt W5300/P713 750,000 3/18 E 2688 Forms/C2118/16.

Instructions regarding War Diaries and Intelligence Summaries are contained in F. S. Regs., Part II. and the Staff Manual respectively. Title pages will be prepared in manuscript.

9th. Battalion ROYAL SUSSEX Regiment.

WAR DIARY
or
INTELLIGENCE SUMMARY.

(Erase heading not required.)

MARCH 1919.

Army Form C. 2118.

Place	Date	Hour	Summary of Events and Information	Remarks and references to Appendices
TAINTIGNIES. Belgium March 1/31.				

For Demobilisation.

T/Captain. D.W.G.May. M.C. To U.K. 16.3.19.
Captain. F.J.Burrows. M.C. To U.K. 16.3.19.
2/Lieut.H.C.Sargent. To U.K. 24.3.19.
2/Lieut.R.A.Dicker. To U.K. 24.3.19.
2/Lieut.F.C.Chew. To U.K. 24.3.19.

Posted to Army of Occupation.

Captain A.V.Rewell. M.C. To 4th. Bn.ROYAL SUSSEX Regiment. 12.3.19.
Lieut.R.S.Heath. do. do.
Lieut.S.J.Chester. do. do. 19.3.19.
Lieut.R.T.Bryan. do. do. 19.3.19.
2/Lieut.M.Taylor. do. do. 23.3.19.
2/Lieut.W.Aldridge. do. do. 23.3.19.
2/Lieut.W.G.Booker. do. do. 28.3.19.

Major.C.F.Goad. M.C. To 52nd. Bn.ROYAL SUSSEX Regiment. 28.3.19.
Lieut.P.W.Chapman. do. do. 28.3.19.
Lieut.R.Hudson.M.C. To 4th. Bn.ROYAL SUSSEX Regiment. 29.3.19.
Lieut.A.G.A.Vidler.M.C. To 52nd. Bn.ROYAL SUSSEX Regiment. 29.3.19.

Appointed General Staff Officer. Grade.3. 24th.Division.

Captain C.V.Newton. M.C.

For a brief period after the departure of the draft to the 4th.Battalion. there appeared little to do and time seemed to go slowly. It was not long, however, before football started again and several who had never played before found that their efforts to master the intricacies of Soccer gave them quite as much amusement as they gave to the usual [illegible] crowd around the goal. The result was that after one or two games keenness had revived and football was played whenever the weather permitted.

D. D. & L., London, E.C.
(10340) Wt W5300/P713 750,000 3/18 E 2688 Forms/C2118/16.

Instructions regarding War Diaries and Intelligence Summaries are contained in F. S. Regs., Part II. and the Staff Manual respectively. Title pages will be prepared in manuscript.

9th Battalion

WAR DIARY
or
INTELLIGENCE SUMMARY.
(Erase heading not required.)

ROYAL SUSSEX Regiment.

M A R C H 1919.

Army Form C. 2118.

Place	Date	Hour	Summary of Events and Information	Remarks and references to Appendices
TAINTIGNIES. Belgium	March 1/31.		Several dances were got up by the civilians and were much appreciated by the men. The month has been one of farewells. Apart from the Officers and men who have already been mentioned, there were many to whom we had to say good-bye. Our sister Battalions were of course breaking up at the same time and at the end of the month the 13th. Bn. Middlesex Regiment left to go to HAVRE for duty. The Brigade Staff also left us - Brig.Gen.R.J.Collins CMG.DSO. to take up an appointment at the Staff College, CAMBERLEY. The Brigade Major. Captain.P.T.Chevalier. D.S.O. M.C. to revert to civil life and the Staff Captain, Captain.R.W.W.Hills M.C. to take up the duties of an appointment at DUNKIRK. In spite of losing so many there are still a few veterans who have been with the Battalion since it was formed and are bent on remaining with it till the finish. H.C. Coleman Captain & Adjutant for Lieut.Col. 3rd. April. 1919. Commanding 9th Battalion ROYAL SUSSEX Regt.	

D. D. & L., London, E.C.
(10340) Wt W5300/P713 750,000 3/18 E 2688 Forms/C2118/16.

Army Form C. 2118.

Instructions regarding War Diaries and Intelligence Summaries are contained in F. S. Regs., Part II. and the Staff Manual respectively. Title pages will be prepared in manuscript.

WAR DIARY
9th.Battalion *or* ROYAL SUSSEX Regiment.
INTELLIGENCE SUMMARY.
(Erase heading not required.)

Vol 44

Place	Date	Hour	Summary of Events and Information	Remarks and references to Appendices
Creplaine, France.	April. 1/30.		During the month the process of reducing the Battalion to Cadre strength was almost completed, the strength being reduced from 14 Officers and 189 Other Ranks to 9 Officers and 65 Other Ranks.	
			The following figures show the numbers who were struck off the strength of the Battalion during the month.	
			DRAFTS.	
			To 4th.Battalion Royal Sussex Regiment. 2/Lieut.S.F.GIBBS. 2/Lieut.F.WALKER and 98 Other Ranks.	
			To 51st Battalion Royal Sussex Regiment. Captain C.H.DUDENEY.	
			To Royal Army Ordnance Corps. 7 Other Ranks.	
			To.Chinese Labour Corps. 2 Other Ranks.	
			DEMOBILIZED.	
			Lieut.S.T.TREW. RSM.B.N.Butcher MC.DCM.(Re-enlisted) and 17 Other Ranks.	
			To England (Regular Officer) Lieut.C.F.EDLINGTON.	
			HOSPITAL etc. 3 Other Ranks.	
			The allotment of leave during the month was good and 2 Officers and 41 Other Ranks were granted leave to England. A number of men were given short leave to BRUSSELS.	
			The work of the Battalion was confined to routine and cleaning Transport at the Vehicle Park BAISIEUX. The only event of interest was the move of the Battalion to CREPLAINE on the 7th. A TAINTEGNIES was left with much regret both on the part of the Battalion and the civilians, but on Sundays there were always a large number of visitors to call on old friends at TAINTEGNIES. The billets at CREPLAINE are not quite so good as those we left, but with the greatly reduced numbers the Battalion was soon comfortably settled.	

B.M.

45 I
2 sheet

garding War Diaries and Intelligence Summaries are contained in F. S. Regs., Part II. and the Staff Manual respectively. Title pages will be prepared in manuscript.

Army Form C. 2118.

WAR DIARY
9th.Battalion *or* ROYAL SUSSEX Regiment.
INTELLIGENCE SUMMARY.
(*Erase heading not required.*)

Place	Date	Hour	Summary of Events and Information	Remarks and references to Appendices
CREPLAINE. France.	April 1/30.		Bad weather stopped football at the end of the month, but during the first half it was played on most days. The Cadre team played the 72nd Field Ambulance in a Divisional Tournament on the 11th, but the weather was very unsuitable. The Battalion lost by 1 goal to 0	
			On the 29th. a very successful dinner was arranged in LONDON and attended by 12 Officers of the Battalion including the Commanding Officer and our old Adjutant and 2nd in Command Major J.L.STOKES.	
			A.C. Coleman Captain & Adjutant. for Lieut.Col. Commanding 9th.Battn.ROYAL SUSSEX Regiment.	

Army Form C. 2118.

Instructions regarding War Diaries and Intelligence Summaries are contained in F. S. Regs., Part II. and the Staff Manual respectively. Title pages will be prepared in manuscript.

WAR DIARY
or
~~INTELLIGENCE SUMMARY.~~

9th. Battalion ROYAL SUSSEX Regt.

(*Erase heading not required.*)

18 45

Ceased

Place	Date	Hour	Summary of Events and Information	Remarks and references to Appendices
CREPLAINE. France.	1919 May. 1st. to 31st.		During the month the Battalion was reduced in strength from 9 Officers and 65 Other Ranks to 6 Officers and 38 Other Ranks. The latter figures include 2 Officers who are volunteers for the Army of Occupation, who are still unposted, and 1 Officer and 3 Other Ranks in Hospital.	
			On 25th. May. Lieut. Colonel. M.V.B. HILL. D.S.O. M.C. left the Battalion for demobilization. He had commanded the Battalion since November 1916 and had served in France since September 1914 with only one break of 3 months in England after being wounded in March 1918.	
			On 26th May Lieut. J.C. WIGGS and 2/Lieut. A.W. CHADWICK left the Battalion to join the No. 337 and No. 319 Prisoners of War Companys respectively.	
			The decrease in Other Ranks is accounted for as follows:-	
			Increase. 1.	
			Demobilized. 12.	
			To. Hospital. 2.	
			To 4th. Royal Sussex Regt. (A of O) 14.	
			To Home Establishment. 1.	
			During the month leave was granted to 1 Officer and 10 Other ranks, but all had rejoined by the end of the month.	
			On Colonel HILL's departure on the 25th. Captain H.C. COLEMAN. M.C. took over command of the Battalion during the absence of Major T. FOSTER on leave.	
			The work of the Battalion was confined to routine.	46 I 2 sheets

(A9175) Wt W2358/P360 600,000 12/17 D. D. & L. Sch. 52a. Forms/C2118/15.

Army Form C. 2118.

WAR DIARY
or
INTELLIGENCE SUMMARY.

9th. Battalion Royal Sussex Regiment.

(*Erase heading not required.*)

Instructions regarding War Diaries and Intelligence Summaries are contained in F. S. Regs., Part II. and the Staff Manual respectively. Title pages will be prepared in manuscript.

Place	Date	Hour	Summary of Events and Information	Remarks and references to Appendices
CREPLAINE. France.	May. 1st. to 31st.		On the 12th. a lorry was obtained and a party of Officers and men spent the day looking over the line at LENS and LOOS and visiting our old billets at BULLY GRENAY and LES BREBIS.	
			On the 19th. a party of Officers and Men left for a 5 days trip to BRUGES and OSTEND. The route taken was through LILLE, ARMENTIERES, BAILLEUL, LOCRE DICKEBUSH, YPRES, PASCHENDALE and ROULERS to BRUGES. Two very enjoyable days were spent at BRUGES and some of the party paid a visit to OSTEND. The return trip was made through ROULERS and MENIN.	
			On the 12th. orders were received that the Battalion would entrain for ANTWERP on XXXXXXX their way to England on the 17th. These orders were cancelled next day.	
			However on the 30th. a further order was received that the Cadre would e entrain about the 2nd of June, and it is hoped that we shall not be disappointed this time.	

A. C. Coleman

Captain.

Commanding 9th. Battalion Royal Sussex Regiment.

(A9175) Wt W2358/P360 600,000 12/17 D. D. & L. Sch. 52a. Forms/C2118/15.

www.ingramcontent.com/pod-product-compliance
Lightning Source LLC
Chambersburg PA
CBHW080913230426
43667CB00015B/2670